About Island Press

Since 1984, the nonprofit organization Island Press has been stimulating, shaping, and communicating ideas that are essential for solving environmental problems worldwide. With more than 800 titles in print and some 40 new releases each year, we are the nation's leading publisher on environmental issues. We identify innovative thinkers and emerging trends in the environmental field. We work with world-renowned experts and authors to develop cross-disciplinary solutions to environmental challenges.

Island Press designs and executes educational campaigns in conjunction with our authors to communicate their critical messages in print, in person, and online using the latest technologies, innovative programs, and the media. Our goal is to reach targeted audiences—scientists, policymakers, environmental advocates, urban planners, the media, and concerned citizens—with information that can be used to create the framework for long-term ecological health and human well-being.

Island Press gratefully acknowledges major support of our work by The Agua Fund, The Andrew W. Mellon Foundation, Betsy & Jesse Fink Foundation, The Bobolink Foundation, The Curtis and Edith Munson Foundation, Forrest C. and Frances H. Lattner Foundation, G.O. Forward Fund of the Saint Paul Foundation, Gordon and Betty Moore Foundation, The JPB Foundation, The Kresge Foundation, The Margaret A. Cargill Foundation, New Mexico Water Initiative, a project of Hanuman Foundation, The Overbrook Foundation, The S.D. Bechtel, Jr. Foundation, The Summit Charitable Foundation, Inc., V. Kann Rasmussen Foundation, The Wallace Alexander Gerbode Foundation, and other generous supporters.

The opinions expressed in this book are those of the author(s) and do not necessarily reflect the views of our supporters.

Conservation for Cities

Conservation for Cities

How to Plan and Build Natural Infrastructure

Robert I. McDonald

ISLANDPRESS

Washington | Covelo | London

Library of Congress Control Number: 2014958640

⊕ Printed on recycled, acid-free paper

Manufactured in the United States of America
10 9 8 7 6 5 4 3 2 1

Keywords: air quality, beautification, biodiversity, climate adaptation, climate change, coastal protection, combined sewer system, density, ecosystem services, flooding, green infrastructure, habitat, health, heat island effect, heat wave, levee, mental health, natural infrastructure, park, particulate matter, recreation, resilience, shade, stormwater, urbanization, water quality

Contents

Acknowledgments

This book would not have happened without the patient intellectual mentoring of Bob Lalasz. Of equal importance, Peter Kareiva fought to give me intellectual freedom to write this book and helped me sharpen its focus. Courtney Lix, my editor at Island Press, helped me focus this book on its core audience. I thank the NatureNet Fellowship for generous support.

Many colleagues have helped me develop the framework for the book, including Jonathan Adams, Sylvia Benitez, Jon Christensen, Bill Toomey, Marty Downs, Teresa Duran, Evan Girvetz, Joe Fargione, Richard Forman, Charlotte Kaiser, Timm Kroeger, Matt Miller, Jen Molnar, Jeff Opperman, Geof Rochester, and Dean Urban. I have also had the pleasure to interview many practitioners and scientists in the course of writing this book, and I'm grateful to all of them. Any mistakes that remain in the book are mine, and any brilliance in the book is due to their kind input: Mike Beck, David Cleary, Aaron Durnbaugh, Jeff Francell, Bram Gunther, Simon Hales, Peter Hill, Kim Jungyoon, Peter Kahm, Frank Kelly, Naill Kirkwood, Carolyn Kousky, Roderick Laurence, Jose Lobo, Gordon MacGranahan, Victor Medina, Jenny Moodley, Joe Nasr, Nicole Maher, Tijs van Maasakkers, Chris Paschenko, Brian Richter, Rebecca Stack, John Tagliabue, Joanne Thrush, Jennifer Turner, Richard Walker, Brett Walton, Patty Zaradic, and Brandon Zatt.

Most of all, I am indebted to my wife, who patiently helped me find time in our busy personal life for this book.

This book is dedicated to my two children. I judge every workday a success or failure by whether or not I've made the world they will inherit a little greener or a little more peaceful. With luck, maybe this book is a little step in that direction.

Chapter 1

Nature in an Urban World

Looking at the skyline, it is hard for me to imagine that just a few decades ago this was a sleepy town by the Fustian River. The skyscrapers of Shenzhen now stretch out to the horizon. Some of the newer towers have a glass façade and fashionable design, but many of the other buildings appear as more or less identical grey concrete blocks, lined up in long rows that shrink toward the horizon. And then everywhere, ubiquitous, are the cranes. The cranes of Shenzhen are always moving, flitting from one building site to another, frantically assembling steel beams into the frames for new skyscrapers. In a few short decades, they have built a city where once there was a small village, and they keep on building. Farmers' fields have disappeared under a forest of skyscrapers, in just one generation. How did this dramatic urban growth happen?

Every city's story, like every individual's life, is unique and full of happenstance. For many decades, the Chinese government under

1

Mao Zedong actively tried to keep cities from growing and in some cases forced urban youth to move to the countryside. With Mao's death and new political leadership, this anti-urban attitude eased a little bit. Shenzhen, then a small town of just 60,000 people (UNPD 2011), was designated one of China's four Special Economic Zones (SEZs), where free market policies and urban development were allowed. All of the suppressed economic development of China began to concentrate in these SEZs.

Shenzhen's location, just across the river from the bustling city of Hong Kong, was perfect. It had a large, deepwater port and, compared with Hong Kong, cheap wages. Manufacturers rapidly set up factories, and during the 1980s the industrial output of the city grew by 60 percent a year (Montgomery et al. 2003). The total population surpassed 10 million in 2010 (UNPD 2011), an astonishing 175-fold increase in its population since becoming an SEZ.

But the dark side of such rapid growth is severe environmental challenges that affect residents' quality of life. Shenzhen's water supply system has struggled to keep pace with its burgeoning population, and providing water of sufficient quality has required significant new infrastructure. Shenzhen's air quality has declined, as industrial production and millions of cars on the road have led to high levels of smog and particulate matter (Che et al. 2011). The rain is so acidic, due to sulfur dioxide and nitrogen oxide from coal-burning power plants, that it sometimes damages the paint on cars. Shenzhen has the distinction of having one of the fastest urban growth rates in the world (UNPD 2011). But while extreme, its story contains themes that are present in many urban areas. Many other cities in both the developing and developed world are experiencing growth (fig. 1.1), and are struggling to accommodate that growth while protecting the environment. All this growth will require new infrastructure, as will the challenge of adapting cities to climate change.

The twenty-first century will be the fastest period of urban growth in human history. In a few decades, more homes will be

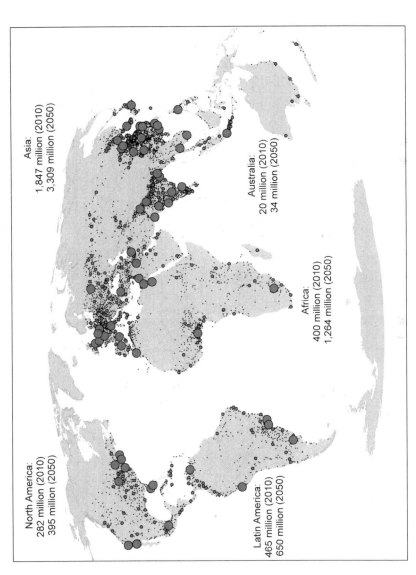

North America:
282 million (2010)
395 million (2050)

Latin America:
465 million (2010)
650 million (2050)

Asia:
1,847 million (2010)
3,309 million (2050)

Australia:
20 million (2010)
34 million (2050)

Africa:
400 million (2010)
1,264 million (2050)

Figure 1.1. Distribution of world cities, with bigger urban agglomerations marked with larger bubbles. Urban population totals, by continent, for 2010 and forecasted totals for 2050 are taken from the UNPD (2011).

built than have accumulated over centuries of urban development in Europe. Rapidly urbanizing regions like Asia and Africa will add billions of people to their cities (fig. 1.1). In a sense, Asia and Africa are catching up with Europe and the United States, which already have substantial proportions of their total populations living in cities. Even in developed countries, however, urban population often continues to expand in some urban areas, driven by overall population growth or shifts in population among cities. Older infrastructure in growing cities needs to be refurbished or replaced. Globally, the twenty-first century will require massive urban infrastructure development, in roads and pipes and power lines and schools.

Ecologists, urban planners, economists, and landscape architects are increasingly asked to consider the role that natural infrastructure—the natural habitat or constructed natural spaces that supply crucial benefits to urban residents—can play in meeting these challenges. Whether it is the role of upstream forests in maintaining water quality in reservoirs, how shade trees keep cities cool during heat waves, or the way parks can contribute to the quality of life and financial success of a city, natural infrastructure is all the rage.

Even in Shenzhen, the concept of natural infrastructure has caught on. By 2000, the city's rapid urban growth had made the Fustian River an open sewer. The river had been channelized, with concrete embankments boxing in the its foul waters for most of its length as it passed through the city. In 2009, the Shenzhen Fustian River project began. At a cost of 300 million yuan (US$49 million), the project first created new pipes to carry stormwater and sewage water to a treatment facility, to limit the release of untreated sewage into the Fustian. But this *grey infrastructure* investment—concrete and pipes and other engineered structures—was complemented by an investment in *green infrastructure*. The concrete embankments were torn down, replaced by sand and mud and pebbles. Eventually, artificial wetlands were created in low-lying areas of the floodplain, to further filter stormwater as it reached the Fustian, as well as to provide a beautiful park along the river (Lide 2013).

Yet for all the excitement about natural infrastructure, guidance on how to plan and implement projects is often hard to come by. How can a city like Shenzhen tell which of nature's benefits—the ecosystem services provided by natural habitat—are most important? How can they map which patches of natural habitat are most important, and quantify the economic benefits they provide? How could planners in the Shenzhen Water Planning and Design Institute, which ran the Shenzhen Fustian River project, find the optimal mix of natural infrastructure and traditional grey infrastructure to solve problems facing a city? Perhaps most important, what are the regulatory and policy tools that a city like Shenzhen can use to help fund and implement natural infrastructure projects?

Conservation for an Urban World

Cities need nature to survive and thrive. And yet the traditional viewpoint of environmentalists concerned with "nature" has been that cities are the enemy. It is true that as cities have expanded, they have affected a lot of biodiversity. One-third of all imperiled species in the United States are in metropolitan regions (NWF, Smart Growth America, and NatureServe 2005), and globally at least one in ten vertebrates is impacted by urbanization (McDonald, Kareiva, and Forman 2008). Conservation planners, wildlife managers, and other practitioners who focus on protecting biodiversity increasingly have to consider the impact of cities on their work and design strategies that limit the impact of cities on wildlife. I call this important work protecting biodiversity in urban areas *conservation in cities* (fig. 1.2). Protecting biodiversity in areas of urban growth is a classic topic in the conservation planning literature (e.g., Groves 2003). The general strategy is to keep urban growth out of areas of high biodiversity, and wherever possible to keep houses clustered at high density, to minimize the total area of natural habitat impacted by urban growth. This book discusses biodiversity conservation in urban areas in chapter 12.

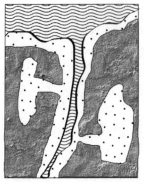 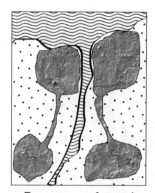 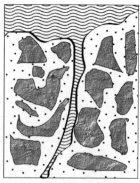

| Biodiversity focused | Resource use focused | Conservation for city focused |

Figure 1.2. Conceptual drawing of urban development (grey areas) *in a matrix of natural habitat* (dotted areas) *for a coastal city, under three types of urban planning: conservation in cities* (left panel), *where important biodiversity areas are protected with corridors between them; conservation by cities* (middle panel), *where compact urban centers are connected by transit corridors; and conservation for cities* (right panel), *where each urban neighborhood is surrounded by natural habitat that can provide benefits to residents.*

I have come to believe that the "black hole" view of many ecologists is myopic, in that it focuses conservationists only on biodiversity protection. Nature needs cities. Cities provide numerous economies of scale, reducing per capita use of some resources. Those interested in promoting resource-use efficiency or the reduction of greenhouse gas emissions will often advocate for an urban form that will maximize the efficiency of the city. I call this important task of making our cities more efficient *conservation by cities* (fig. 1.2). While this book does not focus on how to plan a city to maximize resource-use efficiency, there are numerous other works in the smart growth literature that provide useful tools to planners and ecologists (e.g., APA 2002).

Cities are centers of activity on the landscape, and there are strong bonds between cities and nature, whether inside the city's walls or far away. More and more, conservation biologists, urban planners, and landscape architects are being asked to craft plans that maintain or strengthen these bonds while also allowing for continued urban growth. As the urban century continues, the maintenance of these bonds will become more crucial, both because more people will depend on them and because rapid urban growth, as in the case of Shenzhen, risks severing them.

This book is meant to be a practical guide to this task, which I call *conservation for cities* (fig. 1.2). It aims to guide urban planners, landscape architects, and conservation practitioners trying to figure out how to use nature to make the lives of those in cities better. Rather than focusing on how to protect nature *from* cities, this book is about how to protect nature *for* cities.

Conservation for cities could include the protection of existing patches of natural habitat, their restoration where degraded, or the creation of entirely novel patches of green infrastructure. These patches can be inside the metropolitan region, like a city's parks or street trees. Or they can be far away, like the watershed upstream of a city's reservoir. Humanity is now planning and building the new cities and neighborhoods of the twenty-first century, and this book is about how to incorporate nature into those plans.

Getting Cities What They Need

The patches of vegetation that provide benefits to those in cities are increasingly called *natural infrastructure* or *green infrastructure*. The term originated in the United States as an outgrowth of the greenways movement and at first had a strong focus on preserving biodiversity and the landscape connectivity that allows it to move across the landscape. The term has broadened over time, as an increasing variety of benefits from nature are considered by planners. In particular, *green infrastructure* most often now refers to constructed wetlands and other man-made spaces that help cities reduce the stormwater going into their stormwater drainage system (see chapter 4). In this book, I use the term *natural infrastructure* in its broadest possible sense, for any piece of nature that provides important benefits to those in a city. For man-made spaces, such as a constructed wetland, I will use the term *green infrastructure* to designate that while vegetation is key to this infrastructure functioning, it is an area fundamentally designed by people. Conversely, when I want to specifically refer to natural habitat that serves as natural infrastructure, I will use the term *critical natural habitat*.

But what does it mean to say that a particular way of supplying a benefit to urbanites is more "natural" than another? The distinction may make intuitive sense when we are talking about remnant patches of natural habitat, but what about environments that are clearly human created, like a row of street trees or a constructed wetland? The *Oxford English Dictionary* defines nature as "the phenomena of the physical world collectively, including plants, animals, the landscape, and other features and products of the earth, *as opposed to humans or human creations*" (emphasis mine). Taken too strictly, this definition can imply a fake distinction between cities and nature that isn't there. I find it helpful to think about a gradient of naturalness, from very natural (e.g., a wilderness area) to somewhat natural (e.g, critical natural habitat, their ecosystem processes undoubtedly affected in many ways by nearby urban areas) to a little natural (e.g., green infrastructure such as a constructed wetland) to entirely man-made (a piece of grey infrastructure like an asphalt road). Conservation for cities is about using natural infrastructure, ranging from wilderness areas to green infrastructure, rather than only grey infrastructure.

While sometimes the rhetoric around natural infrastructure may imply differently, the idea of using nature to improve the lives of those in cities is not a new one. More than a century ago, Frederick Law Olmsted tried to use the natural processes of wetlands to guide his design of Boston's Green Necklace series of parks, and the Garden City movement in England tried to bring urbanites in closer contact with nature. Post–World War II, the New Town and the Garden City movements also strove to use nature to better urbanites' lives. In the 1960s, Ian McHarg and others mapped natural areas providing important services and protected them in their plans. More recently, the New Urbanism movement has also paid attention to the role parks and street trees play in a vibrant, walkable city. All of these movements thought about natural infrastructure, although in varying ways and for varying purposes.

Natural resource management has also long focused on at least some of the benefits nature can supply to people, such as timber and opportunities for hunting and fishing. Since the 1970s, with the emergence of conservation planning and landscape ecology as disciplines, a large literature has examined how best to protect habitat to maintain biodiversity. This literature shows it is often best to preserve large tracts of remaining natural habitat as core areas. These ideally would be connected by corridors, sometimes called greenways. Since the 1990s, ecologists have increasingly moved to quantify the other benefits that nature provides to people.

These two strands of thought—one coming from urban planning and the other coming from ecology and conservation biology—have merged. There is increasing recognition of the importance of natural infrastructure to good planning, and an increasing number of tools by ecologists that quantify nature's benefits in either physical or economic terms. While we shouldn't let the rhetoric of natural infrastructure get too out of hand, there is something new here in terms of skill and sophistication. Never before have conservation biologists, urban planners, and landscape architects had so many tools at their disposal to plan how to get cities what they need from the natural world.

What Is an Ecosystem Service?

The central premise of this book is that conservation practitioners, urban planners, and landscape architects can use natural infrastructure to meet some of the needs and desires of those in cities. While the scope of human desires is infinitely variable, and many desires are satisfied entirely with human technology, there are certain things that most urbanites the world over would consider part of the good life that necessarily involve nature. Getting clean water to urban residents depends, in part, on the trees upstream of the reservoir preventing erosion. The air quality of a region depends, in part, on how much canopy cover there is to scrub the atmosphere. Parks and other urban public spaces almost universally contain natural features like vegetation alongside human-created features like playgrounds.

All these things that cities demand from the natural world can be thought of, more positively, as benefits nature provides urban dwellers. Ecologists call these benefits, rather dully, *ecosystem services*. While the core idea is pretty simple, the term has been defined in slightly different ways over the years. In this book, I will use the definition of Boyd and Banghaf (2006), who define ecosystem services as "the components of nature, directly enjoyed, consumed, or used to yield human well-being."

An ecosystem service occurs when an ecosystem function is supplying something that people are demanding. Put another way, ecosystem functions become ecosystem services when they are directly increasing someone's well-being. Note that many goods that increase someone's well-being are made with both ecosystem services and conventional goods. Consider the delivery of clean drinking water to residents. As we shall see in chapter 3, natural habitat in the watershed upstream of a reservoir helps stabilize soil (the ecosystem function), which keeps sediment from getting into the reservoir and maintains the water of high enough quality for human use (the ecosystem service). Human technology then further treats the water, if necessary, and delivers the treated water to urbanites (the market good that people are willing to pay for). Human technology here, as in many cases, is a partial substitute for an ecosystem service: if the water in a reservoir is more polluted, we can use more complicated and expensive technology to treat the water.

There are a myriad of different ecosystem services that are important to human well-being, and so there are a myriad of different kinds of natural infrastructure that a conservation practitioner might have to consider. A short list of ecosystem services most relevant to cities is shown in table 1.1.

The first category of ecosystem services is provisioning services, the products people obtain from ecosystems such as food, fuel, or fiber. Agricultural crop production is a clear example of a provisioning service. Livestock production and aquaculture are two other examples. One of the most important provisioning services for cities is providing sufficient quantity of water. Municipalities supply water to their residents, who need water for drinking, sanitation, cleaning, and irrigating landscaping, among many other uses. Water is also crucial for energy production, particularly the cooling of thermoelectric plants. As discussed in detail in chapter 3, municipal water utilities depend on the natural water cycle to provide sufficient water to their water intake points.

Another category of ecosystem services, recognized by the Millennium Ecosystem Assessment (MEA 2003, 2005), is cultural services, defined as the nonmaterial benefits people obtain from ecosystems. The aesthetic benefits, for example, of natural areas can be very important to urban dwellers. Whether street trees, urban parks, or a view of beautiful mountains, these aesthetic considerations have demonstrated quantified value to the well-being of those in cities (chapter 9). Recreation opportunities for urban residents are another important benefit of urban natural areas, as is the potential value of natural areas, whether near and far, as tourist destinations. There are important health benefits urban residents obtain by being near natural areas, including reductions in obesity rates (chapter 10) and improvements in mental health (chapter 11).

The third category of the MEA is regulating services, the benefits people obtain from the regulation of ecosystem function. For instance, in riparian systems, natural floodplains play an important role in allowing floodwaters to spread out, lessening peak flows and reducing flood risk in downstream urban areas (chapter 5). Similarly, some natural coastal habitats like wetlands, oyster reefs,

Table 1.1. Ecosystem services of greatest relevance to cities, classified according to the Millennium Ecosystem Assessment, the category of economic good they represent, and the spatial scale at which they operate

Ecosystem service	Economic category	Spatial scale
Provisioning services		
Agriculture (crops, live-stock, aquaculture, etc.)	Private good	Regional to global
Water (quantity)	Private good	100s km—upstream source watershed
Cultural services		
Aesthetic benefits	Public or common good	10s km—area of daily travel by urbanites
Recreation and tourism	Public or common good	10s km—area of daily travel by urbanites
Physical health	Public or common good	10s km—area of daily travel by urbanites
Mental health	Public or common good	10s km—area of daily travel by urbanites
Spiritual value and sense of place	Public or common good	Varies—often local, but can be up to global
Biodiversity	Public or common good	Varies—global for existence value, local for direct interaction
Regulating services		
Drinking water protection (water quality)	Public good	100s km—upstream source watershed
Stormwater mitigation	Public good	100s m—downstream stormwater system
Mitigating flood risk	Public good	100s km—downstream flood-prone areas
Coastal protection	Public good	10s km—coastal zone
Air purification (particulates, ozone)	Public good	100s km—regional airshed
Shade and heat wave mitigation	Public good	< 100 m—varies with solar angle

Sources: MEA 2003, 2005.

mangroves, and coral reefs may mitigate the risk of flooding to cities during storms (chapter 6). The natural world plays an important climate regulation role, affecting surface temperature, evapotranspiration, wind flow, and other climate parameters (chapter 7). Finally, natural habitat may help reduce air pollution and regulate air quality within acceptable limits (chapter 8).

Ecosystem Services and Market Failure

If ecosystem services are so wonderful, why are so many of them not successfully provided by the free market to urban residents? Economists would call the lack of natural infrastructure for most ecosystem services an example of market failure, which occurs systematically for certain types of goods and services. To understand further, we need to go into some detail about how economists classify goods (table 1.2) into four categories.

Private goods—the agricultural produce we buy from the supermarket, for example—are rival and excludable (Kolstad 2000): I cannot take home an apple from the store unless I pay (excludable), and my purchase of the apple prevents others from purchasing it (rival). Other important natural resources to cities that function as private goods include wood for timber and meat from ranching.

However, many very important goods are *public goods*, defined as nonrival and nonexcludable. As I write these words, I can look out the window at a beautiful row of street trees, with the US Capitol Building looming in the background. My enjoyment of this aesthetic

Table 1.2. Goods and services defined as rivalrous (consumption by one person prevents another from enjoying it), and/or excludable (access to the good can be limited to those who pay)

	Rivalrous	Nonrivalrous
Excludable	Private goods	Club goods
Nonexcludable	Common goods	Public goods

beauty does not prevent others from enjoying it (nonrival), and this public street is open to all who wish to enter it (nonexcludable). Another important category is *common goods*, which are rival but nonexcludable. Fishing in the open ocean is one example, since anyone can fish (nonexcludable) but any fish I catch and eat are not there for others to use (rival). A rarer category is *club goods,* which are nonrival but excludable. If I decide to purchase access to cable TV or to a paid website, my use imposes little or no cost on other users (nonrival), but the company running such a subscription service can certainly exclude me if I don't pay.

Both economic theory and practical experience suggest private goods are well provided by markets. Firms have financial incentives to bring private goods to market. In contrast, public goods and common goods are generally underprovided by markets, precisely because they are nonexcludable: no firm could make money off the provision of these goods, since free riders (users who haven't paid) would just use the goods for free. Common goods are specifically at risk of degradation via the *tragedy of the commons* (Hardin 1968). Each person has an incentive to use as much of the common good as he or she desires; after all, why not? It is free! However, if too many people reason this way and all of them use the common good, it may be degraded.

Most ecosystem services that cities depend on are public or common goods (table 1.1). As such, adequate natural infrastructure for their provision will not be maintained by the action of the market. The beautiful street trees I can see outside the window were not planted by any private business, since in general the benefits they provide (aesthetic beauty, shade, etc.) are public goods. For similar reasons, urban parks for recreation, a common good (nonexcludable, but rival, since if too many people use a park it can get too crowded to be useful for recreation), will tend not to be provided by private land developers, at least at the level of provision society would prefer.

Solutions to Market Failure

If the private market has little incentive to provide natural infrastructure for most ecosystem services, then governments or other social organizations can step in to ensure provision, either directly through policy or indirectly by giving market actors incentive to consider ecosystem services in their decisions. In short, the solution to market failure is collective action to promote the public good. Urban planning and zoning is one of the key places where ecosystem service provision can be ensured. There are also many laws that try to promote the public good, usually for particular aspects of the environment (e.g., in the United States, the Clean Air Act and the Clean Water Act).

Consider a city that suffers from too much stormwater and wants to use green infrastructure to absorb stormwater and mitigate any stormwater problems the city is having (the subject of chapter 4). It could change its zoning code to require that new developments contain a certain amount of green infrastructure, enough to capture a given quantity of stormwater. Apart from legislative or policy solutions, there are also so-called market-based mechanisms that fix market failure (Hanley, Shogren, and White 2013). These involve either a fee for the damage an action does to society (e.g., an impervious surface charge to pay for actions to mitigate damages caused by increased stormwater) or some system of permits that must be obtained to perform an action that causes damage to society (e.g., a requirement that new development in a city have a permit for any additional stormwater they generate).

Valuation of Ecosystem Services

One of the central tasks of environmental economists and ecosystem service scientists is quantifying the value of ecosystem service provision for a particular set of beneficiaries. The methodology used to value ecosystem service varies between ecosystem services and is discussed in detail for each ecosystem service in chapters 3 through 12. In general, private goods have a market price that provides ready information on the economic value of the good. Sometimes, the good with value is a function of both ecosystem services and other input goods and services, making the valuation a little more complex. For instance, clean drinking water has a market value, and the contribution of ecosystem services to the overall final product (a liter of water clean enough to drink) can be calculated by looking at other grey infrastructure alternatives that could produce the same product.

Ecosystem services that are common goods and public goods lack market prices. But a link can sometimes be made to other economic actions that do have a price. For instance, the role of natural infrastructure in mitigating floodwaters is not something that anyone directly pays for. However, people are willing to spend money to avoid flood damage to their property, so estimates of the economic value of this ecosystem service can be constructed (chapter 5). In some cases with particularly intangible ecosystem services (e.g., aesthetic beauty, chapter 9), economists are forced to ask people hypothetical questions about how much they would be willing to pay to avoid the loss of an ecosystem service, an approach that is called contingent valuation.

This book is concerned with how conservation actions can maintain or create natural infrastructure, ensuring and perhaps enhancing ecosystem service provision. It is important to note that when evaluating a potential conservation action, what matters is how much greater ecosystem system service provision is than what it would have been without the conservation action. For instance, in a city with lots of street trees, it is possible to calculate the total aggregate value of all street trees in terms of providing shade or aesthetic beauty. The total value is, however, unlikely to be of much use in conservation planning. Of more use is what would happen to the population of street trees over time if no further conservation action was taken. In this book, this "what-if-we-don't-act" scenario is called the counterfactual scenario or status quo scenario. In many US cities, for instance, there is a slow decline in the amount of street trees over time, and a new conservation action such as a tree protection ordinance should be evaluated against this status quo scenario.

This book is structured, from chapter 3 on, with each chapter addressing one ecosystem service at a time. However, many conservation actions provide multiple ecosystem service benefits. When the city decided to plant the street trees outside my window, they may have been motivated primarily by the aesthetic benefits. But, the street trees are also providing shade, reducing the urban heat island effect, and intercepting stormwater, thus helping mitigate the city's stormwater problem. Ideally, a smart urban planner would consider all of these *cobenefits* when making decisions.

If it is the sum total of all cobenefits that should be considered, why is this book structured with each chapter considering a separate ecosystem service? For the simple reason that most planning processes or pieces of legislation focus on a single key ecosystem service. For instance, the Safe Drinking Water Act (SDWA) in the United States has rules governing drinking water quality, which affect how a water utility might manage their supply watershed's natural areas, but other ecosystem services from those natural areas (e.g., carbon sequestration) are irrelevant to the SWDA.

Where Ecosystem Services Are Provided

Natural infrastructure needs to be within a certain distance from people for the ecosystem functions it generates to be useful as an ecosystem service (McDonald 2009). One common mistake in urban planning is to focus on areas of ecosystem function, and then treat such zones as simple overlays in planning decisions. This approach misses a very important spatial dimension of ecosystem services, which is the importance of proximity between natural habitat and beneficiary. This zone of provision is sometimes called the "serviceshed" (Tallis and Wolny 2011), after the familiar concept of a watershed. I will also talk about the "transportability" of an ecosystem service (McDonald 2009), which describes the slow decline in service provision with distance from natural habitat. This decline, rather than a sharp boundary, is the case for most ecosystem services.

The transportability of different ecosystem services varies widely (table 1.1), which affects where urban planners and conservation practitioners need to protect or restore natural infrastructure. Some services are very local, operating over the scale of meters, like the shade from street trees. Others, like the provision of parks for day-to-day recreation, operate over the scale of tens of kilometers. Water provision operates within watersheds, which can vary from small to quite large and have a unique element of upstream–downstream directionality: actions upstream affect water quantity and quality downstream; actions downstream do not affect points upstream. Similarly, air quality in a region's "airshed" depends on regional wind patterns, which define an upwind–downwind directionality. As these examples illustrate, the transportability of an ecosystem service is not a simple function of Euclidean distance but is determined by the physics of the ecosystem service in question, which controls how useful a particular patch of natural infrastructure is for a particular person's well-being.

Where to Protect Nature to Benefit Urbanites

Cities characteristically have a dense core and then lower population density as one heads away from the core into suburbs or exurbs. Since by definition ecosystem services benefit people, and most people live and work in cities, cities are centers of ecosystem service demand (McDonald 2009). Natural infrastructure may provide greater ecosystem services when it is closer to the dense urban core than when it is located in a remote rural area. Thus, all else being equal, urban planners or conservation practitioners should take action to maintain or enhance ecosystem services close to where people live and work. For instance, they might prioritize patches of natural habitat in the urban core for protection, as key areas of ecosystem service provision.

Of course, all else is not equal. There is a steep gradient in land prices or rent from the city center to the exterior. For instance, house prices in San Francisco are more than triple that of suburban towns 50 km distant (McDonald 2009). This gradient in land prices reflects the intensity of the competition for land for different uses. Put another way, protecting or creating natural infrastructure in the city center has a high opportunity cost, since the land could be used for many other purposes. Moreover, conservation action in the city center is expensive for other reasons as well. Natural areas surrounded by urban areas are more expensive to maintain, and are more readily ecologically degraded, than are natural areas in rural settings.

To define the optimal place to preserve or protect natural infrastructure for ecosystem service provision, one needs to consider both costs and benefits of preserving or restoring nature in a particular place. This is mathematically parallel to the idea of bid rent theory for cities, which describes why different types of firms, farmers, or households are willing to pay (bid) up to a certain amount to locate at a certain distance from the city center (Alonso 1964). Consider a factory that produces goods that it has to transport to the city center for sale, with the cost of transport depending on the distance to the city center (km) and the transportability of the good ($/km). Its net profit, π, is

$$\pi = PQ - T(m,Q) - R(m)$$

where m is the distance from the city center. This is simply the gross profit, defined as the quantity Q of goods they make times their market price P, minus their costs. Costs include transportation costs T, a function of m and Q, and the rent and the other costs of production R, a function of m. T decreases as you approach the city center, but at the expense of an increase in R. For any firm, there is a zone in which it is profitable to operate: too close and rent is too high; too far and transport costs are too high (Richardson 2013).

Urban planners or conservation practitioners have to make a similar calculation (McDonald 2009). We may take Q to be the quantity of ecosystem services consumed, and P to be their societal value. R would represent the costs of maintaining or restoring natural habitat at a given distance m from the city center. T represents how different distances between the natural habitat and people limit the ecosystem services consumed. Particular ecosystem services have different degrees of transportability affecting the size of the term T.

For any particular ecosystem service, there is a zone in which it is profitable to protect or restore habitat for ecosystem service provision. In the city center, the costs of doing projects may be too high, and in rural areas there may be few ecosystem services provided (i.e., transport costs are too high), but in between there is a zone where conservation is profitable. In a stylized city where the center of the city is a single point, these zones of profitability are concentric circles (fig. 1.3). Since different ecosystem services have different transportability, the zones of optimal protection differ for different services.

All of that math can seem pretty abstract, but this conceptual framework gives some real insight into where ecosystem service projects should be located. Let's say a city is interested in increasing carbon sequestration by natural vegetation, as part of an overall plan to mitigate the city's contribution of greenhouse gases to the atmosphere. Since carbon sequestration operates on a global scale, any projects the city funds could be located anywhere. The opportunity costs of land and the cost of project management are cheaper farther away from the city center, so the city is better off conducting the project in a rural area (fig. 1.3). Indeed, most commercial sequestration projects trying to generate credits for one of the extant markets (e.g., Certified Emissions Reductions under the UN Framework Convention on Climate Change) are in rural areas

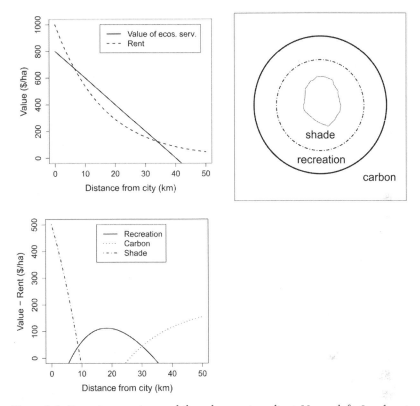

Figure 1.3. Ecosystem services and the urban rent gradient. Upper left: Land rent declines rapidly with distance from the center of a city. Natural habitat located farther from the city center also provides fewer ecosystem services. Lower left: Different ecosystem services have different transportability, so the area with positive net value of conservation (i.e., the value of the ecosystem service provision is greater than the rent) occurs at different distances from the city center for different ecosystem services. Right: A bird's-eye view of a city (grey area). The different transportability of ecosystem services implies that natural infrastructure to supply different kinds of ecosystem services must be located in different places in the city.

on degraded land that has few other profitable uses. Many cities, of course, have programs like New York City's MillionTreesNYC, which encourages tree planting in urban areas. But these programs are focused on a whole suite of cobenefits, some local, and in some cases, directed at government-owned or underutilized land that has low opportunity costs.

For urban parks to provide useful recreational opportunities for urban residents, they have to be located within a reasonable distance from where people live or work (fig. 1.3). Within this serviceshed, an optimal program would try to maximize the ecosystem service benefits of conservation action (creating the park) as compared with the cost of the actions (paying to create and maintain the park). This logic leads to creation of urban parks for recreation at a moderate distance from urban centers and where the costs of land are lower than the center city.

Finally, consider the benefits that street trees or urban parks provide to aesthetics or to mitigate the urban heat island effect. These are very localized benefits, which means natural infrastructure to provide them must be located close to where people live and work—in the city center (fig. 1.3). Working in a city center implies a high cost of conservation action per unit area. Cities often try to avoid this by creatively reusing vacant land or brownfields (land previously developed that is now underutilized), where opportunity costs can be lower.

This book aims to give readers a consistent framework for planning and implementing natural infrastructure projects. After presenting this framework in general terms (chapter 2), the rest of the chapters focus on specific ecosystem services. Each chapter opens with a case study of a real-life city that came to realize that a particular ecosystem service was crucially important to their residents. The chapter then presents the best available tools for mapping and valuing ecosystem services, pointing to more technical documentation where appropriate, and then ends by discussing how the case study city and others like it have successfully set up natural infrastructure projects. While this book can serve as a textbook for courses in urban ecology, landscape architecture, and urban planning, I want it to be above all a source book that practitioners can turn to again and again as they begin thinking about protecting or creating natural infrastructure for cities.

Chapter 2

Figuring Out
What Matters

W HEN I CONVINCED FOLKS in the New York City Department
of Parks & Recreation to give me a tour of their MillionTreesNYC
(MTNYC) project, the last thing I expected was to spend so much
time discussing asthma. The city's goal of establishing a million new
trees along streets or in parks was first announced as part of PlaNYC,
the city's overall sustainability strategy (New York City 2011). The
million tree number was ambitious, but not unprecedented. The
effort was a continuation of what NYC Parks has tried to do for decades: provide trees as an amenity that New Yorkers enjoy. To avoid
any nasty fights between neighborhoods, MTNYC prioritized tree
planting in neighborhoods that currently have fewer trees. Equity
in access to trees and parks was thus given a central role in MTNYC.

I met my tour guides at park headquarters, and we drove north
through Central Park, heading up to Harlem. It was a bitterly cold
January day, but we got out at several spots, looking at entire city

blocks that had been planted with rows of tree saplings. To increase efficiency in planting, the city had focused on transforming entire blocks that previously were barren, blocking off all parking on the street (a big deal in New York!) and bringing in heavy equipment to make the tree planting go faster. Such a radical transformation generated excitement in Harlem and other targeted neighborhoods, but also apprehension.

To reduce this apprehension, NYC Parks began to enumerate the many benefits that street trees can provide, as part of their explanation to the public of the benefits of MTNYC. These transformed blocks in Harlem should have more shade in summer, and the presence of street trees should increase property values. Previously, these neighborhoods with few street trees had some of the highest levels of poverty and, not coincidentally, some of the highest incidences of asthma and other respiratory diseases. NYC Parks gradually started talking more and more about tree planting as a way to improve human health as well.

NYC Parks had gone from focusing on trees as an amenity to thinking of trees as natural infrastructure for the city, supplying a set of key ecosystem services to residents. They had realized the value of "conservation for a city." They started asking themselves hard questions: How much would air quality really increase on the block in Harlem? What trees should they plant to maximize air quality benefits, or any of the other benefits that MTNYC aimed to provide?

This chapter is about what cities do after they encounter the idea of natural infrastructure. The first section presents a simple framework for conservation for cities. I discuss in detail the first two steps of the framework and then describe how the remainder of the book can help practitioners work through the rest of the steps in the framework.

A Framework for Conservation for Cities

Once a city has seized upon the concept of natural infrastructure, how should it go about systematically evaluating the possibilities for natural infrastructure to satisfy the needs of its citizens? The following framework, or something similar, has been used by cities and organizations to plan for the maintenance and creation of natural infrastructure. The steps in my framework are derived from the rational planning model commonly used in urban planning (Berke, Godshalk, and Kaiser 2006), particularly for more technical plans like water and transportation infrastructure plans. Many cities would naturally turn to some planning framework like this even without reading this book, because the rational planning model is an ideal that many cities try to achieve. I have also based the first two steps on the *Manual for Cities* published by The Economics of Ecosystems and Biodiversity program (TEEB 2011), which presents a related framework that cities can use to assess the value of ecosystem services to their residents. The TEEB framework is focused just on analysis, whereas my framework includes planning, implementation, and monitoring of natural infrastructure projects.

In all the steps in this framework, it is important to keep in mind that natural infrastructure cannot and should not be considered separate from grey infrastructure. As discussed in chapter 1, while the two are sometimes substitutes for each other, more often they are complementary. The flood protection value of natural wetlands is only valuable because there are people and property that need protection from floods—the grey gives value to the green. So cities need to align their natural infrastructure planning with their grey infrastructure planning. Note also that a planning framework is only as good as the people who create it. Having a broad set of stakeholders involved throughout is essential to ensuring that the plan will best provide natural infrastructure that meets the needs of all of its citizens. Six stages are presented below, although different cities will have to modify these stages to fit into their unique political, socioeconomic, and ecological context.

1. Define the problem or policy issue.
In the first stage, those leading the planning process need to have a dialogue with key stakeholders about the problem or policy issue that natural infrastructure, in combination with grey infrastructure, should address. A city that evaluates natural infrastructure in the context of climate change adaptation planning will define the problem one way: What actions, using natural infrastructure or grey infrastructure, should the city take to increase our resilience to climate change? In contrast, a government agency in charge of managing coastal hazards might define the problem differently: What actions should be taken to reduce the risk of coastal flooding damages? Getting clarity on the key problem or policy issue to be addressed is essential and will shape the actions taken at all other stages in the framework. This first stage is discussed in more detail later in the chapter, with three examples of problem definition in specific circumstances.

2. Take inventory: What ecosystem services matter?
In this second stage, cities begin broad, considering the full suite of ecosystem services and determining which ones matter for their particular problem or issue. Even when the particular problem or issue seems to point toward one ecosystem service as being of paramount importance, a full consideration of the other ecosystem services that might be important in a city will be crucial, at a minimum, for identifying important cobenefits that should be included as part of the planning process. The goal of this phase is to quickly get from a large list of potentially important ecosystem services to a short list of which ecosystem services really matter and will be further evaluated in the planning process. This phase will be discussed in detail later in this chapter, with a suggestion on how a short workshop can quickly help cities take inventory.

3. What natural infrastructure provides those services?

The next step is figuring out which patches of natural infrastructure currently provide one or more of the important ecosystem services. This map of important patches is the baseline case today. If possible, it is helpful to have quantitative estimates of the ecosystem service benefits provided, either in physical units (e.g., tons of sediment not eroded due to vegetation) or in monetary units (e.g., $). Not all habitat patches are equally important, and having some way to at least rank them is important for later steps in this framework. Having quantitative estimates of benefits provided by each patch allows for a transparent, defensible way to choose which habitat patches to try to protect or to restore. If advanced modeling efforts aren't possible to rank patches, then sometimes expert opinion can help provide a semiquantitative ranking of patches.

4. Identify options for actions.

In this stage, the goal is to figure out what actions the city could take to maintain or enhance ecosystem service provision. Most processes begin by defining the threats that may reduce or destroy the effectiveness of current natural infrastructure. For situations in which the restoration of degraded natural infrastructure or the creation of novel patches of green infrastructure is a possibility, the planning process must consider where spatially restoration or creation would be most appropriate. This step is key because the whole point of natural infrastructure planning is to increase ecosystem service provision relative to a baseline, status quo scenario of no action (i.e., if a city took no action, what would ecosystem service provision be). If there is little threat to an existing natural area, then efforts to protect that critical natural area have little impact on levels of future ecosystem service provision. Conversely, if a piece of critical habitat is very likely to be lost under the baseline, then conservation action significantly increases future ecosystem service provision above the baseline. The effectiveness of a restoration action can similarly be evaluated against what the ecosystem service provision would be without the restoration action, under the status quo scenario.

Next, cities need to identify the opportunities or strategies that mitigate the threats to critical natural systems. One strategy, land protection, has been discussed earlier, but other strategies may also be possible. Incentives to provide natural habitat and ecosystem services on private land, for instance, could be another cost-effective strategy to mitigate threats or even restore some habitat. For situations where restoration or creation of new green infrastructure is a possibility, specific opportunities need to be defined. The outcome of this stage is a finite, well-defined set of proposed natural infrastructure options that seem worthy of further evaluation.

5. Assess options and implement.

Here, the goal is to evaluate the various potential options and pick the best one. Sometimes this is done using formal cost-benefit analyses. In order to evaluate the return on investment of a strategy, an analysis has to integrate information on the economic value of the ecosystem services provided, the threat to those services under the baseline scenario, and the costs of implementing the strategy. Specific techniques to estimate return on investment for particular ecosystem services are discussed in the following chapters. Sometimes, however, a particular opportunity or strategy just makes the most sense to urban leaders and is selected without a formal cost-benefit strategy. After selecting the best opportunity or opportunities, cities have to develop plans to implement the strategy. In many ways this is standard business planning, familiar to most organizational bureaucracies. However, some creativity is often required to figure out how to best correct the market failure that most ecosystem services represent. Once the business plan is finished, the city moves to implementation. This often takes leadership by key municipal officials, since many successful strategies to protect ecosystem services require working across multiple departments in a city, and asking staff to do new jobs that they may be hesitant to do.

6. Monitoring and adaptive management

Monitoring the natural infrastructure program after implementation is a crucial and often ignored step, and helps ensure that the program is achieving its goals. Moreover, information from monitoring programs can help refine management of existing natural infrastructure over time: the so-called adaptive management feedback loop. If the city decides to further expand its portfolio of natural infrastructure, monitoring information can also be very helpful in making these new investments more efficient.

How to Define the Problem

Getting all stakeholders to agree on the problem that natural infrastructure should, in part, solve (stage 1 of the framework) is essential for success in a natural infrastructure planning process. The definition of the problem will shape what ecosystem services are defined as important (stage 2) and will thus shape every decision made during planning and implementation. All too often, however, the exact problem or issue to be addressed is never formally defined but just implicitly assumed because of the political and social context in which the idea of natural infrastructure is encountered. It is worthwhile to always put in writing, however briefly, the key problem or issue that is trying to be solved in the planning process.

Below, I discuss three specific ways that cities might encounter the idea of natural infrastructure, and how they might shape the problem definition chosen.

Via an Existing Planning Process

Perhaps most commonly, cities encounter the concept of natural infrastructure while working on another planning process. For reasons having nothing to do with natural infrastructure, the city has begun to create a new plan or update an existing one. There could be a legal or policy mandate to begin the planning process, or it could just have seemed like a fortuitous moment to city leaders. Regardless, the city begins the planning process by carefully considering the goals and objectives of the plan, which leads to the realization that trees and other natural elements could help realize these objectives. That in turn leads to tricky questions about how to incorporate this natural infrastructure more formally into the planning process.

In some ways, a comprehensive planning process is the best time for cities to encounter the concept of natural infrastructure. Comprehensive plans, also known as master or general plans, aim to provide more specific decisions around zoning, transportation, parks, and the other myriad things a city has to plan for (Berke, Godshalk, and Kaiser 2006). They often have very broad goals. The overall goal of the comprehensive plan thus logically becomes the problem definition adopted for natural infrastructure planning. Because of the broad focus, comprehensive plans can be a perfect vehicle for consideration of ecosystem services. As we saw in chapter 1, there are many different types of ecosystem services, being supplied by many different kinds of natural habitat and operating at different spatial scales. Comprehensive plans have the breadth to consider this full spectrum of benefits from nature, as do sustainability plans like PlaNYC.

In contrast, cities sometimes encounter natural infrastructure when engaged in a sectorial plan for a particular agency or infrastructure system. For instance, many cities in the United States and elsewhere are struggling to deal with stormwater problems. In large rain events, there is either too much stormwater, which can lead to sewage overflows in combined sewer systems, or the stormwater is heavily polluted. As cities plan to deal with their stormwater problems, they may begin to think of natural infrastructure as a solution (chapter 4). Their problem definition will of course be focused narrowly on how to most effectively mitigate stormwater. As the planning process continues, the responsible agency will naturally focus on the specific ecosystem services that matter for stormwater, and a very detailed analysis may be conducted of the amount of stormwater mitigated by different natural features. However, sectorial plans often struggle to consider the full suite of cobenefits supplied by natural infrastructure, since the cobenefits are often defined as beyond the scope of the planning process.

Resiliency Analysis

Many cities are now launching planning processes to estimate how resilient a city is. The concept of "resiliency" is famously difficult to define, and there are many different definitions in use. Good resiliency analyses can answer clearly the question "resilience of what, to what?" (Carpenter et al. 2001). Generally, there is an emphasis on resilience to disasters or large shocks, so a city is deemed resilient if its economy or population stays healthy in response to these shocks.

The Rockefeller Foundation, for instance, is working to increase the resiliency of 100 cities globally. They define resiliency in their City Resilience Framework (Rockefeller Foundation and ARUP 2014). This defines seven qualities of resilient cities: reflective, robust, redundant, flexible, resourceful, inclusive, and integrated. There are then twelve indicators developed to help assess cities' resilience, in four broad categories: Leadership and Strategy, Health and Well-being, Economy and Society, Infrastructure and Economy. There are a broad set of shocks considered, with an emphasis on disasters like earthquakes, hurricanes, and flooding. In some cases, other events like terrorism or economic collapse are also considered.

For resiliency analyses that are broadly defined like this, it is likely that natural infrastructure will play only a small role, as many of the steps needed to achieve resilience will involve the creation of grey infrastructure or changes in its management. Moreover, the kinds of ecosystem services that will be relevant to increasing resilience vary from shock to shock. It is helpful in this case to craft specific problem definitions for each type of shock considered. For instance, when considering flooding, the relevant problem might be how changes in infrastructure, whether natural or grey, could decrease a city's resilience in the face of flooding.

Climate Change Analysis

Many cities are also explicitly planning for a changed climate. One useful guide is the World Bank's Climate Resilient Cities primer (Prasad et al. 2009). It focuses on disaster risk management (DRM). There are four major consequences of climate change that cities are urged to consider: sea-level rise, temperature changes, precipitation changes, and extreme events like large storms. The primer then gives a systematic way to rapidly assess the impact to a set of important sectors in cities, and then identify some mitigation or adaptation actions. The general planning process is to select a Climate Change Team that will then hold a series of workshops with experts and stakeholders. Information from the meeting will be used to fill out a City Typology and Risk Characterization matrix, which collects quantitative indicators in six sequentially completed spreadsheets: city description, governance and management, built environment, political and economic impacts, natural hazards, and climate change impacts.

As with resiliency analyses, it may be helpful to break down the broad climate change analysis into a set of specific problem definitions. For instance, for temperature, the relevant question may be, What infrastructure, grey or natural, could help minimize risks to our population from increased summer temperatures? For precipitation, the relevant question may be, What infrastructure, grey or natural, could help minimize the risks from flooding due to increased stormwater? Notice that each of these different, relevant questions implies different key ecosystem services (stage 2).

How to Take Inventory of What Services Matter

This section of the chapter is focused on the second phase of the conceptual framework, taking inventory of what ecosystem services matter in a particular city. Note that this can only be done after adequately defining the problem that natural infrastructure is to solve (stage 1).

There are many different ways of deciding which ecosystem services matter. Sometimes, if the problem definition is narrow, the answer may seem intuitive and obvious. In other cases, such as sustainability planning where the goal is to create new parks that maximally improve the lives of residents, there is a broad list of potentially important ecosystem services.

The TEEB Manual for Cities (TEEB 2011) provides one way to filter this list down ("take inventory"), essentially presenting municipal staff and key stakeholders with a list of ecosystem services and questions that can elucidate whether they are important in a particular city. In what follows, I present a modified way to take inventory of what ecosystem services matter, based on a one-day *critical ecosystem services identification* workshop. Such identification workshops are also relatively inexpensive to host, and their short duration means the time commitment is not prohibitive for workshop participants.

This approach is necessarily subjective. The outcome of the identification workshop will reflect merely the opinions of those in the room about which ecosystem services matter in their city. However, opinions from local stakeholders and experts are usually good enough in this first stage of identifying important ecosystem services. The latter stages of the framework, requiring detailed quantification and valuation of particular ecosystem services, are not well suited to a workshop and instead require a small dedicated team working over a period of time. It is in these latter stages that detailed economic analyses of the value of different ecosystem services are conducted. Since these sorts of detailed analyses entail a significant amount of resources, both in terms of time and money, one of the goals of the identification workshop is to focus the analytical effort on ecosystem services that matter in a city. Similarly, the identification workshop helps ensure that no important ecosystem services are forgotten and ignored in later analyses.

The identification workshop is best structured as a series of group discussions about specific topics and is similar to structured brainstorming or horizon scanning exercises. Good workshops will follow the best practices identified by the literature on effective brainstorming. One key best practice is the separation in time between identification of ideas and the evaluation of their utility (Rawlinson 2005). During the identification workshop, it is important to keep the focus on which ecosystem services are most important, and to whom, (identification) and avoid extensive discussions of the practical difficulties the city will face in protecting those ecosystem services (evaluation).

Scope

Before the workshop begins, organizers need to define the spatial area that workshop participants should have in mind when they consider what ecosystem services matter to the city. Often the spatial area will be defined by the planning process in which the city encountered the concept of natural infrastructure. The planning process may be focused on the municipality or other political jurisdiction. In one sense, this is a useful definition of the spatial area, since it means the results of the workshop will be directly relevant to the planning process. Moreover, the results will be directly relevant to the political entity with the power to implement any plan developed.

However, there are a few problems with using municipal boundaries or other political jurisdictions as the spatial scope of the identification workshop. Many ecosystem services are supplied from critical natural areas that lie outside the municipal boundaries.

This is particularly problematic for more transportable ecosystem services, where the distance between supply and demand of the service can be quite large. Watershed boundaries, for instance, do not generally follow municipal ones, yet downstream cities are often dependent on upstream areas for a suite of ecosystem services related to water. For this reason, it is often useful to consider during the workshop a slightly larger area than the municipality in question. This enables workshop participants to think about these adjacent, perhaps important, natural areas during the workshop.

Another important issue to define ahead of the workshop is the temporal scope over which to consider ecosystem services. Because ecosystem services are often public or common goods that don't have value in the marketplace, they are often invisible in people's day-to-day lives. For instance, many people would have difficultly answering this question: "How dependent are you on natural habitat for clean drinking water?" It is often easier to answer the question when it is phrased as something like, "Looking ahead a decade, if forests continue to be lost, will the quality of your drinking water be affected?" The workshop moderator needs to make the questions about ecosystem services connect with workshop participants' well-being and to trends they may observe in their lifetime.

Assembling the Team

A diverse set of skills and perspectives are important for the identification workshop. While *ecosystem services* is a wonky term primarily of appeal to ecologists, many different stakeholders may have strong opinion about how nature makes their life in the city better. Urban planners, community leaders, and environmental activists can all play important roles in evaluating which ecosystem services are important in their city.

It is also important that the participants be deeply knowledgeable about the city they are evaluating. Local knowledge is key to identifying which ecosystem services matter in the unique context of a particular city. There is often a temptation by urban planners and municipal staff to skip the identification workshop and move on to stages two through six of the framework, based on the assumption that they know what ecosystem services matter. This temptation should be resisted, since the workshop often brings up other important ecosystem services that were not even contemplated by municipal staff. Local stakeholders and residents are particularly good at identifying relatively intangible benefits from nature, like spiritual or aesthetic values that municipal staff may miss.

Identification Workshop Structure

Once the identification workshop starts, workshop organizers should present to the participants the goals of the workshop, essentially identifying a short list of ecosystem services that are key for solving the problem or issue defined in stage 1, as well as some related information (table 2.1). So, for a climate change resiliency analysis, the goal is to define a short list of key ecosystem services that, if maintained or enhanced, can increase a city's resilience to climate change. Participants should have time for a discussion about the goals of the workshop. It is sometimes helpful to ask participants if there is any way they would prefer to restate or alter the main goals of the workshop, since sometimes the way organizers frame these goals may seem to be confusing or offensive to some workshop participants (Rawlinson 2005).

In the next section of the workshop, participants will work through an initial long list of ecosystem services, identifying those that are most important in their city. It is helpful to start with such a list, rather than simply asking participants to start naming ecosystem services, as many workshop participants will not be familiar with the concept of an ecosystem service. However, let participants know that they can bring up for group discussion any ecosystem services that are not on the initial list. One potential list is shown in

Table 2.1. Key information to be collected during the important
ecosystem services identification workshop

Type of information	Notes
Relevant to problem definition	Does the ecosystem service seem likely to help in answering the key problem or issue?
Number of people	How many people in the city rely on the service?
	Categories: None/Not Applicable, Few, Majority of city, Everybody
Beneficiaries	What specific neighborhoods or groups of people rely most on this service?
	(Open format: Record answers as participants give them.)
Importance	For those relying on the service, how important is it to their lives?
	Categories: Infrequently important, Somewhat important, Very important
Critical places	What places are crucial for the provision of this service?
	(Open format: Record answers as participants give them.)
Threats	Which threats are most likely to degrade ecosystem service provision over time?
	Categories: See table 3.2 for a suggested list of threats.

table 2.1. Other similar tools exist that can be studied by workshop organizers for inspiration, such as the World Resources Institute (WRI) Corporate Ecosystem Services Review (CESR). The CESR helps companies identify which ecosystem services are essential for business operations and develop strategies to maintain or enhance provision of these ecosystem services, in a framework roughly analogous to that presented here for cities (Hanson et al. 2012).

While you have participants assembled for the workshop, it is useful to ask them which natural areas or features are important for the provision of an ecosystem service currently. This is an easy follow-up to the discussion of the importance of a particular ecosystem service, and in essence asks participants to list examples of particular places where an ecosystem service is provided and who benefits from it. Such a discussion will of course not identify all of the critical natural areas for provision of a particular service, but instead it will generate a somewhat idiosyncratic list of exemplar critical natural areas that will be useful in latter stages of the analysis.

There are different techniques for recording spatial information about the critical habitat patches for a particular ecosystem service. Participants can simply list the types of natural habitat (e.g., "forests") that seem important for ecosystem service provision. They can list specific place names (e.g., "Central Park") that are critical natural areas. Alternatively, a large format map of the city could be displayed, either on paper or electronically, and then participants can circle places that seem important.

Another thing worth doing while you have participants assembled for the identification workshop is asking what threats seem likely to negatively impact ecosystem service provision. Participants should be asked to define what threats, if current trends continue, will reduce ecosystem service provision. The goal is to create a list of threats that will be important in the next few decades. At this stage, the threats do not need to be evaluated to quantify their negative impacts or to plan solutions to them. That sort of evaluation will come later and is actually something to avoid during the identification workshop.

There are several effective ways to query participants about potential threats, but one way is to have a list of potential threats available for participants to refer to. Commonly encountered threats to ecosystem service provision are shown in table 2.2. It is usually most efficient for participants to consider threats to each ecosystem service just after they list the crucial natural areas supplying that service. Participants should draw inspiration from the list, but should not be limited to it. Sometimes workshop participants can identify novel threats to ecosystem services that were not even contemplated by the core team that organized the workshop.

Table 2.2. Common threats to ecosystem service provision in an urban context

Type of threat	Examples
Residential and commercial development	Urban areas, suburbs, factories, shopping centers
Transportation and service corridor development	Roads, utility and service lines, shipping lanes
Logging and wood harvesting	Timber harvesting, forest thinning for other management reasons
Human intrusion and disturbance	Overuse for recreation that degrades provision of other ecosystem services
Fire and fire suppression	Inappropriate fire management that alters natural fire regimes
Dams and water management/use	Dam construction, surface water diversion, channelization
Invasive and other problematic species	Invasive nonnative species introduction, overabundant native species such as deer
Pollution	Household sewage and wastewater, other waterborne pollutants, garbage and solid waste, airborne pollutants
Climate change and severe weather	Habitat shifting and alteration, droughts, heat waves, storms and flooding

Source: Adapted from the list of threats to biodiversity developed by the Conservation Measures Partnership and the International Union for Conservation of Nature (Salafsky et al. 2008).

Evaluation

At some point, perhaps several weeks or months after the identification workshop, it is time to begin the process of evaluating the ideas generated. Usually, there is a subset of ecosystem services identified that seemed clearly important to everyone at that workshop (the "keepers"). There is another subset of ecosystem services identified that, upon reflection, seem a little trivial or silly (the "discards"). Much of the challenge of evaluation is to decide what to do with ideas that are in between the keepers and the discards, which identify an ecosystem service that is only somewhat important. Similarly, the list of critical places or the list of threats to ecosystem service provision will also sort into these three camps.

The overall goal of the evaluation stage is to get to a short list of which ecosystem services should be the focus of conservation actions by the municipality or its allies. Cities have finite budgets, and people have a finite amount of time and energy to work on conservation in the city. The people conducting the evaluation, usually the core team who organized the identification workshop, have enormous power, since they are implicitly or explicitly making decisions about what projects the city will work on. Thus, those doing the evaluation should be people invested in implementing ecosystem service conservation projects in the city.

The evaluation process is difficult to standardize and necessarily involves subjective decisions. Nevertheless, the evaluators should have some working criteria by which they evaluate the ideas. Foremost among them is whether the ecosystem service seems essential to solving the problem or issue identified in stage 1. Some other generic criteria are also worth considering, to decide whether an ecosystem service is worthy of further study (table 2.3).

What to Do After You Take Inventory

After the identification workshop, the city will have a short list of important ecosystem services that they should act to maintain or enhance, partially answering the problems or issues identified in stage 1. They will also have a rough list of important natural areas for the provision of those services and the major threats to those services. Now what? How should a city go about moving through stages 3 to 6 of the conceptual framework? The rest of the chapters of this book look at each ecosystem service in detail, and discuss the remaining stages of the conceptual framework in the context of that particular ecosystem service.

There are now often detailed models that quantify the provision of ecosystem services, given a map of natural features and a set of possible beneficiaries (stage 3). These models can be used to define what natural infrastructure is currently providing key services. They

Table 2.3. Criteria used to evaluate the results of the identification workshop and prioritize ecosystem services for action

Criteria

Ecosystem service seems essential to addressing the key problem or issue identified.

Many people in the city benefit from the ecosystem service.

The ecosystem service is very important for at least some people in the city.

There is a significant threat to ecosystem service provision without conservation action.

Conservation action to mitigate these threats seems likely to succeed, politically and financially.

Work on this ecosystem service fits into the broader sustainability goals of the city.

Work on this ecosystem service will fit into ongoing policy or planning processes by the city.

were developed by a variety of disciplines, some of which might not even be aware of the concept of ecosystem services. There are also models that value the provision of ecosystem services in economic terms, although they can have input data requirements. There is a trade-off between model realism and model ease of use. Full ecosystem service modeling and valuation takes staff time and costs money, and they may not be fully needed in many cases. There are some simplified models of ecosystem service provision that can still inform an urban planning process.

The next stage, identifying options for action (stage 4), is more of an art than a science. Finding the best opportunity requires creativity, as well as input from leadership in the municipality. I highlight case studies in each chapter of how a particular city or institution has chosen to protect or restore an ecosystem service, in the hope that it will inspire similar creative decision making by others.

The business planning and implementation phase similarly involves a lot of art (stage 5). It is in many ways the most difficult stage, since it involves finding a creative way to correct market failure. If such a correction were easy to implement, it would have been achieved a while ago, and the market failures that remain are often difficult and intractable to work on. In the case study in each chapter, I present some of the details of how a city or organization has successfully implemented their conservation projects, which will hopefully serve as a guide for other institutions considering similar projects. Finally, I end each chapter by commenting on the methodology for monitoring (stage 6), which varies among ecosystem services.

Chapter 3

Drinking Water Protection

THE *PÁRAMO CAN SEEM LIKE* a world unto itself. These high altitude grasslands sometimes feel remote, separated from the world below. Andean condors, one of more than 700 bird species that live in the páramo, swoop around looking for food. An outside observer could imagine that the grasslands look much as they did centuries ago.

Yet at least one patch of páramo is now intimately intertwined with the fate of Quito, Ecuador, far down the mountain. Quito, a midsized city with a population of 1.7 million people (UNPD 2011), is the second largest city in Ecuador. It draws its drinking water from rivers and reservoirs that have their headwaters up in the páramo. The water moves through a series of canals down to a set of water treatment plants and to the city. The water that flows off the slopes of the páramo has always been relatively pure, reducing the need for treatment at the city's plants.

Starting in the late 1990s, the city began to realize they had a problem. Unsustainable agriculture and grazing practices had begun to degrade the páramo, leaving exposed soil and degraded grasslands. In the massive rainstorms of the region, this soil quickly eroded, washing sediment downstream. On degraded grassland, less water would infiltrate into the soil, instead rapidly moving down the surface. Quito began to worry both about the quality and quantity of its water supply.

In similar situations, many cities choose to expand their treatment plants' ability to remove sediment and other pollutants. More expensive systems for sedimentation and filtration can now clean even fairly dirty "raw water" to acceptable drinking water standards. To deal with a shortage of water, Quito could develop new surface sources, or build dams to store a greater quantity of water. In a real sense, this grey infrastructure is replacing an ecosystem service (e.g., soil stabilization and flow regulation) that used to be provided by natural ecosystems. The problem is that such grey infrastructure solutions do not come cheap.

Quito, however, chose to do something different. They decided to invest in protecting and restoring the páramo. The idea was that this conservation could limit erosion and help maintain raw water quality and quantity. Less sedimentation should reduce the day-to-day operation and maintenance costs of the plant, and hopefully slow the movement of water downhill. "The concept was easy to understand," said Sylvia Benitez, one of The Nature Conservancy staff associated with Quito's source watershed protection program. "When you explain to people, our water comes from high mountains, this is where Quito gets its water, so if we don't protect it, we will have problems—people get it. It's maybe when you get into the details with engineers and scientists it gets hard."

The Quito water utility now puts about 2 percent of their income into an endowment, which is now close to $10 million. The endowment (also known as a water fund) has an independent board made up of large water users and other stakeholders that choose what conservation projects will be funded. The board of course considers the effect that conservation actions will have on raw water quality. But the water fund also has other, secondary goals, including social goals such as providing livelihoods to rural communities. Choosing projects is thus not just about science but a political decision, balancing the needs of different stakeholders.

Cities around the world often turn to conservation to maintain or enhance raw water quality. As we shall see, investments in natural infrastructure can be cost-competitive with grey infrastructure, and provide a host of cobenefits. Source watershed protection is by no means a new strategy for cities. For centuries, cities have tried to protect the source of their water from pollution, and in the late nineteenth and early twentieth centuries many cities like Boston moved to protect significant fractions of their source watershed (Melosi 2008). What is new today is an increased analytical ability to quantify the value that nature provides and choose which conservation strategies will deliver the highest return on investment (ROI).

Source watershed protection is often presented as a simple story of grey versus natural infrastructure. The reality is a bit more complicated. Urban water systems produce clean drinking water, using a combination of ecosystem services and human technology, which jointly produce finished drinking water of an acceptable water quality. When designing an urban water system or considering a major system upgrade, there is indeed a trade-off between ecosystem services and human technology. But once an urban water system is in place, maintaining the flow of ecosystem services becomes crucial for maintaining system functioning. And the presence of an urban water intake thus gives substantial value to the ecosystem functions coming from a natural habitat like the páramo. The existence of the grey infrastructure thus gives value to nature.

This chapter is about how a city in a situation like Quito can figure out the hard details that engineers and scientists need to know. The chapter presumes a city or other institution has gone through an identification workshop and has identified ecosystem services for raw water quality as an important service for the city. This chapter tries to present a how-to guide for the next steps in the conceptual framework laid out in chapter 2. Entire books have been written about source watershed protection (e.g., Alcott, Ashton, and Gentry 2013), and one chapter cannot hope to cover all that material. Instead, this chapter serves as a primer on the major steps a city must go through, pointing toward more detailed technical sources along the way.

Mapping Important Services for Raw Water Quality

After cities have decided that they are crucially dependent on ecosystem services for drinking water, the next step is to map which patches of natural habitat provide this service. A city's dependence on ecosystem services of course depends on where it gets its water: surface, groundwater, or some mix? Conservation actions are much more likely to help improve the raw water quality at surface water sources than for groundwater, although there are some exceptional circumstances in which conservation can help groundwater (see below). Water sources with relatively small upstream areas are, all else being equal, easier to do conservation in than larger basins, simply because it is more costly to implement conservation actions over a larger area. Particularly challenging are basins that cross political jurisdictions, since the legal basis for conservation may not be the same in each jurisdiction. The ideal situation is when one landowner or institution controls land use over a large portion of the basin. Such considerations about basin size and shape may determine whether a natural infrastructure approach is even feasible (McDonald and Shemie 2014).

Source drinking water protection is actually related to multiple ecosystem services (table 3.1). Generally, source water protection is more effective at maintaining raw water quality rather than

Table 3.1. Ecosystem services for urban drinking water provision and where they occur

Ecosystem service	Description	Places
Sediment regulation	Vegetation reduces the rate of erosion.	Areas at risk of erosion: high slopes, highly erodible soils.
Natural water filtration	Vegetation removes pollution, especially excess N and P.	Areas that water moves through: wetlands, riparian areas.
Water yield	Vegetation controls evapotranspiration and water yield (runoff).	Areas with a large difference in evapotranspiration between natural land cover and anthropogenic land uses.
Water retention	Vegetation increases soil infiltration, decreases peak flows and increases base flows.	Areas that water moves through: wetlands, riparian areas.
Increased infiltration to groundwater	Vegetation increases soil infiltration, increases groundwater recharge.	For a confined aquifer, recharge areas. For an unconfined aquifer, areas that water moves through: wetlands, riparian areas.

quantity. Foremost in importance to water managers is preventing contamination by fecal bacteria, which can lead to disease or other serious toxins.

There are now a large number of models that quantify ecosystem service benefits of relevance to urban drinking water supplies. Many of them weren't developed with ecosystem services per se in mind but instead aim to quantify pollution and other factors impacting water quality that are nevertheless mitigated by natural habitat. Despite this diversity of models, many of them are structured in a similar fashion. The important thing is choosing a model that is appropriate for the purposes of the analyses, given the precision required in the quantification of ecosystem service benefits, the quality of available input datasets, and the time and resources the city has available for the analysis (table 3.2).

Table 3.2. Inputs and outputs for ecosystem services models useful for evaluating source watershed conservation activities

	SWAT	VIC	SPARROW	InVEST
Key data inputs				
Precipitation	Daily	Hourly	Yes	Mean annual
Topography	Yes	Yes	Yes	Yes
Land cover	Yes	Yes	Yes	Yes
Soil type	Multilayer	Multilayer	Varies	Single layer
Snow water equivalent	Yes	Yes	Varies	No
Key outputs				
Water yield	Daily	Hourly	Varies (input)	Annual
Evapotranspiration	Daily	Hourly	Varies (input)	Annual
Flows	Daily	w/ routing model	No	No
Sediment retained	Yes	No	Yes	Yes
Nutrient retained	Yes	No	Yes	Yes

Source: Adapted from Vigerstol and Aukema (2011).

Note: SPARROW is a statistical model of contaminant concentrations (weight of contaminant/flow volume) based on empirical measurements at stream gauges, rather than a hydrologic model. However, it is often linked with hydrologic models that estimate river flows.

Sediment Regulation

Another important goal of water managers is to prevent excess sediment from moving off the watershed into the source water body. Increased sediment in raw water increases the amount of time water must be in detention basins and the amount of coagulant that must be added, both of which increase operations and maintenance costs for the utility. Increased sediment also increases the frequency of dredging of detention basins or reservoirs. Above a certain threshold, sediment can cause problems for many filtration and disinfection systems, which is one of the principal reasons most water treatment plants remove sediment prior to these steps (Edzwald and Tobiason 2011). For all these reasons, water utilities have a strong interest in erosion control. This can be achieved through maintaining or restoring natural habitat (Gartner et al. 2013), or through changes in agricultural practices (McDonald and Shemie 2014). For our purpose, soil erosion from rainfall can be divided into two categories (cf. White 2005). Sheet erosion occurs when water on a slope facet falls and begins to move soil particles. Rill and gully erosion occurs when flowing water forms a channel, the banks of which are subject to erosion. Rill and gully erosion can often be minimized by bank stabilization with vegetation. The costs of such bank stabilization and its benefits in terms of avoided sediment are often calculated using simple models, with restoration of a given linear unit of stream channel having a certain cost and benefit per unit length. A good source for methods of bank restoration is the guidance document by the United States Forest Service (Eubanks and Meadows 2002).

Sheet erosion is often modeled using the universal soil loss equation, developed in the 1930s in the United States based upon empirical measurements of erosion rates (Wischmeier and Smith 1978). Average annual soil loss (A) is modeled as the product of five factors:

$$A = RKLsCP$$

R is the rainfall erosivity factor, which describes how hard it rains, how much force the rain exerts on the soil surface. Areas with more intense precipitation have higher R factors, and hence more erosion. K is the soil erodibility factor, which is a function of soil texture and other characteristics. Areas with easily erodible soils (e.g., soils with a high silt content) have higher R factors, and hence more erosion. Ls is a function of slope and the length of the slope facet, and can be calculated from a digital elevation model. Steep slopes that continue over a long distance have higher Ls factors, and hence more erosion. C describes different cropping practices, including the type of crop grown. Some crops have a higher C factor than others, and hence more erosion. Finally, P describes different soil conservation management practices that reduce erosion (e.g., contour tillage, terracing, buffer strips). Farms implementing these practices have a lower P factor, and hence less erosion. In general, source watershed conservation activities aimed at erosion reduction try to alter C and P to reduce erosion. Natural land cover, for instance, has low values of C and P, so any protection or restoration of natural land cover will reduce C and P relative to a base case of no conservation action.

There are several models that try to provide useful implementations of the universal soil loss equation or related equations (table 3.2). The InVEST (Integrated Valuation of Ecosystem Services Tool) Sediment Retention model takes relatively simple input data and calculates sediment transport and the amount that vegetation helps reduce erosion. In principle, it can be run anywhere in the world and is appropriate where input data are limited and/or a more sophisticated, time-intensive analysis is not desirable (Tallis et al. 2013). In the United States, the SPARROW (SPAtially Referenced Regressions On Watershed attributes) model is often used. The SPARROW model uses empirical regression equations of sediment transport and is most appropriate when a detailed analysis, backed by empirical data, is needed by decision makers (Preston, Alexander, and Wolock 2011). One of the most detailed models available for estimating sediment transport is the SWAT (Soil and Water Assessment Tool) model (Waidler et al. 2009). The process of parameterizing a SWAT model can be complex, but some water managers have found the investment worthwhile to enable detailed management decisions.

Natural Water Filtration

Another common goal of urban water managers is reducing nonpoint source pollution into urban water sources. For some—but not all—pollutants, natural habitat can play a role in filtering out a fraction of the dissolved pollutants that pass through the habitat. This filtration ecosystem service is particularly important for the removal of nitrogen (N) and phosphorus (P). N and P are often run-off from agricultural practices such as fertilizer application or animal waste management. Increased concentrations of N and P can directly increase water treatment costs if they reach high concentration. Nitrate (NO_3-) is particularly problematic, since at high concentrations it can lead to human health risks. Excess N and P also increase algae growth, which increases turbidity and causes a host of problems during filtering and disinfection for water treatment plant managers (Edzwald and Tobiason 2011; Kawamura 1991).

Vegetation can retain nutrients like N and P in two ways. First, plants directly uptake some of the nutrients and incorporate them into their cells. Second, the structure of natural habitats, particularly wetlands, tends to slow the movement of water and allow time for chemical reactions to occur. For instance, a fraction of excess N fertilizer that runs off fields is ultimately denitrified, returning to the atmosphere as nitrogen gas (N_2). Phosphorus, on the other hand, does not have a significant atmospheric flux, so a greater fraction of excess P fertilizer tends to flow into surface water bodies.

Most models of N and P transport use the concept of export co-efficients (Reckhow, Beaulac, and Simpson 1980), which is simply the amount of a pollutant exported from a particular unit area in a particular period of time. Average export coefficients vary by land-use type. A forest might export on average 1.8 kg N/ha/yr, while a corn field might export on average 11.1 kgN/ha/yr. Then, as excess N and P flow downhill, intervening patches of natural vegetation have filtration rates that reduce nutrient fluxes by a certain amount. However, most natural vegetation has a limit to how much nutrients can be retained. Beyond this threshold, there is little reduction in nutrient concentration.

As with sedimentation, there are a plethora of different models used to track the movement and accumulation of N and P (table 3.2). The InVEST Water Purification model provides a relatively simple model that can be parameterized anywhere in the world. SWAT is the most sophisticated model, but also the most difficult to parameterize. In the United States, the SPARROW model is frequently used, particularly by the US Environmental Protection Agency (EPA). For instance, the EPA uses the SPARROW model to calculate how changes in nutrient loading in upstream tributaries will ultimately affect the Chesapeake Bay, a water body that suffers from algal blooms due to excess N and P.

Water Yield and Water Retention

Water managers are also sometimes interested in how natural habitat can increase water yield. Water yield is defined as the volume of water per unit area that remains after a fraction of precipitation is returned to the atmosphere via actual evapotranspiration (AET): transpiration, water lost by plants, plus evaporation. Water yield is thus:

$$Y = P - AET$$

AET is affected by numerous factors, including solar radiation, temperature, wind speed, and relative humidity. Since it is time consuming and expensive to measure AET directly, evapotranspiration is commonly estimated using information on potential evapotranspiration (PET), the amount that would evapotranspire if water was not limiting, and the available moisture at a site. At a wet site, AET is very close to PET, but AET cannot exceed available site moisture. There are many equations available for estimating PET, which vary from the simple (Hargreaves) to the complex (Penman-Monteith).

Note that relative to bare ground, natural vegetation typically has a higher PET and thus lower water yield. However, relative to agriculture or nonnative vegetation, natural vegetation may have a lower PET and hence higher water yield. Thus conversion of natural vegetation to other land uses may raise or lower water yield, depending on what the other land use is. Similarly, restoration of natural vegetation in a watershed can either decrease or increase water yield, depending on what land cover that vegetation replaces.

Natural vegetation also commonly alters the timing of flows, helping retain water on the landscape for longer. A fraction of water yield infiltrates into the soil and the remainder moves as overland flow. Natural vegetation tends to allow a greater fraction of rainfall to infiltrate than does bare soil, and thus less water moves as overland flow. This slows down the movement of water on the landscape, reducing peak flows that occur in rivers after a rain event. Of the fraction of water that infiltrates, some water stops in the vadose zone, the unsaturated zone where air is present in pore spaces, and some infiltrates farther down to the saturated zone, where all pore spaces are filled with water. Water in both zones can move laterally, gradually filling up rivers downstream. Thus, natural habitat helps increase the "baseflow" of a river, its flow between rain events.

Many hydrologic models calculate water yield at various time steps, and can be used to evaluate how conservation or restoration of natural restoration can change water quantity (table 3.2). InVEST models are again the simplest to parameterize, but they work at an annual time step and thus do not shed light on changes in timing of water flows before or after a conservation action. The SWAT model can work at a daily time step, and is well suited to studying changes in flow timing. Another model—the Variable Infiltration Capacity (VIC) model—can even work on an hourly time step. Another interesting model is the FIESTA (Fog Interception for the Enhancement of Streamflow in Tropical Areas) model, which focuses on a phenomenon that occurs in only a few places but can be extremely important where it occurs: vegetation increasing precipitation rates by increasing capture of fog.

Increased Infiltration and Maintaining Water Quality for Groundwater

As mentioned, natural infrastructure projects to enhance groundwater quality or quantity are less common than projects that focus on surface water sources. A natural infrastructure strategy is generally considered only when the aquifer has a short mean residence time, so that the water entering the aquifer today will fairly quickly have an impact on the overall characteristics of the aquifer's water. Natural infrastructure projects are also more likely to be considered for a confined aquifer, or just a very small aquifer, which is recharged from a relatively small spatial area that could become the locus of conservation efforts. Determining recharge zones for aquifers is challenging and requires three-dimensional knowledge of the shape of aquifer and surrounding soil layers (Fitts 2012). Models are commonly run by engineering firms specializing in groundwater. Conceptually, conservation interventions for groundwater are similar to those for surface water. Natural vegetation filters out nutrient and other pollutants and prevents them from reaching the aquifer. It can also increase infiltration and, if some of the water makes it down to the saturated zone, thus increase aquifer recharge.

Common Threats and Common Solutions

Once cities have identified which pieces of natural infrastructure supply ecosystem services that help maintain drinking water quality or quantity, they need to identify threats that could reduce provision of those services in the future. For instance, one common threat is land-use change, particularly conversion of natural habitat to anthropogenic land uses. Such a land-use conversion will decrease provision of essentially all the ecosystem services that help ensure raw water quality and quantity. This threat is often analyzed by having land-use change scenarios that describe how land cover in a watershed is likely to change with and without conservation intervention. Another common threat to raw water quality is the creation of point sources of pollution in a watershed. Again, scenarios can help evaluate whether ecosystem services help mitigate this new source of pollution, or if other actions might be needed.

After potential threats are identified, cities have to identify which strategies will help them continue to cost effectively deliver finished water of acceptable quality to their customers (table 3.3). There is a large literature on source watershed protection, and cities researching potential strategies should consult this literature for ideas (Edzwald and Tobiason 2011; McDonald and Shemie 2014). The US Environmental Protection Agency designates source watershed protection and conservation as part of a multibarrier approach to water quality and provides guidance on how utilities should develop source watershed protection plans (EPA 2002). Another useful report is Protecting the Source (TPL 2004). One software program developed by the Natural Capital Project, RIOS (Resource Investment Optimization System), is designed to help users evaluate potential strategies for watershed conservation, with a special focus on Latin American watersheds.

Table 3.3. Common strategies for source water protection and their likely positive or negative effects on ecosystem services that benefit urban drinking water

Threat	Sediment regulation	Natural water filtration	Water yield	Water retention	Increased infiltration to groundwater
Habitat protection	+	+	+/−	+	+
Revegetation					
High slope areas	+				
Riparian areas		+	+/−	+	+
Ranching protection					
Prevent overgrazing	+			+	
Riparian area fencing		+	+/−	+	+
Cropping practices					
Soil conservation	+			+	
Fertilizer management		Benefits raw water quality			

Note: Effects are compared with the results of no conservation action taken and continued urban and agricultural development. Only the main intended effects are listed. For instance, revegetation on high slope areas is a targeted way to reduce erosion and is usually done primarily to increase sediment regulation.

Perhaps the most common strategy used by utilities is land protection, either fee-simple or easement. A global survey of the water sources of major cities and the land cover in upstream contributing areas found that more than 60 percent have some degree of land protection (McDonald and Shemie 2014). Protection prevents land cover change, and hence prevents degradation of ecosystem service provision and raw water quality. It also keeps incompatible land use from occurring in sensitive areas in the source watershed, such as by preventing point sources of pollution like septic tanks from being located in these areas (Edzwald and Tobiason 2011). Land protection in urban source watersheds is thus often motivated by the people it keeps out rather than the nature it keeps in, and in this sense is often not motivated by ecosystem services per se. Nevertheless, the natural habitat that usually exists in protected areas also supplies ecosystem services that further ensure raw water quality. In cases where ecosystem service provision has been degraded, a water utility might opt for site restoration. This usually involves the revegetation of problematic areas in the watershed (table 3.2). Generally, it is wise to prioritize problematic areas with low ecosystem service provisions, like high slope areas with bare soil (if erosion is a problem) or riparian buffers (if an increase in natural filtration capacity is desired). As a strategy, restoration is generally more expensive than simply protecting areas of remnant natural habitat. Significant questions have to be answered by land managers: What should we plant during restoration, and who will pay to maintain the site over time?

Another common strategy for source water protection is paying or otherwise motivating ranchers to change their practices. A common tactic is to avoid grassland degradation, often caused by overgrazing. Healthier grasslands have lower levels of erosion than areas of exposed soil, potentially reducing the sediment that reaches the urban water source. Another common tactic is fencing that keeps livestock, particularly cattle, out of riparian areas. This helps prevent bank erosion, and keeps fecal matter from livestock from reaching the stream.

Similarly, changing agricultural practices is another common way that water utilities try to maintain raw water quality. Depending on the particular raw water quality problems facing a utility, different agricultural practices may be advocated. For instance, where erosion is a problem, getting producers to switch from till to no-till agriculture may help reduce sediment transport. For watersheds where excess N and P are a raw water quality problem, fertilizer management may be advocated. Fertilizer management essentially involves changing the amount, timing, and manner of application of fertilizer to allow suitable uptake in the crop but minimize nutrient pollution in the surrounding landscape. While these changes in agriculture practice do not necessarily utilize ecosystem services for their effectiveness, they are part of what has traditionally been called natural resource conservation.

Valuation of Source Water Protection

After identifying potential strategies that can maintain or enhance source water quality and quantity, cities want to evaluate the costs and benefits of implementing each strategy. They will then usually choose the solution with the highest return on investment (ROI). More accurately they end up choosing a suite of strategies, some green and some grey, that collectively have a high ROI. In an earlier section, we discussed the methods for quantifying and mapping in physical units the benefits that nature supplies to source water bodies. This section talks about how you value those benefits in economic terms.

Whether measured in physical or economic terms, the benefits of conservation action must be measured against a reasonable baseline scenario, where there is no conservation action taken but where other major temporal trends occurring in the watershed continue as expected. For instance, the ROI of protecting a particular parcel of land should be compared to a baseline development scenario, in which current trends are extrapolated over time. Then, the effect of these two land-use change scenarios (the conservation action and baseline scenario) on some parameter of the environment, such as erosion, can be estimated using hydrologic models.

One important question to consider before a valuation calculation begins is, value to whom? Often the main focus of the analysis is on the value to the water utility's bottom line. But if there are other important stakeholders in the watershed, then the ecosystem services provided to them can also be important. In the Quito water fund, for instance, there are multiple goals for conservation, and so a broad set of stakeholders is involved in decisions on what to implement. While achieving raw water quality goals are important, so are other improvements in the lives of rural dwellers.

Even when the scope for a valuation analysis is narrowly focused on a water utility, it can be difficult to quantify exactly how changes in ecosystem service provision affect costs. There is clear evidence from many studies that decreases in raw water quality increase operations and maintenance costs for a water treatment plant, but the amount of the increase depends on which pollutant is problematic and what technology is in use at the treatment plant. For instance, increased sediment in new water increases the time it must be in detention basins before the sediment settles out and increases the amount of coagulant that must be added to water. Increased sediment also increases the frequency of dredging of reservoirs and basins. Increased concentrations of N and P also increase operations and maintenance costs, particularly during filtration.

One often quoted study of thirty-five US water utilities found that a 10 percent increase in forest cover in a source watershed decreases treatment costs by 20 percent (Enrnst 2004). Note that forest cover here is a proxy measurement of the value of both ecosystem service provisions and the exclusion of sources of pollution from a watershed. However, research with data from a broader panel of water utilities suggests more modest effects, with a 10 percent reduction in sediment or nutrient associated with around a 5 percent reduction in water treatment costs (McDonald and Shemie 2014). Even with this more modest average effect, we found that one in three cities can make investments in source watershed conservation that have an ROI greater than 1, that is, the benefits to the utility outweigh the cost. Watershed size is key, with small source watersheds being much more likely to have an ROI greater than 1 than large source watersheds.

There are also important threshold effects in raw water quality. A given water treatment plant usually works only when raw water quality is in a certain range. If it decreases and falls outside this range, the water utility might need to install new, more expensive, water treatment technologies. For instance, increased sediment makes it difficult to conduct filtration and disinfection, and past a certain point, may begin to overwhelm a water treatment plant. Such excess sedimentation might necessitate a new system for sediment removal to salvage the existing plant, the construction of a new treatment plant, or the abandonment of a particular urban drinking water source.

New York City (NYC) is the now famous example of watershed conservation alleviating the need for construction of an expensive new water filtration plant. NYC had historically had relatively high water quality, so they have never had a filtration plant. Under the rules of the Safe Water Drinking Act (SWDA), passed in 1974 but significantly amended in 1986 and 1996, most United States utilities must filter their water unless they get a Filtration Avoidance Determination (FAD) from the EPA. The EPA had concerns that water quality in NYC's source watershed would continue to drop and required NYC to have a plan to maintain raw water quality to obtain a FAD. By getting a FAD, NYC avoided the need to build a filtration plant at an estimated cost of more $4 billion, which makes the hundreds of millions of dollars of conservation action the city committed to seem like a bargain (Alcott, Ashton, and Gentry 2013).

Note that for the purposes of valuation of conservation, the baseline scenario for NYC included the construction of a filtration plant to meet the requirements of SWDA, and it is only against this baseline that large investments in conservation make sense.

Estimating the costs of conservation actions sometimes gets less analytical attention than estimating ecosystem service benefits but is as important in calculating ROI. Costs are often estimated using average per-hectare cost values taken from a similar conservation project that had occurred somewhere else (e.g., costs of riparian buffer restoration per hectare). Care must be taken that these average per-hectare cost values are from sites that are similar ecologically and economically to the source watershed under analysis. It is also tricky to know the long-term maintenance costs of conservation actions. For instance, conservation easements are cheaper to establish than fee-simple land protection but require that money be set aside for legal enforcement of the easement in coming decades.

Often, the most cost-effective solution is a mix of green and grey infrastructure strategies. It can be a challenge to create these mixed solutions, since it requires conservation between engineers and conservation practitioners, often housed in different governmental agencies or companies. It also requires an understanding of the trade-offs between raw water quality and grey infrastructure. For instance, if the goal is to minimize a water utility's treatment costs, how much erosion control is optimal (none, a little, or a lot) depends very much on the water treatment technologies in use and the marginal effect of an increase in sediment on operating costs, which is sometimes unclear even to engineers who manage the plant.

To allow more rigorous evaluations of the economic value of a particular ecosystem service benefit, it is crucial to have information on the quantity of benefits generated over time. To see why this is important, suppose a land protection project requires a significant capital outlay now but will only significantly reduce deforestation in the watershed decades from now. Generally, decision makers choose among strategies by evaluating their ROI either over some finite time horizon (e.g., twenty years) or using net present value (NPV). NPV discounts future costs and benefits by a discount factor. The time horizon or discount factor chosen will make a big difference in the results of the valuation analysis, perhaps even changing the rank ordering of ROI from different strategies. Large discount factors mean the future matters less and will tend to favor strategies that minimize up-front costs and deliver benefits quickly (e.g., annual payments to farmers to implement agricultural practices that reduce erosion). Conversely, small discount factors mean large up-front investments are acceptable if they deliver a sufficiently large cumulative stream of benefits over time (e.g., fee-simple land protection that will prevent the slow accumulation of suburban development in a watershed).

Implementation

Finding funding for conservation activities that protect source drinking water is often fairly straightforward, at least relative to other urban conservation strategies. There is an entity, the water utility, which has a direct financial incentive to pay for ecosystem service provision. Projects to maintain or enhance ecosystem service provision are easiest when there are relatively few buyers and providers of the ecosystem service. While the former is often the case for source watersheds, the latter varies depending on the watershed. In some cases in the United States, for instance, the federal government owns a substantial portion of an urban area's source watershed, and thus there is a single landowner that can enter into negotiations with the city over source water protection activities. Conversely, in some watersheds there are hundreds of thousands of individual landowners, making implementation of a program to maintain or enhance raw water quality difficult.

Funding by water utilities is often only part of the financing for source watershed conservation. Because of the substantial cobenefits of a natural infrastructure approach, other institutions may also be motivated to finance some conservation activities. For instance, in Connecticut, water utilities traditionally owned and protected much of their source watershed. After passage of the Safe Drinking Water Act, which with rare exceptions requires water filtration by large water utilities, new treatment plants reduced the need for source watershed protection, and utilities began to sell off their land. Eventually the state of Connecticut and environmental NGOs moved in to purchase these remnant patches of natural habitat to maintain their biodiversity and recreational values (Alcott, Ashton, and Gentry 2013). If, in principle, financing source watershed conservation is simple, in reality there are myriad different models used by different cities. Some water utilities may take money from user fees to pay for conservation activities directly. However, sometimes a water utility does not have the expertise or resources to implement such a project. They can then transfer money to another agency to conduct the work. Alternatively, as in our Quito example, a new independent entity can be created to implement conservation work in a basin.

Particularly in the United States, cities sometimes borrow to finance source water protection activities. These bonds may be created as part of a broader bond package. Since these packages are often designed to achieve multiple goals for a municipality or other political jurisdiction, they often explicitly or implicitly factor in the other cobenefits to society of a natural infrastructure approach. For instance, San Antonio needed to protect areas of recharge to the Edwards Aquifer, the source of water both for San Antonio and for some federally endangered wetland species. By taking out $135 million in bonds, approved by ballot initiatives in 2000 and 2005, the city aims to protect raw water quality and provide recreational parkland.

Finally, some cities use legal requirements to influence land-use or agricultural practices. Where cities have this legal authority, it is a cheap and effective way to maintain raw water quality. Zoning rules, for instance, may keep development out of riparian areas. Governments may issue rules for new construction projects to limit erosion and stormwater from sites. These legal tools are, however, difficult to use when the source watershed extends beyond the municipality's jurisdiction.

Monitoring

Monitoring actions help ensure that conservation actions are increasing raw water quality as promised. During the design of monitoring protocols, focus should be paid to the stated goals of the conservation action. Often, these goals are not just water quality related, so there are a suite of outcomes to monitor. For instance, if cobenefits such as recreation and aesthetic values are promised, than ideally such outcomes would be monitored as well. A good first introduction to designing a source water protection monitoring plan can be found in *A Primer for Evaluating Monitoring Funds* (Higgins and Zimmerling 2013). The first data collected for monitoring is often simple implementation metrics collected in the field. Was the conservation practice implemented? How many acres in the watershed have been affected? How many dollars have been spent implementing the conservation practices? These simple metrics are cheap to obtain, and are essential for basic project evaluation. They can be supplemented by remote sensing imagery, which can provide an easy way to track changes in land cover over time.

What matters more to water utilities, of course, is changes to water quality itself. Stream-level measurement of water quality downstream of conservation actions can be used to show water quality benefits over time. The water quality at a particular point in a river is some integrated measure of everything going on upstream, both in areas impacted by conservation action and other, untreated areas. It can be difficult to detect the effect of conservation action in streams with large contributing areas. Moreover, there can be lag times between when a conservation action occurs and when benefits can be expected to be observed in a stream. For instance, in large streams N and P cycle in and out of sediments, so a reduction in fertilizer inputs may not reduce aqueous concentration of these nutrients for years or decades. There is also the challenge of when to collect water quality measurements to obtain all the information needed to monitor a program. For instance, often much sediment and pollutant transport occurs in a short interval of time after major rain events, so measuring during these periods is crucial.

Summary

In Quito and New York, investments in source watershed conservation continue. There are many other examples of cities that have invested in maintaining and enhancing water quality and quantity in their source watersheds. My own organization, The Nature Conservancy, works in more than twenty cities on such projects, from restoring the Atlantic Rainforests of Sao Paulo's watershed to protecting the aquifer recharge areas of San Antonio's groundwater source. It appears that there are many more cities that could make a profitable investment in source watershed conservation. Recent research suggests that one in four cities could get a positive return on investment from source watershed conservation, meaning the costs of conservation are more than outweighed by the benefits in terms of reduced treatment costs (McDonald and Shemie 2014). Moreover, the tools for ecosystem service valuation and quantification are quite well developed for the field of source watershed conservation. At this point, the limiting barriers to greater adoption of this strategy are primarily institutional and financial, rather than scientific, but as the section on implementation discusses, there are ways smart cities have found to get past these barriers.

Chapter 4

Stormwater

PUTTING IN THE PLANTS IS THE EASY PART. What takes time is jackhammering concrete, breaking up pavement, churning up soil. Yet throughout Washington, DC, it's happening: newly constructed wetlands or other pieces of green infrastructure are appearing where there were once only parking lots, sidewalks, or roads. As I walked up First Street NE, municipal officials in charge of the city's stormwater mitigation program showed off with pride the new green infrastructure lining the road. Just in front of the DC Department of the Environment building, the sidewalk had been modified to make a small wetland that would take some of the stormwater runoff from the street and detain it long enough to allow it to infiltrate down below the soil's surface. Across the street, an upscale office and condo building had a similarly functioning but much more stylish wetland, with vivid green horsetails all standing straight at attention. A few blocks away on North Capitol Street, you could see the new headquarters of National Public Radio, which was surrounded by a moat of green infrastructure for stormwater mitigation.

If these new urban wetlands are beautiful, the problem they are supposed to solve is very ugly: sewage. Washington's old core, like that of most cities built before World War II, combines sewage—what you flush down the drain—and stormwater, letting both of them flow downhill together in pipes until they reach the sewage treatment plant. This type of combined sewer system works fine, most of the time. But when it rains hard, the massive flush of stormwater is too much for the system, and the excess water, a nasty mix of sewage and stormwater, is dumped directly into the Potomac River, where it floats downstream to the Chesapeake Bay and then out to the Atlantic Ocean. Apart from being gross, it is also illegal to dump raw sewage like this: every time there is a combined sewer overflow, the District of Columbia could potentially owe the US Environmental Protection Agency a large fine for violating the Clean Water Act.

Washington, DC, is far from the only city having stormwater problems. In just the United States, more than 700 cities have combined sewer systems that could overflow when it rains (EPA 2014a). No comprehensive global figure exists to my knowledge, but out of the tens of thousands of cities that exist globally, the majority likely has combined sewer systems. And even cities that use separate sanitary sewer systems are still plagued by concerns about the water quality of stormwater that is being dumped in rivers and streams. Stormwater mitigation has become one of the central urban challenges of the twenty-first century.

Because combined sewer systems are so problematic, most newer neighborhoods have separate sanitary sewer and stormwater systems (Melosi 2008). In DC, these newer metropolitan, separate, sanitary sewer and stormwater systems (MS4s) serve all of the newer parts of the city, including the garden apartment building where I live. But even with a separate sanitary sewer, stormwater can be a problem. The stormwater that the city dumps into rivers and streams is so dirty it violates rules under the Clean Water Act. And if stormwater flows too quickly into the stormwater system, localized flooding can result.

Replacing combined sewer systems with separate sanitary systems is far too expensive an option for most cities even to contemplate. Many cities have tried therefore to find ways to reduce the amount of stormwater entering a system. If they can do that, then they can reduce combined sewer overflow (CSO) events. Slowing the flow of water also reduces the rapid flush of contaminants and sediment after a big rain event, improving stormwater quality. The standard grey infrastructure solution to the problem is large concrete basins to detain stormwater, or a tunnel to shunt excess stormwater quickly downstream.

But, increasingly, cities like Washington, DC, are trying something different, using green infrastructure to mitigate stormwater. Wetlands and other constructed natural habitats can slow the flow of stormwater and increase infiltration into the subsurface. Natural infrastructure also acts as a filter, reducing concentrations of some pollutants. In essence the city is restoring bits and pieces of the ecosystem that once was there, so that they can receive its stormwater mitigation benefits.

Finding enough space for enough green infrastructure to significantly reduce stormwater can be a challenge, requiring action by thousands of landowners. Washington, like many cities, offers both carrots and sticks to private landowners. Every month, my condo association gets a bill (the stick) for our impervious surface fee. Such fees are roughly proportional to the amount of impervious surface on a property. The idea is that since greater amounts of impervious surface correlates with greater stormwater runoff, those landowners that cause more of the problem should pay more. However, there are now incentives (the carrot) to create green infrastructure. If my condo association installed green infrastructure, we could get up to a 55 percent reduction in our fee. So there is now a strong financial benefit to installing green infrastructure, in terms of fees avoided.

New developments in Washington, DC, are regulated a bit differently. A new development must show it is able to detain the first 1.2 inches of rain on-site for twenty-four hours to receive a building permit. Alternatively, if it is too expensive to have this much green infrastructure on-site, then the developer may buy Stormwater Retention Credits (SRCs). An SRC is issued to a landowner who has built a certified green infrastructure project, who in turn may sell it to developers. Suddenly, a market for nature's benefits is emerging in Washington, DC, as it is in other American cities.

This chapter is about how a city like Washington can plan to use the power of nature to solve its stormwater problems. I begin by discussing how cities can find the best places to build green infrastructure and then present the different types of natural infrastructure that could be built. I present techniques for valuing stormwater-related ecosystem services and then discuss project monitoring and implementation.

Mapping Important Services for Stormwater Mitigation

This chapter assumes that a city has identified stormwater mitigation as an important ecosystem service that it relies upon, or could rely upon after green infrastructure creation (see chapter 2 for more details on this identification process). After having identified stormwater mitigation as a crucial ecosystem service, the city needs to begin mapping the current and potential future distribution of ecosystem service provision. The first step is to define the scope and spatial distribution of the stormwater problem.

The stormwater problem should be defined with as much specificity as possible. Often in cities with combined sewer systems the problem is too much water entering the system during large storm events, leading to CSOs. In this case, a useful goal is to reduce the number of CSO events that occur to an acceptable level under current regulations. This is often translated to a goal for natural infrastructure to absorb or at least detain a certain volume of rainfall in a reference storm event of a particular intensity.

Alternatively, stormwater quality may be the problem. In this case, the goal is to have measurable improvements in water quality after it flows off the natural infrastructure. Often this translates into a simple metric of the ability to capture or detain a certain volume, such as the first inch. While relatively few rainstorms may be large enough to cause CSOs, the first flush of rain in many smaller rainstorms can transport a lot of pollutants. Thus, designing green infrastructure for improving water quality often requires a strategy to deal with the first flush of rainfall, whereas green infrastructure for limiting CSOs often also requires strategies to deal with the larger volumes of stormwater generated during big rain events.

Based on their specific definition of the problem, cities may set an overall target for natural infrastructure. For instance, to reduce overall stormwater volumes by a certain quantity of liters to avoid CSOs, the city may set a target of a certain number of hectares with natural infrastructure, using simple average metrics of the effectiveness of natural infrastructure. Similar areal targets are often set for programs to increase stormwater quality using rules of thumb about the filtration effect of natural habitat. For cities facing regulatory limits, either on the number of CSOs or on the quantities of pollutants (e.g., limitations on total maximum daily loads, TMDLs), convincing regulators that a given areal natural infrastructure target will achieve regulatory compliance is often a hard sell. Regulators may only agree if more complicated ecosystem service modeling suggests the areal target is adequate, or if a monitoring system will be designed to ensure the natural infrastructure is working as planned.

Once cities have clarity on exactly what their stormwater problem is, they can move on to map the ecosystem service benefits that natural infrastructure can provide. Since most cities focusing on using natural infrastructure for stormwater mitigation are looking to increase ecosystem service provision, cities often map the potential for new patches of green infrastructure, rather than focusing on the ecosystem services provided by existing natural habitat. These new patches of green infrastructure may involve the restoration of a site back toward original habitat conditions, or may involve wholly novel constructions. Regardless, the city needs to expand its supply of particular ecosystem services to meet their goal and wants to know the optimal places within the city to put green infrastructure. These are several kinds of ecosystem services of importance for stormwater mitigation, and exactly which to map depends on a city's stormwater goal.

The most common goal of stormwater natural infrastructure is simply slowing the rainwater down, with the goal of reducing peak flows. Impervious surface leads to fast runoff overland. Natural habitats can slow the movement of water over the surface, reducing peak flows and spreading out the hydrograph of a storm event (figure 4.1). The effectiveness of natural infrastructure in providing this service thus needs to be measured, implicitly or explicitly, over a time interval (e.g., amount of rainfall that natural infrastructure can detain on-site for twenty-four hours).

Another common goal for natural infrastructure is increasing infiltration into subsurface flow. Infiltration of water generally greatly reduces the speed with which water travels into river channels, and may allow stormwater to avoid entering into the stormwater drainage system entirely. Additionally, increasing infiltration may help with recharge to some groundwater aquifers, which may be a benefit for over-withdrawn aquifers. The effectiveness of natural infrastructure in providing this service is often evaluated as either the volume of water that infiltrates or the fraction of stormwater that infiltrates.

Finally, cities may be interested in natural infrastructure for filtering out pollutants. As discussed in chapter 3, this filtration service of natural habitat is only effective for some ecosystem services, not for others. Biologically active molecules such as N and P may be

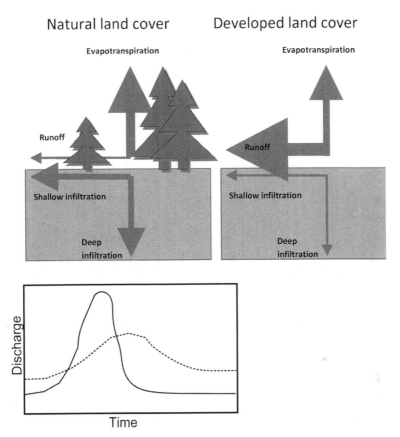

Figure 4.1. The effect of loss of natural vegetation on stormwater runoff and stream discharge. (Top) In areas of natural vegetation, the majority of stormwater either returns to the atmosphere through evapotranspiration or infiltrates into the soil, moving laterally in the soil (shallow infiltration) or downward toward the water table (deep infiltration). In developed areas, by contrast, surface runoff is greatly increased, and evapotranspiration and infiltration are decreased. (Bottom) The effect of loss of natural vegetation on stream discharge during a storm event. When natural habitat dominates the basin (dotted line), several things are systematically different than when that habitat is lost by urban development (solid line): peak flows are less, there is a greater lag time from the precipitation event to peak flow in the stream, and the base flow (the flow before and after the rain event) is greater.

incorporated into the plants. Effectiveness of natural infrastructure in providing this service is often measured as the amount of fraction of the pollutant that is absorbed.

Note that there are limits to what natural infrastructure can do. Natural infrastructure for stormwater is most useful for dealing with the first increment of rain that falls. It can prevent the first flush of pollutants that occurs during any rain event. However, in very large rainfall events when the soil is saturated, most rain will move as overland flow. Thus, if there is a risk to the city from large rainfall events, natural infrastructure may not be helpful in mitigating that risk.

There is a plethora of different models that cities can use to map the current and future provision of ecosystem services for stormwater mitigation. They range along a gradient of complexity of the inputs required and the outputs generated (table 4.1). Cities should decide how much detail is needed for the predictions of the model. Are citywide estimates of the average effectiveness of particular classes of natural infrastructure enough, or are site-specific predictions needed? Cities must also realistically appraise the time and resources available for the modeling effort, since the more complex tools can be quite time intensive. Moreover, in many cases, cities may not be able to use site-specific projections of effectiveness in their programmatic work. For instance, it may be politically infeasible to pay different urban residents different rates for the installation of the same amount and type of natural infrastructure, even if very different levels of ecosystem service provision occur on the two parcels.

The simplest models for stormwater natural infrastructure are merely spreadsheets that multiply the area of certain natural infrastructure types by their per-unit effectiveness in mitigating stormwater. They often use the so-called Rational Method (EPA 2011) to calculate peak flows and runoff volumes in a watershed:

$$Q = CiA$$

Table 4.1. Inputs and outputs for ecosystem services models useful in evaluating natural infrastructure for mitigating stormwater problems

	Green Long Term Control EZ Template	WERF-BMP SELECT	National Stormwater Calculator	SUSTAIN (SWMM)
Key data inputs				
Precipitation	Yes (basin total)	Yes	Yes	Yes
Topography and watershed characteristics	Nonspatial watershed info	Nonspatial watershed info	Yes (nonspatial)	Yes
Land cover, soils	No	No	Yes (nonspatial)	Yes
Total Area of BMPs	Yes	Yes	Yes	Yes
Spatial map of BMPs, streams, stormwater sewers, etc.	No	No	No	Yes
Key outputs				
Watershed-level estimate:				
Water storage	Yes	Yes	Yes	Yes
Natural filtration	No	Yes	No	Yes
Spatial maps of benefits of BMPs				
Water storage	No	No	No	Yes
Nature filtration	No	No	No	Yes
Optimization of placement of sites for BMPs	No	No	No	Yes
Other notes	Designed for small US communities struggling with CSO discharges that violate the CWA.	Designed to meet stormwater quality targets. Includes financial calculations.	Designed for small sites, to forecast the effectiveness of BMPs. Calculator takes data from many online sources.	A decision-support framework that uses SWMM for calculations, with model parameters preloaded.

Note: Users who do not need spatial maps of the benefits of best management practices (BMPs) are encouraged to use one of the simpler models. For instance, for those in the United States interested in evaluating at a site level the effectiveness of BMPs in reducing water quantity, the National Stormwater Calculator is a good first choice. For users who want to evaluate over a whole watershed the effectiveness of BMPs in reducing stormwater, and optimally place BMPs where they will be most helpful, the SUSTAIN model is a good first choice, although users outside the United States will have to alter default parameters to match local conditions.

where Q is the runoff in a period of time (e.g., cubic meters per hour), i is the rainfall intensity (e.g., meters of rainfall per hour), and A is the watershed area (e.g., square meters). The factor C is the runoff coefficient for a given land-use type, the fraction of rainfall that becomes surface runoff. The volume of stormwater reduced by natural infrastructure (V) is then often estimated simply as

$$V = QR$$

where R is the average volumetric fraction of stormwater reduced by a particular best management practice (BMP). See table 4.2 for a list of average volumetric fraction for various types of stormwater BMPs. Note that in the literature on stormwater mitigation, BMPs are also called Low Impact Development (LID) controls.

The US Environmental Protection Agency (EPA) maintains a good list of spreadsheet methods (EPA 2013a). For cities with CSO problems, an obvious first choice is the EPA's Green Long Term Control EZ Template, which provides output metrics relevant to avoiding CSOs. All spreadsheet methods are nonspatial, so they cannot supply site-specific estimates. However, they are useful for setting overall municipal targets for natural infrastructure and are so quick to use that it is often worthwhile to run them before running more complex models. Another similar spreadsheet tool is WERF BMP SELECT. This model requires the user to input effectiveness parameters for the various stormwater BMPs, which is more work but makes the model flexible enough to be tailored to cities outside the United States. It also supplies a calculation of the net present value (NPV) of natural infrastructure and other useful financial calculations.

The next level of complexity is models that are simple to run but take into account some of the spatial context of the city's stormwater system. Models in this category sometimes come preloaded with input data to make them relatively user friendly. EPA's National Stormwater Calculator is a good model in this category for those located in the United States. It is based on the more complex SWMM

Table 4.2. Types of natural infrastructure best management practices (BMPs) for mitigating stormwater quantity or quality

Practice	Description	Average percent of runoff avoided by the BMP
Constructed wetlands and rain gardens	Man-made landscape depressions that store water and allow for increased infiltration	40–80
Vegetated swales	Vegetated open drainage channels designed to slow the flow of stormwater and allow for infiltration	40–60
Green roofs	A roof partially or completely covered with vegetation	45–60
Rain barrels and cisterns	Systems for collecting rainwater for later use on-site	10–40
Permeable pavement	Pavement that allows water to infiltrate into the soil	45–75

Source: Adapted from EPA 2011.

Note: The maintenance of natural habitat is not included in this list, since it is often not considered a BMP per se. However, the stormwater benefits of maintenance of natural habitat are substantial. For instance, the average forested site has 60–80 percent less runoff than a developed site.

model (Storm Water Management Model—see below), but many common parameters come preloaded, with the user only having to supply a land cover map and a map of where particular stormwater best management practices (BMPs) are applied.

The most complex models may require substantial input data and calibration, but also give the most detailed output. For users in the United States, the SUSTAIN model (System for Urban Stormwater Treatment and Analysis Integration) may be most helpful. It is designed to be a decision-support tool for urban water managers that defines not just how much natural infrastructure is enough but also where it should optimally be placed. The user inputs spatially explicit information of land cover, hydrology, and different categories of BMPs. The model then outputs estimates of ecosystem service provision (e.g., infiltration). SUSTAIN uses the SWMM model internally, providing a set of useful postprocessing routines to SWMM output.

Many other models exist, such as the Source Loading and Management Model and ITree (discussed more in chapter 7). Some of the models mentioned in chapter 3, such as SWAT and SPARROW, can also output information on water quantity and quality. To avoid being overwhelmed by this broad selection of models, it is helpful to think carefully about what data the model needs to produce. Is information on water quantity reductions from natural infrastructure all that is needed, or is information on water quality effects needed as well? Are nonspatial predictions of effectiveness okay, or does the user need spatial predictions of the effectiveness of natural infrastructure across a whole stormwater system? Often the combination of a city's geographical location and output data needs will point to just a couple of candidate models (table 4.1).

Common Threats and Common Solutions

Natural infrastructure to deal with stormwater is often different than for source water protection (chapter 3). Often for source water protection there is a regulatory or technological limit that might be breached with continued degradation of ecosystem service provision. In contrast, with stormwater that limit has often already been breached, and the only question for the city is how to most cost effectively get back on the right side of the limit. In the United States, the common limit violated is the Clean Water Act. There are some 7,000 municipalities in the United States with regulated MS4 systems. Another common limit violated is CSO events—more than 700 cities in the United States have combined sewer systems that occasionally overflow (EPA 2014). In other countries, there are often parallel regulations that lead cities to begin thinking about creating stormwater green infrastructure. For instance, the European

Union requires all wastewater to be treated, so CSOs are similarly forbidden.

Some cities, to their credit, do begin thinking about stormwater problems proactively, often out of a concern about the scope and pace of new development. Development almost invariably leads to an increase in impervious surface, which will lead to an increase in peak stormwater flows that may exceed the capacity of the system to handle it. Proactive land-use planning and zoning can prevent such an outcome from occurring.

Similarly, a city might be concerned that climate change might make stormwater problems worse. In some areas, climate change is predicted to increase average rainfall. The Intergovernmental Panel on Climate Change's 5th assessment (IPCC 2013) predicts that it is very likely that average rainfall will increase in already wet climates at high and midlatitudes, such as the northeastern United States, northern Europe, and northern China. At the same time, some dry climates, like the arid western United States and Mexico, southern Europe, and much of Australia may decrease in average rainfall. This general pattern extends to seasonal variations in precipitation: wet seasons are generally projected to get wetter, and dry seasons drier. Perhaps more important, the IPCC predicts that the intensity of heavy rain events will likely increase in most places. If climate change drives an increase in peak rainfall intensity, many cities will find their stormwater management systems overwhelmed and may have to rely on new green infrastructure to solve part of the problem.

The geography of a stormwater system often means that runoff problems are localized in specific areas, where there are high pollutant loadings to stormwater or where the volume of stormwater gets high enough to cause a CSO. Some of the detailed models (e.g., SUSTAIN) point the way to a site-specific valuation of stormwater mitigation ecosystem service provision. But in many cities there is a fundamental disconnect between this level of detail and the political reality of running an urban stormwater program. Many programs must be opportunistic, building green infrastructure where landowners volunteer. Furthermore, for reasons of equity or fairness, it is often difficult to differentially impose fees or burdens on parts of the city where stormwater problems are most acute. The philosophy of many cities is that stormwater management is a common good they supply to their citizens. The exception to this philosophy is new neighborhood development, which may be charged a disproportionately large fee if it is in a particularly problematic stormwater management location.

Cities often begin their stormwater green infrastructure programs by working on municipal or other public land. This land can often be used for green infrastructure for little or no cost to the city. However, only a small fraction of land in urban areas is publically owned, limiting green infrastructure to small spaces like sidewalks. The exception may be the local road network, which occupies a significant fraction of the urban area and generates significant stormwater runoff. While public land is where many municipal stormwater green infrastructure programs start, it is by no means easy to work on public lands. Negotiations among municipal departments can be a big barrier. In Washington, DC, for instance, green infrastructure on a sidewalk has to meet not only the regulations for stormwater but also zoning regulations, and if the green infrastructure is on public land, it has to be maintained by a different department.

Thus in most cities actions by private landowners are needed to reach a scale of natural infrastructure that can adequately mitigate stormwater problems. Private land occupies more than two-thirds of the urban area in many cities. One of the central challenges for municipal officials, therefore, is to find a way to motivate action by hundreds or thousands of private landowners. Most landowners have little knowledge about where the stormwater that falls on their property goes, so education campaigns are often needed to raise landowner awareness of the potential benefits of natural infrastructure.

There are a variety of types of natural infrastructure that can mitigate stormwater problems. Some of the most cost effective involve protecting existing wetlands from development. Many cities also promote planting of trees or other native vegetation, which provides stormwater benefits. Since these sorts of habitat protection and restoration programs also provide many cobenefits (aesthetic beauty, increase in property values, etc.), the evaluation of their return on investment (ROI) needs to consider these cobenefits. There is also an institutional hurdle in many cities, with the protection and care of natural areas left to the parks department, which often has no institutional mandate to help solve the city's stormwater problem.

Maintenance or restoration of existing wetlands with some natural land cover is often most cost effective, but most cities also have to construct novel "green" systems to store and filter rainwater. This can include constructed wetlands (sometimes called bioretention cells), which are often little more than detention basins where vegetation is established around the edges. If unplanned and unmaintained, such vegetation tends to become dominated by species of low biodiversity value, such as cattails and purple loosestrife. However, with proper care and maintenance, much more is possible. Cities have taken to calling particularly attractive displays of wetland plants "rain gardens." Washington, DC, installed just such a rain garden downhill of the pool deck of my apartment complex, and it is as pretty as any other piece of landscaping. There is a whole list of other specific types of natural infrastructure that similarly contain some natural vegetation, such as vegetated swales and green roofs (table 4.2).

There are other ways to mitigate stormwater that may serve cities well but are arguably not natural infrastructure as defined in this book, in the sense that no natural vegetation is involved. Rainwater catchments like cisterns can store stormwater for future use. This is not a particularly new idea: many nineteenth-century homes contain cisterns to store rainwater to use for watering gardens. Permeable pavement is another technique in this category. Permeable pavement is simply asphalt concrete with less fine aggregate incorporated into it, so there are air spaces in the asphalt concrete that can allow some rainwater to percolate through. Because of the large surface area of pavement in most cities, this is an appealing technology that could really reduce stormwater on a large scale. However, porous pavement remains generally more expensive than regular pavement and less durable, and hence more appropriate for use in low traffic areas. While using permeable pavement for new developments is straightforward, it is much more complex and costly to replace existing pavement, since substantial work would be needed to break up the road bed and allow for infiltration.

Valuation of Stormwater Natural Infrastructure

As with all types of natural infrastructure investments, the storm-water mitigation benefits provided must be evaluated against what would have happened in the status quo scenario of no conservation action. For stormwater, this requires comparing the amount and quality of stormwater after the city's actions with what would have occurred without any municipal stormwater natural infrastructure program. The status quo scenario would have had more, or dirtier, stormwater, which would have imposed more costs on the city, but these avoided costs must be balanced against the expense of the city's natural infrastructure program.

For many cities already in violation of government regulations for stormwater, the status quo scenario might include continued fines for violations. For instance, fines against a MS4 system that has not taken adequate steps to increase stormwater quality can be tens of thousands of dollars per day. Fines for CSOs can be even bigger: San Antonio had to pay a $2.6 million civil penalty for illegally discharging raw sewage (EPA 2013b). Moreover, the regulatory process may require cities to achieve a certain goal (e.g., reduction in number of CSOs). In this case, the relevant baseline scenario is the amount of money the city would have spent to achieve this regulatory requirement entirely with a grey infrastructure solution. This can often be very expensive. In Washington, DC, the estimated cost of using grey infrastructure to comply with EPA rules was estimated at $1.2 billion in 2002 (DC Water and Sewer Authority 2002). It is only against this large baseline expense that the construction of green infrastructure can seem comparatively cheap. A full analysis of the status quo scenario would consider the cost to society at large of continued water pollution. For instance, the discharge of sewage by Washington, DC, contributes to the further degradation of the Chesapeake Bay, one of the nation's most threatened aquatic ecosystems. An increase in this degradation will damage fisheries and oyster reefs in the Bay, with real economic impacts to coastal communities. However, these sort of broader social costs are often ignored by municipal stormwater officials, who reason that their mandate is solely to help the city solve its stormwater problem.

Moreover, natural infrastructure also brings with it substantial cobenefits. For instance, street trees can dramatically increase property values along a street (see chapter 9). Conservation organizations, like the one I work for, may be happy with the way natural infrastructure can support biodiversity in an urban region. Ideally, these broader societal benefits of natural infrastructure should be counted in an analysis of the ROI of a natural infrastructure strategy.

The long-term maintenance costs of natural infrastructure for stormwater mitigation remain uncertain. Many pieces of natural infrastructure are relatively cheap to install up front but require maintenance to remain effective over time. Sometimes the city can push maintenance costs on to others: my apartment complex must maintain our rain garden, or we risk losing our modest reduction in DC's stormwater fees. This transfer of maintenance costs can be a source of friction between municipal agencies, if one agency wants to install natural infrastructure but another agency would have to maintain it. In general, it is wise to dedicate a source of funding for the long-term maintenance of green infrastructure at the time it is created. Such a move, however, is often resisted by municipal budget makers who find part of the appeal of natural infrastructure in its delay of maintenance costs to future years.

One challenge in valuation analyses is to compare different possible mixes of grey and natural infrastructure. This is usually addressed by designing a set of scenarios with a different mix of natural and grey infrastructure, and then using ecosystem models to evaluate the costs and benefits of each scenario. The scenarios developed should be constrained by the political, economic, and hydrologic realities in a city. For example, in Washington, DC, the consent decree with the EPA on limiting CSOs requires a mostly grey infrastructure solution, making analyses of scenarios that are predominately green a somewhat theoretical exercise. Projects done to improve MS4 stormwater quality have comparatively more administrative flexibility, and in these cases a broader range of scenarios could be considered.

Implementation

Often, the biggest implementation challenge is just convincing regulators that natural infrastructure works and can help a city hit its regulatory limits. In the United States, the EPA has moved strongly toward allowing natural infrastructure to be considered as part of the stormwater solution and even provides tools (e.g., SUSTAIN) to make natural infrastructure easier to plan for. However, regulators in some state governments remain less convinced of the utility of natural infrastructure. Outside the United States, some national regulators remain skeptical too. There is often a perception that natural infrastructure is a cop-out: simply a way to avoid making the big capital expenditures that will definitively solve the problem. For instance, in Washington, DC, some environmental groups

argue that the city simply needs to spend billions on its grey infrastructure fix, and that any discussion of using natural infrastructure
to meet the goal of reducing CSOs is simply delaying much-needed
investment in the ultimate solution.

Another implementation challenge that has already been mentioned is getting to scale. Many cities have bought into the idea
of natural infrastructure for stormwater mitigation but few have
implemented projects at a scale to substantially change the quantity
or quality of stormwater. Getting to scale is a problem for many
natural infrastructure strategies but is particularly acute for natural infrastructure for stormwater. The generally small parcel size
in downstream urban areas means that each green infrastructure
project is small, so actions by thousands of landowners might be
needed (NRDC 2012). Moreover, any ecosystem service benefits
from the natural infrastructure are often not appreciated by urban
landowners. The exception in many cities seems to be high-end
development for people who might view a green aesthetic as an
amenity they want in a building.

The strategy used by most cities involves an approach similar
to that of Washington, DC: a big stick and a bundle of small carrots. The stick is putting a fee on the stormwater that comes off a
parcel. Often this fee is structured as proportional to the amount
of impervious surface area. If the fee per-unit area is set equal to
the marginal cost of the extra stormwater produced by a unit of
impervious surface, then the fee should on average provide an appropriate incentive to landowners to consider the stormwater implications of their actions. However, such a constant fee per-unit
impervious surface is rarely optimal since the location of the parcel
controls its stormwater impact. While a spatially varying fee on impervious surface would theoretically be more efficient, it has rarely
been implemented.

A true impervious surface fee can often be a large price hike
over historic practices where stormwater was essentially untaxed,
so even if there is a rational reason to put a price on a negative

externality, there can be substantial political resistance. Political realities may require that such a fee be implemented slowly over many years, to give landowners time to adjust their land-use plans for their parcel. Often, small preexisting landowners are "grandfathered," so these landowners are not overwhelmed with the new fee. By a similar political logic, it is often easier to apply stricter rules to new structures than to existing structures.

The small carrots are financial incentives to use green infrastructure, either by reducing the impervious surface fees or by direct incentives. Financial incentives are almost always based on the practices followed, rather than their actual impact on stormwater quantity or quality. This is simply because it is far cheaper to monitor whether landowners are conducting certain practices (e.g., maintaining a functioning bioswale) than to conduct hydrologic monitoring.

Most private landowners simply don't have sufficient time or knowledge to construct green infrastructure on their property. Some studies have found this to be one of the biggest single barriers to widespread construction of stormwater green infrastructure (Valderrama et al. 2013). One way around this problem would be an "aggregator" company. In Washington, DC, for instance, an aggregator might approach landowners, convince them to allow the installation of green infrastructure, finance its construction, and then sell the Stormwater Retention Credits generated at a profit. The idea of a stormwater aggregator is borrowed from energy efficiency retrofits, where aggregator companies have proved essential in certain contexts.

Another common issue is that even with a large, impervious-surface, fee-motivating action, the payback time (also called the breakeven point) for stormwater natural infrastructure can be quite long (Valderrama et al. 2013). It can take more than ten years for the money saved from the reduction in impervious surface fees to equal the cost of installing the green infrastructure. Put another way, the NPV of investing in stormwater green infrastructure is low, particularly with high discounting rates, since an up-front cost is only slowly paid back by a stream of benefits. There is also what is called regulatory uncertainty: the city might change its fee structure, and promised future savings in impervious surface fees might disappear. Or the landowner might sell the property, and any benefits from the natural infrastructure would transfer to the new landowners.

One way around these problems is a source of financing for natural infrastructure that alleviates the need for landowners or aggregators to pay up-front costs. One model is energy efficiency retrofits via Property Assessed Clean Energy (PACE) financing. In PACE, energy efficiency projects (e.g., installing more insulation to minimize heating and cooling costs) are financed by a loan. The loans are repaid through an annual assessment on the landowner's property bill. Thus the landowner enjoys the benefits (reduced energy use) of a retrofit at the same time he is paying for it. The existence of an aggregator company and a market for stormwater credits can similarly help solve this conundrum. If a municipal government can loan at relatively low interest rates to an aggregator, it can conduct projects that generate credits it can sell immediately while only having to pay back the loan over a period of years.

Monitoring

While many cities are rushing to build green infrastructure to solve stormwater problems, relatively few have monitoring schemes in place. There is, however, a large scientific literature on the average stormwater benefits that different BMPs provide. Most cities thus focus on collecting information on simple implementation metrics, such as the area over which a particular practice is being implemented. Ideally, this involves an annual check that ensures that the BMP for which a landowner is claiming credit is indeed still in place.

It is crucial that cities measure actual stormwater quantity or quality, at least at a few sites, to ensure that actual stormwater mitigation benefits are in line with average estimates assumed during project development. Stormwater is notoriously hard to sample, since storms are so episodic, and the greatest flux of water and pollutants happen over a short period of time. Often, therefore, the recommendation is to concentrate monitoring resources in fewer sites, but to invest in a system that can continuously monitor stormwater quality or quantity over time. Water quantity is usually cheaper to measure than water quality and is thus the focus of many monitoring efforts.

Information on implementation metrics, combined with estimates of the average benefits of BMPs, can be joined with models to estimate overall program effectiveness citywide. This is a particularly valuable approach when site-level measurements can be compared with model predictions to validate the models. If model predictions provide reasonably accurate predictions of site-level measures, then this strengthens confidence that the overall modeled benefits of a stormwater program are actually occurring.

Occasionally, municipalities will have monitoring metrics that are farther downstream. For instance, a city could track the number of CSOs at a particular CSO outfall. Because the amount of stormwater that reaches that point in the pipe is the integration of all land use upstream, it can be difficult to see much of an effect. This is particularly true given everything else that could vary over time in the catchment: new development could have increased impervious surface area, for example.

Summary

Washington, DC, is moving forward with setting up the Stormwater Retention Credit (SRC) market. At least dozens and perhaps hundreds of cities in the United States are also considering the utility of green infrastructure to help mitigate stormwater, all driven by a goal of complying with the provisions of the Clean Water Act. There are more than 700 cities that have consent decrees with the

US Environmental Protection Agency around stormwater. Green infrastructure for stormwater is less actively used outside the United States, but it is increasingly common in many countries with strong clean water standards. The tools and methods for quantifying the benefits of stormwater green infrastructure are relatively well characterized. However, the actual scale of construction of green infrastructure has to date been limited in many cities. Working at scale requires motivating action by hundreds or thousands of landowners, which is a different coordination challenge for many cities.

Chapter 5

Floodwater

It all started with Hardin Bigelow. The city of Sacramento had only been in existence for a year when in January 1850, the Sacramento River flooded its banks and wiped out most of the town. Immediately after the flood, city leaders, led by Hardin, agreed to tax their citizens $250,000 to build a levee to protect Sacramento from its namesake river. And for a while, Hardin's levee seemed to work. Just a few months later, the river rose again, but the city was spared. Hardin was a hero, and went on to become mayor (Kelley 1989).

Over the next fifty years, Sacramento, like many cities all over the world, kept building levees, yielding to an understandable sentiment: make the banks higher, keep the floodwater in the river channel, and move it as quickly as possible downriver. But downtown Sacramento was never really safe. A few years after Hardin's levees were installed, the town raised every city street, burying the old first floor of buildings beneath tons of dirt and turning them into basements. Yet the floods kept coming, and when Hardin's levees were occasionally overtopped by water, all the floodwater was trapped in downtown Sacramento. Finally, after an extreme flood in 1907, city and state leaders slowly began to realize they had to try something new.

Instead of fighting to contain the raging floodwater within the river channel, they decided to let the river flood its banks. The city built the Yolo Bypass, which allows floodwaters to spill on a floodplain safely out of town. When a large flood comes down the Sacramento River, 80 percent of the floodwater is dumped on to this floodplain, saving the town from destruction. The rest of the time, a lot of the land on the floodplain, with its rich productive soil, is used for agriculture. And the river and its floodplain have become habitat for important fish species, like the Sacramento splittail and the Chinook salmon, and for migrating ducks (Salcido 2012). The Yolo Bypass is now seen as one of the smartest urban water investments in natural infrastructure of the twentieth century, precisely because it uses nature rather than fighting against it.

On the other side of the globe, a similar story is playing out in the Netherlands (Room for the River 2014). The Rhine is one of the world's most economically important rivers, flowing more than 1,000 km before draining into a large delta in the Netherlands. Flooding in the Rhine has been a problem for centuries. The Netherlanders have massively engineered the Rhine, building high levees along its length and even changing the course it takes to get to the sea. The dendritic drainage pattern of the delta was simplified, as land was reclaimed for farmland.

But damages from flooding continued to increase. Massive floods in 1993 and 1995 devastated the delta. The Netherlanders decided to reverse course and created a new policy called Room for the River. The levees would be moved back from the Rhine, creating space for the river to flood. This retreat means that in a few places vulnerable infrastructure, like buildings and roads, will have to be removed from the floodplain. There is even a proposed flood by-pass, to protect the villages of Veesen and Wapenveld, that will function very much like the Yolo Bypass.

The mistake of Hardin Bigelow is being repeated in rapidly growing cities throughout the developing world. The coastal areas are some of the fastest growing cities globally, and hundreds of millions more people will move into these cities. This chapter explores when and how natural infrastructure can be at least a partial solution to the risk posed by freshwater flooding. Maintaining or restoring floodplains may not be a solution everywhere, but it can be a promising solution for some cities. This chapter tells how to determine if it would work for your city.

Mapping Important Services for Flood Mitigation

The Hardin Bigelow strategy is to keep floodwaters in the river channel wherever possible. The levees simply raise the wall of the channel, increasing the channel's cross-sectional area and, thus, the volume of water the channel can carry (figure 5.1). As a logical corollary, the strategy advocates moving water rapidly down the river, so that the volume of floodwater never exceeds the carrying capacity of the channel. The logical endpoint of this strategy is the Los Angeles River. It has been channelized with concrete for much of its length. On the rare occasions when the Los Angeles River floods, its water moves extremely fast toward the ocean. The river has become, essentially, one giant stormwater pipe.

Room for the River is the opposite of the Bigelow strategy. Water is allowed to spill out of the river channel onto flood plains that have natural land cover or human land uses that are compatible with occasional flooding. By allowing the water to spill on to the floodplain, it gives floodwater someplace to go, decreasing pressure on levees downstream. In effect, society designs its use of the floodplain to match its flood frequency, rather than controlling flood frequency to allow more intense human land uses in the floodplain.

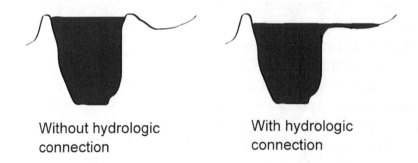

Without hydrologic connection

With hydrologic connection

Figure 5.1. Schematic of river cross section for a given flood event. Left panel is where levees have severed the hydrologic connection between the river and the flood-plain (status quo scenario). The right panel is where one levee is not present and the floodplain is hydrologically connected to the river (conservation action scenario). Note that the flood elevation (the height of the water, black) is lower with reconnection, as some of the floodwater is now stored on the floodplain. This may reduce flood risk downstream.

Vegetative cover in river floodplains, relative to impervious surfaces, increases infiltration of rainwater to the subsurface and groundwater. This decreases surface runoff. As discussed in chapters 3 and 4, natural habitat also slows the movement of surface runoff to river channels. The net effect of natural habitat is to slow the movement of water to the river channel, reducing peak flows and spreading the flush of stormwater over a longer period. For headwater basins, this can be an important ecosystem service that reduces flooding risk. However, for many floodplains of large rivers, this ecosystem service is of relatively little importance. The amount of water entering the floodplain through overland flow is dwarfed by the amount of water entering from riverine flow.

A more crucial ecosystem service for the Room for the River strategy is the ability of a floodplain to convey and store water. A floodplain covered in natural habitat can perform this service, but so too can any other land use that can withstand occasional flooding (Opperman et al. 2009). Farming and ranching are two common compatible land uses in floodplains. While these activities are disrupted by floods (crops may be lost, livestock may have to be moved temporarily), the economic impact is generally modest compared with the damage to buildings and hard infrastructure.

Cities for which flood management is a priority might be interested in quantifying the amount of flood storage that currently connected floodplains are providing, or the potential for hydrologically connecting former floodplains to increase flood storage. There are three major analysis steps. The first is to quantify the relationship between rainfall and runoff (Bedient, Huber, and Vieux 2012). Information is usually needed on the statistical distribution of rainfall magnitude, intensity, and duration. Additionally, information on the spatial distribution of rainfall is helpful if there is substantial variability in rainfall across the basin. This is certainly true for big basins, and sometimes even for small ones, particularly during spotty thunderstorm events.

Empirical rainfall/runoff curves are often estimated from river gauges, which can directly measure flow velocities and height and can be used to calculate discharge. There are also a variety of mechanistic models (table 5.1). The Hydrologic Engineering Center's Hydrologic Modeling System (HEC-HMS) is one commonly used in the United States. Other similar models are discussed in chapters 3 and 4 (e.g., Soil and Water Assessment Tool [SWAT]). All these models simulate the movement of water downhill until it reaches the river network in a basin.

The second task is relating a given level of runoff to how high the water level will be. This is often called hydraulic modeling, since it is the hydraulics of the river system that are modeled: how water flows down the river network. The height of floodwaters is called the flood elevation. Flood elevations are often evaluated for a certain "base flood," such as the amount of discharge that has a 0.01 probability of occurring in a year (the "100-year flood"), and are then called the base flood elevation. Hydraulic models describe the movement of water according to the laws of fluid mechanics. For

Table 5.1. Inputs and outputs for ecosystem services models useful for evaluating natural infrastructure for flood mitigation

	Rainfall/runoff models: HEC-HMS, SWAT	Hydraulic model: HEC-RAS	Hydraulic model: GSSHA	Hazard models: HAZUS, HEC-FDA
Key data inputs				
Precipitation (intensity, duration, distribution)	Yes	No (takes discharge as input)	Possible (can also take discharge as input)	No (takes flood elevation as input)
Topography and water-shed characteristics	Yes	No	Possible	Yes
Land cover, soils	Yes	No	Possible	No
River cross section	No	Yes	Yes	No
2-dimension bathymetry information for river	No	No	Yes	No
Detailed property maps	No	No	No	Yes
Key outputs				
Discharge	Yes	No	No	No
Vulnerability: Flood elevation:				
At cross sections	No	Yes	Yes	No
Throughout river	No	No	Yes	No
Exposure: property at risk	No	No	No	Yes
Other notes	Other models in this category include SWMM, VIC, and HSPF. Note that GSSHA can be run as a rainfall/runoff model.	A 1-dimensional hydraulic model. Other models in this category include Quick 2.	A 2-dimensional hydraulic model, which can also be used for rainfall-runoff modeling. Other models in this category include FESWMS-2DH.	Calculates what property is damaged for a given flood elevation.

Note: Models of rainfall/runoff are used to estimate discharge to the stream network (see chapters 4 and 5 for discussion of more models of this type). Hydraulic models can be used to estimate flood elevation for a given amount of discharge. Hazard models are used to estimate the number of people and amount of property within the area inundated at a given flood elevation.

open channel flow of water however, where water can be assumed to be a constant viscosity and density, the equations of fluid mechanics simplify considerably. Gravity pulls water down the river channel, giving the water momentum as it builds up speed. However, viscosity and friction with channel walls act to slow the water.

The effectiveness of natural infrastructure is usually evaluated by having two scenarios of channel configuration. One scenario is the status quo scenario, where a floodplain is disconnected hydrologically from the river due to a levee. The other is the natural infrastructure scenario, which describes a situation where the floodplain is connected hydrologically with the rivers. A hydraulic model is then used to evaluate base flood elevation under these two different scenarios. One measure of the effectiveness of the proposed conservation action is, therefore, the difference in base flood elevation between the scenarios.

Many hydraulic models do their calculations of flood elevation for a series of cross sections of the river, so-called one-dimensional models. In the United States, the most commonly used is the Hydrologic Engineering Center's River Analysis System (HEC-RAS). While measuring river depth at multiple river cross sections would be time consuming, this information is readily available for many river systems in developed countries. Some hydrologic models are two-dimensional models, which use a grid representation of the river network. One of the most common is the Gridded Surface/ Subsurface Hydrologic Analysis (GSSHA) model. For both HEC-RAS and GSSHA, a useful support tool is the Watershed Management System (WMS), which can format inputs and display model outputs. Because determining base flood elevations is important legally, most countries have a limited list of approved hydraulic models, and readers are encouraged to consult experts about the requirements in their jurisdiction.

The third and final analysis task is mapping what area would be inundated for a given base flood elevation. This requires digital elevation information with sufficient resolution in the Z-dimension (elevation). A good global first stop is Hydrosheds information (Lehner, Verdin, and Jarvis 2008), although much finer resolution DEMs can be obtained from LIDAR (LIght Detection And Ranging) remote sensing (NAS 2009). Once the area flooded in the base flood is delimited, one can estimate what the damage from inundation could be. Damage can be estimated in monetary terms, or in terms of people affected or other metrics of social vulnerability.

Most scenarios of conservation action involve not just hydrologic connection of floodplains but also the installation of a compatible set of land uses in the connected floodplain (Kousky and Walls 2013). The hope is that the flood storage on the connected floodplain reduces base flood elevation and hence the area inundated and economic damages downstream, relative to the status quo scenario.

For a simple assessment of damage, an overlay in a GIS (geographic information systems) may be sufficient. If detailed property maps are available, there are several models that can help with this task. The Hydrologic Engineering Center's Flood Damage Analysis (HEC-FDA) is used often by the US Army Corp of Engineers, while HAZUS is used by the US Federal Emergency Management Agency. Both evaluate whether a property is flooded based on its elevation, then quantify the cost of partially or completely rebuilding the damaged property.

Common Threats and Common Solutions

Most cities begin thinking about flooding by trying to clearly define the risk they face. Risk is often defined as the vulnerability (the probability that a site will be flooded) multiplied by exposure (the damage that will occur if a flood happens). This quantification of risk may require a detailed study, along the lines described in the preceding section. Alternatively, government officials may have already defined base flood elevations and associated flood polygons, and cities can evaluate their risk under the status quo scenario with a simple GIS overlap to quantify exposure.

Smart planners will also consider how risk will change in the future under the status quo scenario (Kousky et al. 2011). If future development is likely in floodplains, this will increase the exposure of people and property to floods. Moreover, climate change may alter the frequency or intensity of rainfall events, increasing the vulnerability of a site to flooding.

The examples from Sacramento and the Netherlands illustrate the hydrologic reconnection of floodplains to their rivers. However, there are conservation solutions that stop short of this drastic solution. For instance, a city may focus on protecting areas of natural land cover in currently hydrologically connected areas in the river's floodplain. This protection maintains ecosystem service provision of increased infiltration and flood storage. Natural areas also provide numerous other cobenefits to society. Many cities, for instance, make the protection of natural areas in the floodplain a central part of their open space and parks master plan, because of the recreational benefits they provide. Protecting these natural areas ensures that this stream of cobenefits continues into the future.

Another, related solution is to limit further development in floodplains (figure 5.2). This can be done by protecting natural habitat, of course, but it can equally be achieved by maintaining agricultural land uses and limiting construction of new buildings. While this is not strictly a strategy that relates to ecosystem service provision (any land use that is compatible with occasional flooding provides this "service"), it fits in well with the open space and farm preservation movements.

If the risk analysis for a city reveals substantial risk, a city may consider hydrologic reconnection as a way to increase flood storage along a river system. Sometimes a quantitative goal is set. In the case of the Room for the River program in the Netherlands, this goal is expressed as a lower base flood elevation after hydrologic reconnection. Equivalently, the goal can be expressed as a reduction in the spatial area or number of buildings downstream that are at risk for floods. Regardless, the goal is usually set so that after

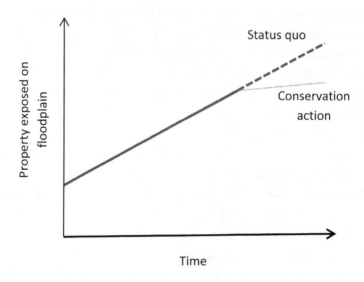

Figure 5.2. Development over time in a floodplain may increase property exposed to floodwaters (solid line). Continued development in the future will further increase exposure (status quo scenario, dashed line). Land protection or zoning restrictions might limit future floodplain development, reducing property exposure (conservation action scenario, dotted line).

hydrologic reconnection the remaining risk for people and property is acceptable.

Hydrologic reconnection also often implies a retreat from the reconnected floodplains, or at least a shift to a more compatible land use. For instance, floodplains might become part of a waterfront park, or they may be revegetated to become a new forest. Smart planners will try to make these newly reconnected floodplains an amenity for those who live nearby.

Valuation of Flood Mitigation Natural Infrastructure

Once a city has well-defined scenarios of the status quo and at least one potential conservation action, valuation is relatively straightforward. For each scenario, the risk (exposure × vulnerability) is calculated, in terms of expected flood damages. The reduction in expected damages in the natural infrastructure scenario is the benefit of implementing that scenario (Kousky et al. 2011). Note that natural infrastructure will likely not reduce the risk to zero, and significant flood damages may still be expected under the natural infrastructure scenario.

Exposure is generally quantified using maps of property and information about their value, although other metrics should also be considered as a supplement to a measure of expected property damage. Particularly for marginal populations, such as the poor or elderly, other metrics that capture their specific exposure may be useful to policymakers.

Vulnerability should be considered over a range of storm events (NAS 2009). The tendency is to use predefined base flood elevations for only one return interval; in the United States, there is an excessive focus on the 100-year floodplain. This tendency can blind planners to truly catastrophic events. Climate change may also increase vulnerability, making what used to be a 500-year flood occur more frequently. Another consequence of using predefined base flood elevations is that, while their use makes evaluation of risk under the status quo scenario relatively easy, it can be impossible to calculate the risk under a conservation action scenario that involves hydrologic reconnection. This information imbalance can push urban planning processes away from considering hydrologic reconnection, so it is worthwhile to quantify the flood storage benefits of the conservation action scenario wherever possible, even if it involves new hydraulic modeling.

Any benefit in reduction in risk from hydrologic reconnection must be weighed against the cost of implementing the conservation action scenario. There are substantial costs to any reconnection project, both in altering water management infrastructure and in altering land use in the newly connected floodplain. Similarly, the status quo scenario may involve the construction of new status quo infrastructure. For instance, new development in the status quo scenario may necessitate the construction of new levees, which may be quite expensive. Indeed, sometimes it is only against the cost of these large grey infrastructure expenses in the status quo scenario that the conservation action scenario makes sense.

In general, the return on investment (ROI) of efforts to keep new development out of floodplains is high. This is particularly true from the standpoint of municipal officials, who may bear some of the financial responsibility of rebuilding. On the other hand, banning development imposes an opportunity cost on landowners in the floodplain but not necessarily on municipal officials or society at large.

In comparison to the avoided development strategy, retreat and reconnection is generally expensive and may have a lower ROI. Developed property is worth a lot of money and may be expensive for municipalities to acquire. It is also expensive to remove vulnerable grey infrastructure from the soon-to-be-reconnected floodplain. For these reasons, the Yolo Bypass was in a certain sense easier than the current Room for the River project on the Rhine, since the Rhine River is more developed than the Sacramento River was when the Yolo Bypass was constructed.

Implementation

One of the most common ways cities try to limit development in floodplains is through their zoning codes. While such an alteration of zoning codes may be politically controversial, at least to property owners in the floodplain, it has little financial cost to municipalities. At least in the United States, it is relatively rare to bar all development in the floodplain, which could be seen as a "taking," requiring compensation. More frequently, zoning codes limit the amount of development and the types of structures that can be built, with the goal of limiting the cities' exposure to floods.

To further limit development in a floodplain, cities may purchase land outright (fee-simple) through voluntary transactions.

This land can then be used for a variety of compatible land uses. Frequently, it becomes part of a state or municipal park. Parkland, whether it is forests or ball fields, can deal with occasional flooding, although any structures at the park, like restrooms, must be able to withstand floodwaters. More rarely, governments use the power of eminent domain to compel sale of properties at risk of flood and remove buildings at risk. Whether voluntary or forced, transactions to protect natural habitat is likely to be less controversial than transactions that move people from the floodplain. In the Netherlands, for instance, the government has struggled to remove enough grey infrastructure to make hydrologic reconnection a real possibility.

Alternatively, a city could pay landowners in the soon-to-be-reconnected floodplain to accept flooding risk. This type of "flood easement" is used in the Yolo Bypass for instance. Legally, the state has the right to flood properties along the bypass, and this easement is considered superior to other land uses. California never had to purchase these flood easements but just made acceptance of the easement a condition of owning and using the land near the bypass (Salcido 2012). Depending on the legal structure of the country, officials may be able to compel landowners to accept compensation for a flood easement, or may have to work with purely voluntary transactions.

Governments also try to influence the land-use decisions of private landowners by influencing flood insurance policies. Much flood insurance is run by the public sector, because the private sector views much flood risk as uninsurable. Flooding events tend to be correlated (many policyholders are simultaneously affected by one event) and potentially catastrophic (cumulatively expensive enough that they could bankrupt many insurers), so the necessary premiums for an insurance company to accept this risk would be so high as to be difficult to market. Unfortunately, the public sector tends to offer flood risk at premiums that do not adequately cover the government's assumption of risk. In effect, these public sector flood insurance programs have the perverse effect of subsidizing development in floodplains (Kousky 2014). Governments may therefore try to raise flood insurance premiums to end this subsidy, a move that is theoretically very defensible but may be politically controversial.

Generally, floodplains that flood frequently are easier politically to take action in. Everyone in the area will have seen the flooding and understand the risk. Taking action gets harder when the flooding is more infrequent. For instance, the Mississippi River has two large spillways (the Bonnet Carré and the Morganza) that can be used to divert water during extreme floods. They operate much like the Yolo Bypass does but are used much less frequently. Landowners in the Morganza spillway knew that their property could be flooded but still brought a lawsuit after the spillway was opened in 2011 during a massive flood.

Monitoring

There are multiple types of monitoring a city could conduct. First, they could examine whether discharge in a river after a precipitation event matches that predicted by rainfall/runoff models. This is an important step in model validation, and provides an important check on whether the calculated likelihood of a given discharge event is correct.

Cities almost always track implementation metrics. Was the floodplain reconnected? Is appropriate land use in place? If gauge data is available, it is also possible to compare the actual flood elevation for a given discharge with what was predicted by the hydraulic models. And if a large enough flood event occurs, the city will be able to check if the newly reconnected floodplain was inundated to the expected depth.

The ultimate goal of these floodplain reconnection projects is to reduce flood risk downstream on the river. If a properly calibrated and verified hydraulic model is in place, then gauge data from before and after the reconnection can be used to see whether during flood events the extra flood storage has reduced flood elevation. For reconnection projects, however, where the design flood occurs infrequently, this kind of monitoring may be infeasible. For instance, on the Mississippi, the Morganza spillway has only been opened twice since its construction in 1954. One would have to wait a long time to directly monitor the Morganza spillway's effect on downstream flood elevations.

As with other natural infrastructure strategies, the counterfactual can pose a problem during monitoring. This is particularly problematic when a conservation action is merely limiting floodplain development over time. In this case, there is not a dramatic change in river hydraulics, as with floodplain connection. Rather, the conservation action limits the amount of people and property exposed during floods relative to a counterfactual case, that is, what development would have been without the conservation action. For instance, a study by Resources for the Future that evaluated the ROI of floodplain conservation in Missouri constructed a counterfactual scenario, assuming development on currently protected parcels would have been of a similar type (residential) and density (single-family homes) as other nearby parcels (Kousky and Walls 2013). They then calculated avoided property damage relative to this counterfactual scenario.

The ultimate in monitoring would be to detect a reduction in flood damage due to implementation of a conservation action. But because insurance claims are stochastic and highly variable, this can be challenging. Such an approach would ideally examine flood damage claims over time, both before and after the conservation action. It would also examine claims over time from other nearby basins. These pseudocontrols would help to detect, for instance, if there has been a general increase in damage claims, simply because there has been an increase in property values. In this case, natural infrastructure might only reduce the rate of increase in claims.

Summary

Sacramento continues to use the Yolo Bypass, and the Dutch continue to make Room for the River. In recent years there has been increasing attention by government agencies to how conservation solutions can help mitigate freshwater flooding problems. However, in many cases the distortions of faulty national flood insurance programs have been difficult to correct, and the rapid urban growth occurring globally has increased the total exposure of people and property to floods. Moreover, while the science of quantifying the benefits of conservation action to mitigate floodwater is clear, the more sophisticated tools that involve hydraulic modeling are complicated and require specialized knowledge. For all these reasons, while natural infrastructure solutions to freshwater flooding are becoming increasingly common, there is a less rapid pace of deployment than is the case for drinking water protection or stormwater mitigation.

Chapter 6

Coastal Protection

Iₙ ᴛʜᴇ ᴇᴀʀʟʏ ʜᴏᴜʀs ᴏꜰ Oᴄᴛᴏʙᴇʀ 30, 2012, a massive storm made landfall on the coast of New Jersey. Hurricane Sandy's impacts were felt up and down the United States Eastern Seaboard. Even my home in Washington, DC, was affected: I spent the early hours of October 30 trying to drive my very pregnant and very much in labor wife to the hospital through gale force winds and flooded streets. In the end, it worked out fine. By the time the storm was over, we had a happy and healthy baby to bring home. Farther north along the Eastern Seaboard, however, things were very much *not* fine.

The epicenter of Hurricane Sandy's impact was the New York City metro area (Associated Press 2012). Storm surge was greater than thirteen feet. Hundreds of thousands of homes were flooded. Floodwaters knocked out power for weeks, and caused the combined sewer system of the city to dump billions of gallons of untreated sewage (Schwirtz 2013). Almost fifty people died in the New York metro area during the storm.

There has been a tendency since to talk about "Superstorm Sandy," as if the storm was wholly unprecedented. Indeed, some were quick to blame the storm on climate change. In a certain sense, this is correct. Everything is now altered; we live in an altered climate world. Sea level was higher in the Atlantic than it would have been without climate change, which meant the storm surge into New York City was even higher. The Atlantic was warmer than it would have been without climate change, which gave the hurricane more strength.

In reality, though, Sandy had precedents. Nicole Maher and colleagues worked before Sandy to map where sea-level rise and storm surge would cause flooding in Long Island. When the map was presented to Long Island communities, Maher described how "some folks reacted by saying that is totally unreasonable." But previous storms had flooded similar places. "Folks who were here in the 1938 hurricane said what flooded then matched up with our map," said Maher.

And Maher's map predicted well what flooded during Sandy. Many other groups had also studied coastal flooding in the New York metro area and knew that substantial flooding was possible. The tragedy of Sandy is not that it was unprecedented; the tragedy is that it was entirely predictable, yet New York City was still not fully prepared for the flooding that came.

Maher works with many colleagues on a project called Coastal Resilience that aims to help coastal communities understand and plan for coastal flooding hazards (Gilmer and Ferdaña 2012; Beck et al. 2013). Their website (coastalresilience.org) presents spatially explicit data on where sea-level rise and storm surge might lead to flooding, and this information has slowly started to be used by the communities making planning decisions, such as the town of Southold out on Long Island.

Maher has also been studying how natural habitats like marshes can help prevent erosion. Marshes hold the soil together and slow down the water moving through their grasses, which prevents erosion from occurring every day. Because they slow down water, they also encourage sediment deposition, which can actually raise the marsh over time. Other natural habitats are important too. Dunes can keep storm surges at bay. Oyster reefs can help limit erosion over time, and provide multiple other benefits to people.

Hurricane Sandy has given new urgency to coastal communities trying to figure how to make our coasts more resilient in future storms. The New York governor appointed a commission on how to rebuild the coastline of the state, and a similar New York City task force has worked on how to increase the city's resilience. Much of the work of these commissions is about financing the rebuilding of homes and infrastructure. But they are also working to make sure the tragedy of Sandy is never repeated.

Part of the plan for increasing coastal resilience will be hardening shorelines with new grey infrastructure. New, higher seawalls will help keep storm surge away from people and property. Vulnerable grey infrastructure may be raised to a higher elevation, or moved farther inland. But part of the plan will also be maintaining natural habitat. Keeping the marshes maintains the coastal protection services they supply. Moreover, preventing more development on marshes means there aren't new homes in harm's way during the next storm.

Mapping Important Services for Coastal Resilience Mitigation

A coastal region is often represented with a one-dimensional transect that shows the beaches' profile (Tallis et al. 2013). The ocean has a mean sea level (MSL). At any moment in time, the actual stillwater elevation (the water level ignoring waves) is either higher or lower, depending on the tide. During storms, storm surges can substantially increase stillwater elevation, as water is pushed toward the shore. Waves are then the movement of water a certain height (H) above and below the stillwater elevation. Wave energy will push water on a beach to an even higher elevation, called wave runup (R). A couple of typical beach profiles are shown in figure 6.1. Note that the shape of the beach profile has a great effect on the size and position of the foreshore and backshore.

For temperate regions like where New York City is located, beaches are usually sandy in the foreshore and backshore up to some dunes (or on some beaches lacking natural dunes, just a small berm of sand). Tidal wetlands like marshes occupy low positions on the landscape and get a mix of saltwater from the ocean and freshwater from a stream. Oyster reefs are located near or below MSL, and are frequently or continuously submerged by ocean water. In tropical regions, the set of natural habitats is a bit different. Mangroves often occupy the foreshore and backshore. Coral reefs are located near or below MSL like oyster reefs, but they can get quite large, sheltering a lagoon from some of the wave energy from the open ocean.

Natural habitats provide several important coastal protection services, and identifying which ones are important for a particular location is key for good urban planning. Wave attenuation is one ecosystem service provided by natural habitats. Relative to bare soil on sand, natural vegetation has more friction, which causes wave energy to dissipate, reducing wave height. This is true for a submerged habitat, like in oyster and coral reefs: as a wave passes over these habitats, some of its energy is dissipated. It is also true for emergent vegetation like marshes and (especially) mangroves, which have significant drag and dissipate energy as water moves around their stems.

A second ecosystem service of importance is shoreline stabilization, the way natural habitat will limit the day-to-day erosion from a site. Erosion during storm events is less due to wave attenuation discussed. Rather, the roots of vegetation like marshes and mangroves bind sediments together, preventing erosion.

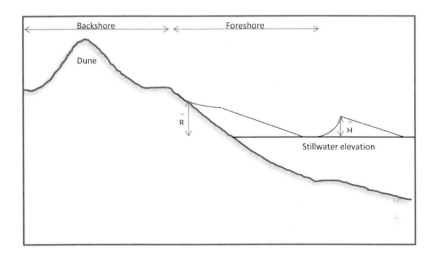

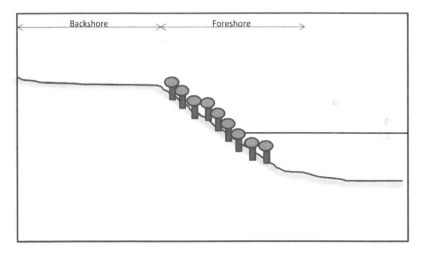

Figure 6.1. Beach profiles for a sandy shore in a temperate climate (top) and coastal mangroves in tropical habitats (bottom). The ocean level is shown at stillwater elevation, which is mean sea level plus the effects of tides and storm surge. Waves have a certain height (H) above and below that stillwater elevation. When breaking on a beach, wave runup (R) is generally greater than H.

Finally, marshes and mangroves play an important role in flood-water attenuation. This floodwater could be freshwater from upstream (see chapter 5) or saltwater from the sea. These habitats are located on large areas of relatively flat land that can "store" a lot of floodwater. In the case of coastal hazards, by providing a safe place for water pushed up by storm surge to go, the habitats attenuate flooding events for sites farther uphill.

The first step for many cities is to map the spatial distribution of coastal hazards (table 6.1). One easy-to-use model is the Coastal Vulnerability Model (CVM) of the Natural Capital Project (Tallis et al. 2009), which produces a semiquantitative estimate of the vulnerability of coastal communities to erosion and inundation. It also produces a simple index of the number of people who would be exposed to a coastal hazard at a particular site. Overall risk at a site is defined as vulnerability multiplied by exposure.

User-supplied inputs to the Coastal Vulnerability Model are easy to find, since many of the necessary data sources are freely available on the web. Key input information includes information on bathymetry and topography as well as land cover and the locations of natural habitat. Climatic information, such as wind speed and direction, and MSL are also needed. The estimated vulnerability index ranks sites from 1 (very low vulnerability) to 5 (very high vulnerability). Similarly, the number of people potentially exposed to coastal hazards is estimated. While crude, these metrics can allow policymakers to quickly assess patterns of vulnerability and social exposure. For instance, a study of the entire Gulf of Mexico showed that key places with high vulnerability and social exposure were the coast of Florida, Houston, and New Orleans.

After cities identify coastal communities that seem vulnerable, they might turn to estimating how much natural habitat provides ecosystem services that reduce vulnerability. To answer this question with any specificity, the city must know which ecosystem service (wave attenuation, shoreline stabilization, or flood attenuation) is most needed at a site. For quantification of wave attenuation and shoreline stabilization, a good next step might be the Coastal Protection Model of the Natural Capital Project (Tallis et al. 2009). The first step in the model is called the Profile Generator. It takes detailed information on topography and bathymetry to construct a one-dimensional beach profile (e.g., figure 6.1). If such detailed information is not available, there are a variety of ways to estimate a beach profile. The current or proposed natural habitat also needs to be located in this profile (e.g., Where exactly are the mangroves located?). Users will often want to construct two profiles: the status quo case (where natural habitat is missing or degraded) and the conservation case (where there is more or better quality natural habitat).

The second part of the Coastal Protection Model calculates the effect of the beach profile and its natural habitats on Nearshore Waves and Erosion, given an initial wind speed and stillwater elevation of a storm the user wishes to model. Essentially, the model estimates wave height (H) and runup (R), based on the beach profile, after accounting for any dissipation of wave energy due to natural infrastructure. Then the model estimates erosion for that wave height and runup. To see the effectiveness of natural infrastructure under this storm event, one compares wave height and erosion between the status quo and conservation beach profiles. Note that users of the tool will want to consider the effectiveness of natural infrastructure for a variety of wind speeds and storm surges. Natural infrastructure is often more effective at preventing erosion for small to moderate storms; intense storms like Hurricane Sandy may have such high wind speeds and storm surges that natural infrastructure offers little additional protection.

There are many other models used for calculating storm surge associated with a given storm, and then estimating wave height and erosion (Maidment et al. 2009). Some of these models require more engineering experience than most municipal staff have on hand, so this work is often contracted out. Their principal advantage is the two-dimensional, high-resolution spatial forecasts

Table 6.1. Inputs and outputs for ecosystem services models useful for evaluating natural infrastructure for coastal protection services

	Coastal Vulnerability Model (CVM)	Coastal Protection Model (CPM)	SLOSH, ADCIRC	CHAMP (WHAFIS), SWAN, STWAVE	HAZUS
Key data inputs					
Climate information (wind speed and direction)	Yes	Yes	Yes	Yes	Yes
Topography (foreshore)	Yes	Yes	Yes	Yes	Yes
Bathymetry (nearshore)	Yes	Yes	Yes	Yes	No
Map of coastal natural habitat	Ideally	Yes	Yes	Yes	No
Detailed beach profile, including location of natural habitat	No	Yes	No	Yes	No
Storm surge	No	Yes	Not an input	Yes	Yes
Key outputs					
Risk assessment					
Vulnerability	Yes	Yes	Not applicable	Yes	No
Exposure	Yes	Yes	Not applicable	Yes	Yes
Storm surge	No	No	Yes	No	No
Wave height (H) and runup (R)	No	Yes	No	Yes	No

Table 6.1. continued

	Coastal Vulnerability Model (CVM)	Coastal Protection Model (CPM)	SLOSH, ADCIRC	CHAMP (WHAFIS), SWAN, STWAVE	HAZUS
Quantitative damage estimates	No	No	No	No	Yes
Other notes	Calculates a semiquantitative index of risk from coastal hazards. Links to easily available data inputs.	Calculates H and R given a beach profile, including effect of natural habitat. Also calculates erosion.	Calculates storm surge for a given storm event. SLOSH is simpler, while ADCIRC is more sophisticated.	Calculates H and R, given a beach profile. More sophisticated than CPM, but harder to parameterize for natural infrastructure.	Calculates property damage, for a given storm surge, H, and R.

Note: Users are encouraged to start with a simple model for evaluating vulnerability and exposure to coastal hazards (CVM) before moving on to more complex models that can quantify ecosystem services provision (CPM, or some combination of models that can quantify storm surge, wave height and runup, and damage estimates).

they can provide. A medium complexity model of storm surge is the Sea, Lake, and Overland Surges from Hurricanes (SLOSH) model. If more sophistication is desired, the Advanced Circulation (ADCIRC) model is used. Wave height can be estimated with the Simulating WAves Nearshore (SWAN) model or the Steady state spectral WAVE (STWAVE) model. Another common model is the Coastal Hazard Modeling Program (CHAMP), which incorporates parts of the Wave Height Analysis for Flood Insurance Studies (WHAFIS). Natural infrastructure can in principle be incorporated into these models by treating it as another land cover type, although the models were not designed with that purpose in mind.

Once there is an estimate of storm surge and wave height, numerous models are able to calculate area inundated, based on topography. Somewhat more challenging is the estimation of damage to people and property. The HAZUS Hurricane Model takes as input maps of storm surge and wave height and then combines this information with user-supplied building inventory to estimate which specific buildings will be inundated and their economic value.

Common Threats and Common Solutions

Maher and her colleagues stress that Coastal Resilience is an approach, rather than a tool (Gilmer and Ferdaña 2012; Beck et al. 2013). The ultimate goal is to make coastal communities more resilient in the face of future coastal hazards by planning and adapting for those hazards before the next big storm arrives. The Coastal Resilience approach has four steps. The first step is assessing the risk that coastal hazards pose to communities, which is what the Coastal Vulnerability Model of the Natural Capital Project tries to do (Tallis et al. 2009). Sea-level rise, due to climate change or other factors, is a threat itself to low-lying sites, and also increases the vulnerability during storm surges, since the overall stillwater elevation is higher than it would have been without sea-level rise. Climate change may also alter the frequency or intensity of storms, thus altering the vulnerability of coastal sites. Sites can be vulnerable to erosion, either day-to-day erosion or large erosion events during big storms. Sites can also be vulnerable to inundation during coastal storms.

The distribution of vulnerability for one region, the Gulf of Mexico, is shown in figure 6.2. An intensive study used the Coastal Vulnerability Model to calculate vulnerability for the whole Gulf. The coast of Louisiana is most vulnerable to coastal hazards. Exposure, as measured by population, is limited on much of the coast of Louisiana but is high in major population centers like Houston, New Orleans, and Tampa. Policymakers must consider both vulnerability and exposure when evaluating the risk to coastal communities in the Gulf of Mexico.

The second step in the Coastal Resilience framework is identifying solutions that can reduce the risk to coastal communities. Potential solutions depend very much on what the problem is. For instance, a city might have a lot of its existing infrastructure threatened by sea-level rise, and might consider a seawall to protect that infrastructure. Alternatively, a community might be trying to plan for future growth, and decide to require that new buildings in coastal flooding zones be elevated on stilts at a certain height.

One common natural infrastructure solution is simply protecting any remaining natural habitat in the coastal zone. This is much cheaper than restoring already degraded sites. It ensures that the ecosystem services provided by the habitat continue into the future. Moreover, in many communities, wetlands remain only in the most low-lying areas. Since these are generally the sites most vulnerable to coastal hazards, protecting these wetlands ensures that no new developments are built in such risky sites.

Another option is restoring natural habitat. While expensive, restoration can increase the coastal protection services available to coastal communities. For instance, many communities are experimenting with restoring oyster beds, which might reduce day-to-day erosion risk and provide other cobenefits. Of all the restoration

Vulnerability

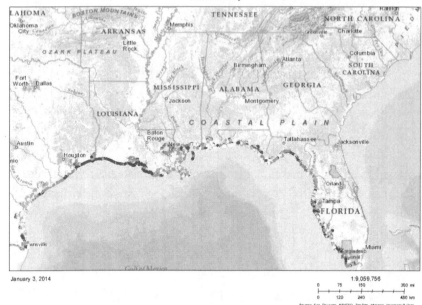

January 3, 2014

1:9,059,756

0   75   150   300 mi

0   120   240   480 km

Sources: Esri, DeLorme, NAVTEQ, TomTom, Intermap, increment P Corp,
GEBCO, USGS, FAO, NPS, NRCAN, GeoBase, IGN, Kadaster NL,

Risk (Vulnerability x Exposure)

January 3, 2014

1:9,722,289

0   80   160   320 mi

0   130   260   520 km

Sources: Esri, DeLorme, NAVTEQ, TomTom, Intermap, increment P Corp,
GEBCO, USGS, FAO, NPS, NRCAN, GeoBase, IGN, Kadaster NL,

options, restoring dunes is arguably the most common. Indeed, sometimes dunes are created on beaches that have never naturally had them, where they can nevertheless substantially reduce erosion and inundation risk. Dunes ideally are more than just piles of sand, waiting to be eroded in the next storm; vegetation on their surface can substantially stabilize a dune.

Habitat restoration is obviously constrained by what natural habitats are suited to a particular climate and site. Mangroves, for instance, are an excellent way to stabilize sediment in the forest shore but only grow in tropical zones. Marshes are the dominant coastal wetland type outside of the tropical zone but cannot grow in the foreshore. Coral reefs and oyster reefs have similarly restricted ranges. While both habitats are located in the ocean, near or below MSL, a site in Long Island might be ideal for oysters but never could support a coral reef.

Cities will certainly need grey infrastructure solutions to provide coastal protection as well. Seawalls are often built to stop the landward movement of ocean water. There are a whole suite of other related technologies, such as groynes—which stop the lateral movement of sand along a beach—and breakwaters, which protect shores and harbors from wave energy. These grey infrastructure solutions are relatively expensive to implement but can substantially reduce risk. Indeed, they can reduce risk so much that they often enable more coastal development near the ocean, increasing the number of people exposed to a hazard if, for example, a seawall ever failed.

One big but controversial solution sometimes considered is

Figure 6.2. Coastal vulnerability (top) and risk (bottom) for the Gulf of Mexico, United States, based on the Coastal Vulnerability Model of the Natural Capital Project. Maps were created using the custom mapping tool at coastalresilience.org (TNC 2014). Darker grey is higher values on the index (more vulnerable or more at risk), while lighter grey is lower values (less vulnerable or less at risk). Risk is defined as vulnerability multiplied by exposure, where exposure in this case is the total population in the coastal zone.

coastal retreat, moving people and property away from the coast and coastal hazards. In the center part of a city, like Manhattan, retreat is often unthinkable. But for more sparsely settled suburban or exurban areas, retreat may be a possibility: there is less property to defend, so a large expenditure on grey infrastructure may not be justified. A retreat also allows for the potential for more natural habitat restoration, increasing coastal protecting services to the remaining human developments.

The trickiest part of retreat is getting enough people to agree to move. Most democracies use voluntary means whenever possible, making financial offers to pay people to leave. For instance, New York State has set aside $171 million to buy out coastal residents (Kaplan 2013). It can be difficult, however, to get enough people to participate in such a program, which limits the effectiveness of a retreat. To encourage entire communities to leave, New York State is targeting buy-out dollars to specific locations and is willing to pay more when a substantial fraction of a neighborhood agrees to leave.

Valuation of Coastal Protection Natural Infrastructure

The value of natural infrastructure is usually measured as the expected damage under two scenarios, the conservation action and status quo scenarios. Expected damage is just a quantitative measure of risk, the probability of an event occurring multiplied by the economic damage if it occurred. For instance, if under the status quo scenario the probability of $100,000 in flood damage occurring is 0.1, then the expected damage is $10,000. If natural infrastructure can reduce the probability of property damage to 0.04, the expected damage falls to $4,000. So the benefit of having natural infrastructure is $10,000 – $4,000 = $6,000. To see whether this benefit is worth it, it must be compared to the cost of implementing the natural infrastructure scenario.

In the example above, exposure is measured in dollars of property damage, a metric of great interest to insurers. Many other types of losses can also be expressed in dollars, making economic damage a useful, integrated measure of the various types of losses. However, it can be difficult to measure. For instance, if a house worth $500,000 is inundated by a foot of water, what will it cost to repair the house? To avoid answering these difficult questions, in simple studies exposure is often just estimated as the total value of property at risk. This is a very useful metric to estimate and is perfectly fine as long as it is remembered that for small storm events damage will be less than full replacement cost.

There are of course many other things that matter to people who are negatively impacted by storms but are difficult to quantify in dollar terms. For this reason, exposure can also be a measure of socioeconomic vulnerability. In the Gulf of Mexico study mentioned above, population was used. Some surveys might focus on the population of vulnerable people at risk, such as the elderly or the poor.

Hurricane Katrina provided a clear example of why the poor might be particularly vulnerable to a coastal storm (Brinkley 2007). Most people with a car evacuated New Orleans. Only those who didn't have a car, or didn't know a relative they could ask for help, were stuck in the city. These were overwhelmingly the poor and elderly. Those who went to storm shelters in the city were safe, but they suffered horrible conditions. Those who tried to stay in their homes were put at risk of injury or death, as levees collapsed and neighborhoods flooded.

Good quality population maps are available globally and can be used to quantify exposure to coastal hazards. The Coastal Vulnerability Model of the Natural Capital Project helps calculate a few simple metrics of socioeconomic exposure, and can be another good first way to quantify exposure. More sophisticated mapping of exposure generally requires detailed property maps, with information on the spatial distribution of property, its value, and any characteristics that could increase or decrease its susceptibility to damage. For most developed countries, this information is relatively easy to obtain, but it is missing for many developing countries. This is especially true for informal settlements, where the lack of legal title to the land means many governments do not accurately census or survey them.

Many countries have maps that delineate areas prone to coastal flooding. These maps are then often used to set rules for what can be built where, or to set the flood insurance rates. For instance, in the United States, the Federal Emergency Management Agency (FEMA) creates a set of Flood Insurance Rate Maps (FIRMs) and related Flood Insurance Studies (FISs). New structures in areas designated on a FIRM as in a Special Flood Hazard Area (SFHA) then usually need to have flood insurance. In principle, the presence or absence of natural infrastructure should affect inundation risk and hence the boundaries of the flood area, but in practice most current flood maps were drawn without any consideration of the role natural infrastructure plays.

Similarly, many insurance and reinsurance companies use hazard models to determine their odds of facing a particular amount of total claims after a storm. Many of these hazard models focus on empirically relating characteristics of past storms to insurance claims. They do not generally incorporate the role of natural infrastructure in reducing vulnerability, although this is an active area of scientific research.

Implementation

Step three of the Coastal Resilience framework (Gilmer and Ferdaña 2012; Beck et al. 2013) is to take action to make coastal communities more resilient. For shaping future development, many cities turn first to their zoning codes. This may involve excluding development from areas now deemed to be at flood risk. Development always involves some public infrastructure—roads, power lines, and so forth—and it makes sense for cities to refuse to put public infrastructure in harm's way. There is also an implicit or explicit promise to protect the life and property of urban residents, and during a storm police and first responders have to risk their own lives to save flooded residents. Therefore, there is a strong rationale for limiting development, both public and private, on flood-prone land. Similarly, there is strong rationale for using zoning codes to protect natural habitat that provides coastal protection services.

In the United States, municipal zoning codes interact with the federal government map of flood risk and the rules of the federal flood insurance programs. The overall trend has been, perversely, for new structures built in flood-prone areas to be able to obtain flood insurance, with premiums that are far below what would really be needed to compensate the government for the risk of having to pay for rebuilding after a flood. FEMA is in the process of updating the FIRMs, which helps, but the new maps still won't generally consider sea-level rise or climate change, so they are likely an underestimate of risk (Maidment et al. 2009).

One of the biggest barriers to protecting or restoring natural habitat is funding. Few coastal communities have large amounts of money set aside for maintaining or creating natural infrastructure. Sometimes funding is drawn from property taxes. More commonly in the United States, funding for natural infrastructure is taken from bonds, often related to parks and natural resource conservation.

It is, sadly, often easier to find funding for coastal resilience after a catastrophe, since coastal hazards are on people's minds and there are defined government programs for reconstruction. However, it is often far more expensive to rebuild a coastline than it would have been to protect it beforehand. More than $1.4 billion in grants and $2.4 billion-low-interest loans have been spent by FEMA after Hurricane Sandy (FEMA 2013). Almost all of this money has been spent on an emergency basis, to repair damaged buildings and roads. However, some money has been set aside for natural habitat restoration, especially rebuilding sand dunes.

Monitoring

The fourth step of the Coastal Resilience framework is measuring effectiveness (Gilmer and Ferdaña 2012; Beck et al. 2013). As with most natural infrastructure projects, monitoring schemes can vary from the very simple to the very complex. The simplest schemes involve implementation metrics: was the natural infrastructure built? This can mean ensuring that protected pieces of natural habitat still remain, or ensuring that contractors who are restoring natural habitat have completed their projects. Field surveys may be needed, particularly for small natural habitat features. Remotely sensed imagery may be very helpful for larger features, helping to track the amount of marsh or mangrove present over time.

At a medium level of complexity, a city might aim to evaluate the environmental impact of their conservation interventions. Environmental impact is the reduction in erosion or inundation risk at a site due to a conservation action. For instance, in Florida a study evaluated whether an oyster reef restoration was effective (Milbrant et al. 2013). This information is now being used to make the design of future man-made oyster reefs better.

The most sophisticated monitoring schemes look at the socio-economic impacts of a city's conservation interventions. Because coastal hazards are infrequent, it is rare to actually observe natural infrastructure reducing inundation of particular buildings. It is also hard to know how much worse the storm would have been without the natural infrastructure (the counterfactual case). Sometimes models are used to evaluate this counterfactual case. Sometimes, nearby similar stretches of coastline without natural infrastructure can be treated as controls. Then the relative socioeconomic impact of both stretches is evaluated. While this level of monitoring is crucial for academic studies, it will often be too expensive and time consuming for many municipalities.

Summary

The greater New York City metro area continues to recover and rebuild from Hurricane Sandy. While there has been good consideration of natural infrastructure, and some pilot projects are underway to protect or restore habitats that provide coastal protection services, the bulk of recovery money has gone to rebuilding grey infrastructure, especially housing, and making it less vulnerable to future storms. It is an understandable human desire to rebuild what was lost, and the default recovery trajectory of many towns is to rebuild in a similar urban form to what was there before. Notwithstanding these practical realities, there has been a drastic increase in the discussion about "resilient cities," and often resilience to coastal storms is front and center in that discussion. For instance, the Rockefeller Foundation's network of 100 Resilient Cities has focused much of its attention on disaster risk reduction, both through grey and natural solutions (Rockefeller Foundation and ARUP 2014). The science for quantifying the value of natural habitat for coastal protection is well advanced, and there are a good range of models available to users, from the simple to the complex. There is every reason to hope that projects that maintain or increase coastal protection services will become increasingly common for cities around the world.

Chapter 7

Shade

WHEN JOHN TAGLIABUE RECALLS the summer of 2003 in Paris, one thing comes to mind. "The main thing I remember were the bodies," said Tagliabue. In early August temperatures began to rise, day after day of record-breaking heat. In some parts of France, the daily temperature was 15°F greater than usual (NASA 2003). "The problem was," Tagliabue remembered, "Northern Europe has a fairly moderate climate. You don't get 100 degree temperatures here, or fairly rarely." But this August was different. Nighttime temperatures did not fall much below the day's highs so the beautiful stone buildings of Paris and other French towns heated up in the morning and stayed hot. The ability of stone to resist temperature changes, which would usually keep the stone cooler than the air on a typical summer day, began to be a problem, as the stone began to store heat. The buildings of Paris became ovens, baking their residents.

The next week, the deaths started in earnest. Many buildings in France do not have air-conditioning, and temperatures inside began to get life threateningly hot. Building residents huddled around fans or fled to the shade of street trees outside, where a passing breeze might alleviate their misery. Hospitals and morgues began reporting back to Paris dozens and dozens of deaths. A later analysis found that mortality rates in Paris were 142 percent higher in August than normal (Vandentorren et al. 2004). In France, the most impacted country, that amounted to 11,000 deaths (Hémon and Jougla 2003). The total for all Europe was greater than 70,000 dead (Robine et al. 2003).

The European heat wave of 2003 is now one of the most studied heat waves in history. Meteorologists, epidemiologists, and government officials all launched inquiries into what exactly happened. One interesting risk factor kept showing up in the research studies of the heat wave's impact. Microclimate, the temperature of particular neighborhoods, was a strong predictor of death rates (Vandertorren et al. 2006). Warmer neighborhoods were more likely to be fatal. Each increase in temperature of 1 degree Celsius (around 1.8°F) raised the odds of death by 21 percent. Cities are generally hotter than the surrounding countryside because they become "urban heat islands" (EPA 2012). Concrete and asphalt that are exposed to the sun's rays can be 50°F–90°F hotter than the surrounding air. This heat then slowly radiates back into air, raising daytime air temperatures by 2°F–5°F and nighttime temperatures by more than 20°F above normal.

France and then the European Union as a whole launched commissions to figure out how to make society more resilient to heat waves (Lefebrve 2003). Many of their recommendations were straightforward. A city needs emergency shelters with air-conditioning or at least fans, and then a system to get elderly residents who live alone into those shelters. While these shelters were recognized as the primary public health response to the tragedy, there was also a recognition in the reports that a long-term commitment to tree planting could help decrease the urban heat island's intensity. Simply shading a piece of concrete or asphalt reduces its temperature by 20°F–45°F (EPA 2014b). Trees provide that shade all through the year, making the city a more pleasant place to be, and this ecosystem service becomes even more important in a world of altered climate.

For a very different example of a municipal program trying to provide shade, we could travel halfway around the world to Sacramento. The Sacramento Municipal Utility District (MUD) has been providing free tree saplings to property owners. The owners must agree to maintain the trees, but in return Sacramento MUD helps plant them. Trees are often positioned on the western edge of a house, to provide maximum shade during the hot afternoon. Having shade trees around a house makes it more attractive, and these aesthetic benefits add tangible value when a home is resold (see chapter 9). But more important for the utility, the trees reduce the houses' electrical use, particularly on summer afternoons when the air conditioners are running strong.

The link between Paris and Sacramento is shade and the benefits it can bring. This chapter is about how natural vegetation can provide shade, although I also discuss grey infrastructure alternatives to vegetation. I present models for quantifying shade provision over time and space, as well as techniques for valuing the economic benefits of that shade.

Mapping Important Services for Shade Provision

Air temperature is just an expression of how energetic and fast-moving gas molecules are on average, and this type of energy is called "sensible heat," since our bodies can sense the difference between warm and cold air. In the atmosphere above a city, as everywhere, energy is conserved; neither created nor destroyed, but simply transformed. Oke (1982) first described the energy balance as

(Equation 1.) $Q^* + Q_F = Q_H + Q_E + \Delta Q_S + \Delta Q_A$

There are two inputs of energy into urban atmosphere: Q^* (the net amount of energy from solar radiation) and Q_F (waste heat emitted by people, such as the hot air your air conditioner puts outside your home). Some of that energy can get stored somewhere, like in concrete or asphalt (ΔQ_S), and wind can carry some of the energy away from the city (ΔQ_A). The remaining energy has to go somewhere. It can increase sensible heat, Q_H, which increases air temperature. It can also go to latent heat, Q_E, which, for our purposes, we can think of as the energy water needs to get from its liquid to its vapor phase (evapotranspiration).

The above equation describes the energy in a small column of air in a city, extending from the ground up to the boundary layer. Above the boundary layer, generally a few hundred meters above buildings and trees, winds rapidly mix the atmosphere, whereas below the boundary layer air is less well mixed (i.e., ΔQ_A is relatively small) and increases in air temperature can persist for some time. Moreover, in cities, with their large areas of impervious surfaces, a relatively large amount of energy (ΔQ_S) is stored and later released, just as happened with those stone buildings in Paris. This release is lagged in time, taking hours for the energy to be fully released.

What is called the surface urban heat island (UHI) intensity is simply the difference in surface temperature between urban and rural areas (EPA 2014b). Surface temperatures are primarily a function of albedo, the amount of the sun's energy that is reflected from a surface. Many urban surfaces are black, such as asphalt, and have a higher albedo than tree leaves. Surface temperature is also a function of the ability of a substance to store heat and the rate at which that stored heat is reemitted. Concrete and asphalt have enormous capacity to store energy and only emit it slowly, compared with natural vegetation. Cities increase the amount of impervious surfaces and so, on average, have higher surface temperatures than rural areas, particularly in the middle of the day and in the middle of the summer, when Q^* is greater.

Air temperature matters more to people's comfort than does surface temperature, so often the atmospheric UHI intensity is of more interest. Air temperature is only loosely coupled with surface temperature, as heat stored is slowly released from concrete and asphalt to become either latent or sensible heat. The atmospheric UHI intensity is greatest at night, when stored energy is released, and in winter, when ΔQ_s is proportionally more of the total energy budget. Air temperature, of course, is still an imperfect measure of human comfort. Numerous indices, combining information on air temperature, humidity, wind speed, and other factors, have been designed to more accurately measure human comfort.

Apart from affecting human comfort, the urban heat island also affects electricity use. Humans use heat pumps and air conditioners to alter the temperature and humidity inside a building to make being inside more comfortable. How hard this task is depends on the atmospheric conditions outside. When it is hotter out, more electricity is needed for air-conditioning. Of equal or greater importance in many homes is the direct input of energy from solar radiation, which can transfer a significant amount of energy (Q^*) to the building. This direct transfer of energy happens through windows, of course, but it can also happen through the roof.

Research into urban heat islands has identified some factors that consistently increase the atmospheric UHI intensity (Arnfield 2003). Table 7.1 lists some of the major findings of this research. The UHI intensity would be greatest in cities with high solar input (e.g., low cloud cover) with lots of impervious surface (e.g., large population or urban area). The UHI intensity is greatest when the energy has nowhere to go except to sensible heat, Q_H. Therefore, cities with low humidity (less potential for latent heat) and low winds (less potential for ΔQ_A) have greater UHI intensity.

From the perspective of a municipal official, there are only a few

Table 7.1. Factors that increase the atmospheric urban heat island intensity

Factor	Explanation
Low cloud cover	Fewer clouds allows for more solar input (Q^*), increasing the heat balance of a city.
Greater solar input	Cities at lower latitudes have greater solar input (Q^*), increasing the heat balance.
Sky factor	Sites within a city that have a higher fraction of their view of the sky unimpeded by buildings have greater solar input (Q^*), increasing the heat balance.
City size (population or area)	Bigger cities have more impervious surface, and hence greater potential to store energy (ΔQ_s) that is later released into the atmosphere.
Anticyclonic conditions	Under these conditions, air is dry, reducing the possibility for some of the incoming energy to be transferred to latent heat (Q_E).
Lower wind	With less wind, the potential for heat energy to move laterally away from the city (ΔQ_A) is reduced.

Source: Adapted from Arnfield 2003.

Note: Atmospheric heat island intensity is the difference in air temperature between urban and rural sites.

terms in equation 1 that can be influenced. The official can't reduce solar input or change overall wind patterns. Increasing building insulation can reduce the anthropogenic sources of heat, Q_F, but this is of relatively little importance during hot summer months. Most strategies to combat the urban heat island therefore focus on reducing heat storage, ΔQ_s, or increasing latent heat (Q_E). Maintaining or increasing vegetation cover can maintain or enhance shade provision. Trees that are tall enough to create a large shaded area under their canopy are more useful than short vegetation. This shade keeps surface temperature low, preventing heat storage. Trees also transpire water as they grow, increasing latent heat storage. From the perspective of mitigating the UHI, this latent heat storage is a good thing, although in some dry climates the loss of water from planted trees may put a strain on scarce water supplies. For projects aimed at decreasing electricity demand, the most important thing is shading part of the building from incoming solar radiation.

One relatively simple modeling task would be to estimate how a given increase in vegetation would decrease surface temperature. There are empirical average estimates for how much shading reduces surface temperatures of different substances (table 7.2). Using such estimates, cities often set simple programmatic goals: a 20 percent increase in canopy tree cover, for instance, or requiring all new parking lots to have at least some minimal canopy cover. As discussed in the monitoring section, changes in canopy cover and surface temperature are relatively easy to see from remote sensing. Thus cities can easily evaluate over time the impact of their programs.

It is more challenging to model the effect of surface temperature on air temperature. A set of empirical regressions exist that relate urban form to atmospheric UHI intensity (Oke 1982). Both population size and impervious surface area are good predictors of maximum UHI intensity, and can be used to estimate the citywide UHI intensity for cities even without direct air temperature measurements. At the scale of individual city blocks, the sky view factor—the fraction of the sky that is unobstructed from a point on the ground—is a good predictor of the maximum UHI intensity.

Table 7.2. Surface temperatures during peak summer heat for unshaded surfaces

Material	Reflectance[a] (%)	Temp. without shade (°F)
Asphalt	5–15	165–185
Concrete	30–40	158–176
Bare metal	30–50	150–165

Source: Based on data in EPA 2014b.

Note: Shade will reduce surface temperatures of these materials by 20°F–45°F.

[a]Reflectance is the percentage of the sun's energy that reflects back to the sky. Albedo is the complement of reflectance, because energy that is not reflected is absorbed.

Blocks with low sky view factors (i.e., "urban canyons" with tall buildings on either side) have greater UHI intensity. Given a dataset on building height, sky view can be estimated in a GIS (geographic information systems) for all the blocks in a city, which can help planners prioritize which blocks have the greatest UHI and where perhaps they should concentrate tree planting.

The standard model (table 7.3) used to calculate the value of shade for reducing electrical costs is I-Tree (USFS 2013). I-Tree is a suite of software modules that quantify various ecosystem services and contains code from previous models by the US Forest Service called UFORE and STRATUM. One module estimates electricity savings due to tree planting using geometrical estimates of a tree's shadow and empirical data on the effect on heating and cooling electricity use. Basic inputs to I-Tree include climate type; the tree species planted; its orientation to, and distance from, the building; and the type of heating and cooling system. A related, similar module called I-Tree Streets (formerly called STRATUM) provides ecosystem services estimates of more relevance for street trees. I-Tree is easy to use, but the empirical relationship used may not hold in other countries with different climates or building standards.

Finally, in rare cases a city might be interested in modeling air temperature evolution over time and space. This is often done by linking the Town Energy Balance model (Masson 2000), essentially an implementation of equation 1, to meteorological models that simulate the movement of air, energy, and water on a three-dimensional grid. For instance, Wouters and colleagues (2013) provide an interesting example, modeling the air temperature of the greater Paris region during a heat wave. They used the Advanced Regional Prediction System (ARPS), and estimate the maximum UHI intensity during the heat wave as 11°F. These kinds of micrometeorology models are rarely necessary during the planning or monitoring of a tree planting program but provide academics important insight into how the UHI changes in shape and intensity during a weather event.

Common Threats and Common Solutions

Urban development necessarily increases impervious surface cover and tends to decrease vegetative cover. Even in cities that are not expanding in size, there is often a slow loss of canopy cover. For instance, Nowak and Greenfield (2012) showed that the average US city lost 2.7 percent of its forest cover over a decade. The loss of canopy cover poses a real threat to urban livability and, because of the reduction in shade provision, makes the urban heat island intensity greater. At the same time, cities are beginning to realize the threat posed by climate change, which in many locations will increase the frequency and severity of heat waves.

There are both grey and natural infrastructure responses to this threat (EPA 2014b). Some of the grey infrastructure responses are focused on ensuring human comfort through air-conditioning and fans, but they take energy to run.

Other grey infrastructure responses work similarly to shade provision, in that they are focused on preventing surface heat storage. So-called cool roofs work by increasing the albedo of roof surfaces, tiles, and shingles, thus ensuring that most incoming solar radiation is reflected back out to the sky. A variety of affordable cool roof technologies are available, depending on the shape and configuration of the roof, and they are so effective at preventing heat transfer to a building that they substantially reduce heating and cooling costs. Similarly, "cool pavement" technologies aim to prevent heat storage by pavement through increasing albedo. Permeable pavement, which is occasionally used as a stormwater mitigation strategy (chapter 4), also reduces heat storage, since the water in its pore space provides plenty of opportunity for latent heat transfer, and hence minimizes sensible heat buildup.

These grey infrastructure strategies generally serve a single purpose. In contrast, shade trees provide multiple cobenefits. They are of substantial aesthetic value, often increase property values, sequester carbon, mitigate stormwater, provide wildlife habitat, and

Table 7.3. Inputs and outputs for ecosystem services models useful for evaluating shade provision of natural infrastructure

	Mitigation Input Screening Tool (MIST)	I-Trees	Shademotion	Town energy balance models
Key data inputs				
Canopy cover	Average proportion cover needed only.	Yes. Contains a tool, I-Tree Canopy, to help in estimation.	Yes	Yes
Detailed tree data	No	Ideally. Contains tools (I-Tree Canopy and I-Streets) to help in mapping. Can use both a sample or complete inventory data.	Yes, for the region of interest, usually small areas where detailed analysis is needed.	Depends on scale of analysis.
Impervious surface data	No	No	No	Yes
Weather data (temperature, wind, humidity, etc.)	No	Climate zone needed	No	Yes
Key outputs				
Surface temperature (average)	No	No	No	Yes
Air temperature (average)	Yes	No	No	Yes
Electrical savings	Average value for city	Yes	No	No

Table 7.3. (continued)

	Mitigation Input Screening Tool (MIST)	I-Trees	Shademotion	Town energy balance models
Spatially and temporally explicit maps of air temperature	No	No	Provides detailed map of what is shaded when by trees.	Yes
Other notes	A web-based screening tool that is a simplification of results from a more complex meteorology model. Only works for US cities.	Contains models formerly called STRATUM and UFORE.	An ArcGIS tool that allows easy visualization of the area shaded by a planted tree.	There are dozens of meteorological models in this category including Advanced Regional Prediction System (ARPS) and Temperature of Urban Facets (TUF3D).

much more. Aesthetic benefits, in particular, are often central motivations for municipal tree planting programs and are discussed in more detail in chapter 9. Nevertheless, this chapter focuses on the benefits of shade per se, since that is increasingly a stated goal of tree planting programs.

To expand tree canopy cover, municipal tree planting programs have to plant trees at a faster rate than they are lost due to development or mortality. It is often an easy first step to plant trees on city owned or controlled land, especially sidewalks and street corridors. To affect a large fraction of the city's area, the city has to mobilize tree planting on private land. This often takes the form of voluntary programs run by cities or their partners. Urban forestry programs, for instance, try to enlist community members to maintain current trees. Some cities like Washington, DC, use municipal funds to buy the trees but then enlist partner organizations or citizens to plant and maintain them.

Cities may also create financial incentives to increase compliance with voluntary programs. Utilities may give financial payments to customers who plant shade trees that reduce their electrical demand. More frequently, utilities give rebates on electrical bills, which are easier to handle administratively than having to process payments and mail checks. These types of payments by utilities approach a true payment for ecosystem services. The challenge is that since often only one ecosystem service (shade's role in reducing electrical bills) is paid for, rather than the full suite of cobenefits, the magnitude of the payment is often far less than the full value of the trees to society.

Other ways to maintain or enhance tree cover are involuntary, utilizing the zoning or regulatory power of the municipal government. Tree protection ordinances are one of the most common solutions and can serve to slow the average decline in canopy cover recorded by Nowak and Greenfield (2012). Municipal building code requirements and zoning laws affect a city's urban tree canopy cover as well. Cities may require new developments to minimize tree clearing or require new subdivisions to have adequate street trees planted. Certain zoning provisions, especially requirements for setbacks and minimum lot sizes, influence the total amount of nonimpervious surface area in a city, where tree cover can be maintained or enhanced. Note that there is a potential tension between maintaining canopy cover through tools like large minimum lot sizes and the goal of creating a compact, walkable city. Zoning regulations that limit density of new development may provide space or substantial tree cover, but at the environmental cost of less dense development.

Another way to increase vegetative cover in cities is through green roofs, where planters are used to grow some vegetation on top of buildings. Roof surfaces make up a large fraction of the area of a city, so in one sense there is a lot of scope for implementation of this solution. Green roofs can substantially reduce heating and cooling costs, just as cool roof technologies can. They also provide several significant cobenefits, as aesthetics amenities and stormwater mitigation structures. However, they are generally relatively expensive to install, so strong municipal incentives, such as from stormwater programs, are needed if a city wants to foster their widespread adoption.

Valuation of Coastal Protection Natural Infrastructure

Similar to the evaluation of other natural infrastructure strategies, the first step when evaluating shade provision is to define the amount of shade provision that would occur under some status quo scenario. As we have seen for US cities, there is often a decline over time in urban tree canopy. Extrapolating this decline into the future provides one type of status quo scenario. For rapidly developing cities, a build-out analysis is often conducted instead, quantifying what tree cover will likely be left after parcels are developed to the maximum allowed by the current zoning code. However the status quo scenario is constructed, it becomes the baseline against which one or more scenarios of conservation action are measured. For instance, a city may set a goal of increasing canopy tree coverage by

5 percent, and then work out how many trees must be planted to meet that target. Using empirical rules of thumb or the ecosystem service models alone, the effect of shade on economic value can be estimated, for both status quo and conservation scenarios.

Compared with other types of natural infrastructure, the valuation of the benefits shade trees provide to human health and comfort more often tend to be based on simple empirical relationships. Partially this is because the meteorological models necessary to translate a reduction in surface temperatures to a reduction in air temperature are quite complex and time consuming to run. But even if such models of air temperature are run, the link between air temperature and human health remains a difficult link to quantify. Epidemiological studies often estimate empirical equations describing the various risk factors. For instance, the probability of mortality during the Paris heat wave is a function of the person's age, whether they lived alone, the height of their apartment building, and the structural characteristics of a building, as well as the air temperature (Vandertorren et al. 2006). If the city under study is similar enough to a published epidemiology study, one can apply the empirical equation to this new city to get a rough understanding of how a decrease in air temperature might save lives. Increased mortality and morbidity can then be, if necessary, valued in economic terms using estimates of the statistical value of a life.

In the case where shade is supposed to reduce electrical demand, I-Tree (USFS 2013) can be used to calculate an estimate of energy savings from shade in status quo and baseline scenarios. Often the electrical utility can supply information on their marginal cost of supplying electricity. Often most relevant is the marginal cost of producing electricity during summer peak loads, when marginal costs are highest and when shade trees provide their greatest benefit. To calculate the amount saved by the utility by pursuing the natural infrastructure strategy, multiply the difference in electrical demand between the two scenarios (status quo and conservation action) by the marginal cost of the electricity production.

Note that the relevant cost to the electrical utility may not be the marginal cost of producing a kilowatt-hour of energy. Often utilities are worried about peak summer demand overwhelming their system, necessitating the construction of new electricity generation capacity. In this case, the largest financial benefit of using natural infrastructure may be helping the utility avoid future capital costs. See the discussion of the parallel case of avoided capital costs for water treatment plants in chapter 3.

The return on investment (ROI) is, in general, the difference in benefits between the two strategies divided by the difference in costs. Note that for energy savings, these benefits are relatively well characterized (table 7.4). One consideration for shade trees is the cost of long-term maintenance. Cities often try to minimize these costs by getting citizens to agree to maintain street trees.

A cursory reading of table 7.4 shows that if electricity savings were the only goal, then cool roof technologies have the highest ROI. However, cities are usually using tree planting as part of an overall program of urban beautification and will be interested in quantifying cobenefits as well. The I-Tree model can quantify multiple ecosystem service benefits, which could in principle be linked with different municipal programs. Green roofs might, for instance, qualify as a stormwater retention technology in Washington, DC, and also as an energy efficiency measure under the federal tax code.

Implementation

Cities face several challenges in implementing tree planting programs to increase shade. The largest challenge is getting thousands of private landowners to participate in a tree planting program. This is a form of a collective action problem, which occurs for many types of natural infrastructure, but it is a particularly thorny challenge for tree planting campaigns. Because of the small parcels of most urban landowners, tree planting campaigns must influence the decisions of thousands. Cities often launch broad public

Table 7.4. Costs and benefits of common strategies to mitigate the urban heat island effect

Material	Cost	Benefit relative to grey alternative	ROI[a]
Shade tree	$15–$65 per tree per year average	Annual cooling savings vary from 1% to 50% depending on orientation, tree shape, and building factors. Annual heating savings 2%–8%	1.5–3.0, if cobenefits to society are considered
Traditional roof	$0.5–$2.1/ft²	Reference grey alternative	Reference grey alternative
Cool roof	Generally 0%–20% greater than traditional roof technologies	Annual cooling savings 10%–70%. Heating costs may actually increase, due to lower solar input.	Above 1 just due to energy savings[b]
Green roof	For a new building, $10–$25/ft² additional to install above standard roof[c]	Annual cooling savings 6%–10%; heating savings 10%	Above 1 only if cobenefits to society are considered
Traditional pavement	Asphalt $0.10– $1.50/ft². Concrete $0.30–$4.50/ft²	Reference grey alternative	Reference grey alternative
Cool pavement	Porous asphalt $2.00–$2.50/ft². Porous concrete $5.00–$6.25/ft²	Can reduce overall air temperature, but no direct effect on electricity use for heating and cooling	Above 1 only if cobenefits to society are considered

Source: Adapted from EPA 2014b.

[a] Return on investment (ROI) is the ratio of benefits to cost of a conservation strategy. Values above 1 have greater benefits than cost.

[b] A California study found positive NPVs of $95–$537 per year of installing a 1,000 /ft² cool roof.

[c] For installation on existing building, double the cost of installing traditional roof.

education campaigns to win citizen support for tree planting. They also will interact with community groups and neighborhood institutions that can help win buy-in from many property owners at once. As noted above, municipal tree planting programs often avoid this landowner cooperation problem by working on municipal land where possible, for there the city is able to act at will.

Another logistical challenge is negotiating who maintains the trees once they are planted, and who pays for that maintenance. To avoid committing their parks department to long-term maintenance of hundreds of thousands or millions of trees, cities often require those receiving trees to commit to maintaining those trees. From the perspective of ecosystem service provision, this is justified, since many of the cobenefits of tree planting accrue to the private landowner. If Sacramento MUD's tree planting program helps plant a shade tree to reduce electrical bills, then that tree will also increase the beauty of the house nearby, and perhaps its property value. However well justified, passing maintenance responsibility off to landowners often creates other problems, because many landowners fail to maintain their trees and mortality rates are high. One study in Sacramento found that trees planted under the MUD's program had a relatively high mortality rate, reducing the ROI of the utilities investment. To avoid this excess mortality of neglected trees, some cities turn to community groups, which might agree to maintain the trees and prove more likely to honor their promise over time.

Another implementation challenge is what benefits one agency or actor may impose a cost on another. A tree planting program might benefit an electric utility but impose costs on the parks department. Or a city's tree protection ordinance might conflict with the desire of urban planners for dense, walkable neighborhoods. Many cities struggle to harmonize the goals and actions of different agencies. For instance, a stormwater management agency and an electric utility may both love the idea of tree planting and natural infrastructure but differ wildly in where and how they want to plant trees. Often comprehensive plans or sustainability plans are a good place to reconcile these competing visions of what an urban tree planting program should look like.

Finally, a large challenge to planting trees to provide shade for human health is that in many cities there is often no clear payer for this service. Even if increasing shade provision can decrease mortality rates during a heat wave, what agency will fight to plant the trees that supply that shade? Health agencies, whether at the municipal, state, or federal level, are not really used to conceiving their role as changers of urban landscaping, and their budgets are often stretched just to provide preventive health care for their citizens and conducting disease surveillance. Generally, the link between human health and shade provision is put into the urban planning process during comprehensive or sustainability planning. However, most of the time a "champion" agency is still needed to translate the broad commitments of a plan into action.

Monitoring

Most cities will maintain records of how many trees they plant and where, which provides simple implementation metrics of success (e.g., number of trees planted). There is a module in I-Tree, called I-Streets, that is designed to facilitate this sort of tree inventory and can be used to ensure that the information collected on each tree (e.g., species, height, etc.) is sufficient to run I-Tree's ecosystem service provision modules. Remote sensing provides an easy way to assess the percent canopy cover of a city over time. Note that it can take ten to fifteen years for a tree canopy to reach maturity, and remote sensing images are thus less likely to detect smaller saplings. Landsat imagery is the standard way to map tree cover, as it is free and of moderate (30 m) resolution, although other higher resolution platforms are available (e.g., Aster, SPOT, Iknonos). One free web database maps global forest cover over time from 2000 to 2012 (Hansen et al. 2013). This database provides an easy preintervention baseline for canopy cover.

The Landsat sensor, as well as others, measures thermal infrared radiation on one band. There is a relatively straightforward link between the amount of radiation a surface emits and its temperature, so Landsat imagery can be used to monitor surface temperature. However, note that such an approach only measures the surface temperature of the top-most surface: for situations where tree canopy covers impervious surface, remotely sensed imagery is generally insufficient to measure the temperature of the impervious surface, and other technology must be used on-site. Nevertheless, because of its relatively low cost to acquire and because it can cover a whole city, thermal imagery can be a good way to monitor surface temperatures over time in a city. Furthermore, this kind of thermal data is useful to have on hand in case more detailed modeling using meteorological models is desired.

Directly detecting lower air temperatures as a result of conservation action is very difficult. First, it takes a lot of natural infrastructure to make a noticeable change. For instance, a modeling study found that even if all roofs in New York City were converted to green roofs, average temperatures would be reduced by only 0.2°C (EPA 2014b). Second, many of the long-term monitoring stations for air temperature are at airports or in large open fields, which makes them unlikely to be affected by new canopy cover that is relatively far away. Third, there is the counterfactual problem, which requires accounting for other temporal trends in temperature due to land-use change or climate change. A Before/After Control/Intervention (BACI) experimental design is often helpful, which requires designating comparable "control" sites where trees will not be planted. For instance, if some streets are going to be subjected to "block planting," where many trees are planted at once on a single street, then nearby streets that are not block planted can be the control. For these block-scale studies, small inexpensive portable temperature loggers can be used.

It is also difficult to detect differences in electrical demand because of planting shade trees. At the level of an individual building, electrical meter data before and after a tree planting often shows a clear impact of the shade on electricity demand. When coupled with information from nearby comparable houses that did not have trees planted, a BACI design gives researchers great inferential power. At the level of a whole city, by contrast, showing the effect of tree planting on overall electrical demand is very challenging, unless the counterfactual, status quo trend in electricity consumption is well known.

Similarly, for human health effects it is difficult to quantify how many more people would have died in a heat wave without the tree planting. Sometimes all that can be done is to apply rules of thumb that relate mortality rates to air temperature, which would allow a rough estimate of program effectiveness.

Summary

Paris, Chicago, and many other cities continue to plan to make their cities resilient to an increase in the frequency and intensity of heat waves. Part of this is increasing shade provision and decreasing the urban heat island effect. In the United States the Environmental Protection Agency has done an admirable job of promoting this strategy in its documents. The science for quantifying the decrease in surface temperatures and energy use from shade provision is quite well defined, although the link from surface to air temperatures and thus to human health impacts remains complicated to model. Lack of a government entity to promote and champion natural infrastructure creation can limit its installation. Unlike with drinking water protection or stormwater mitigation, where you have utilities willing to pay, or with flooding risks, where there are government agencies with a clear mandate to reduce risk, there are no agencies in most cities that have as their primary goal the reduction of urban heat islands. It has thus proven difficult to finance large-scale tree planting solely motivated by shade provision, with the notable exception of tree planting to reduce electricity costs, where electric utilities have a clear incentive to do so.

Chapter 8

Air Purification

Along the A501 highway, city workman have sprayed sticky "dust suppressant," coating the pavement with calcium magnesium acetate. To the London municipal workers doing it, the task must have seemed rather bizarre. Compared with their usual very solid tasks—filing potholes, paving streets—this one must have seemed ethereal, an attempt to catch a near invisible menace threatening London's residents. The hope was that the resin would literally glue air pollution to the road, capturing particulate matter out of the air (BBC News 2011).

Cities in Europe and the United States have struggled for decades to limit particulate concentrations in the atmosphere, since they cause cancer and asthma and respiratory distress. London has always been affected particularly badly because of its foggy weather that traps air pollution near the city. In 1952, London's air got so toxic that it once killed more than 4,000 people in a single week in an event known simply as the Great Smog (Bell, Davis, and Fletcher 2004).

Things have gotten a lot better in London since then, as the city removed some of the worst sources of pollution by banning the burning of coal for heating personal homes and by requiring coal-burning power plants to have large filters on their smokestacks. But the number of cars and buses on London's roadways keeps increasing, which is causing a resurgence of particulate concentrations. At the same time, doctors around the world are accumulating more evidence about just how bad particulate matter is for human health. As Frank Kelly, professor of Environmental Health at King's College London, puts it: "It became apparent that for particulate matter there is no safe level." This led the European Union (EU) to keep tightening its rules for maximum allowable particulate matter concentrations.

"Because London was exceeding the standards," explained Kelly, "the challenge fell upon the mayor's desk to come up with a strategy. There was a need to identify any measures that could work quickly." Out of desperation, London decided to get out the glue.

As cities around the world search for some affordable way to reduce particulate levels, many of them find part of the answer in a humble place: street trees. Compared with installing a filter on a coal smokestack, planting a tree is incredibly cheap. Trees function as filters, as particulate matter settles on their leaves in a process called dry deposition. One study found that the urban tree canopy of London removes 800 to 2,100 tons of particulate matter annually (Tallis et al. 2011). This is a relatively small fraction of the total London particulate matter problem, but every little bit helps the city as it struggles to meet EU standards.

The leaves of trees can even absorb ground-level ozone and some of its precursors, helping solve another chronic air pollution problem for many cities. Trees reduce not only concentrations of ozone and its precursors, but also air temperature, which slows the rate of ozone formation. This has led Houston and other cities to explore whether large-scale plantings of whole forests can help solve this city's ground-level ozone problem. The US Environmental Protection Agency (EPA) has capped the total emissions of chemicals that cause ground-level ozone and then issued permits for allowable emissions that are now traded among factories. Since planting trees helps reduce ozone concentrations, it can help the Houston region meet its obligations to the EPA and may even be cost-competitive with grey infrastructure strategies the factories could use to decrease their emissions.

In this chapter, I take a close look at the prospects and limits of programs like these that try to give value to the air purification services trees provide. I present the best models for mapping and quantifying how trees can reduce air pollution, paying particular attention to the I-Tree model, and then I discuss how existing regulations on air quality can provide financial incentives for cities or industries to invest in tree planting.

Mapping Important Services for Air Purification

Particulate matter (PM) is defined as any molecule or particle that can be transported in the atmosphere. PM is classified by the size of the particle, usually measured in micrometers (μm), which is one thousandth of a millimeter. Size matters because it determines how easily humans inhale the particle into their lungs. Standard measurements are PM_{10} (smaller than 10 μm) and $PM_{2.5}$ (smaller than 2.5 μm) (NRC 2004). PM, particularly the smaller $PM_{2.5}$, can cause coughing, asthma, bronchitis, irregular heartbeat, nonfatal heart attacks, and in extreme cases, premature deaths in sensitive people (Donahue 2011).

PM is directly emitted from both mobile sources like automobiles and stationary sources like factories and power plants (figure 8.1). For the larger PM_{10}, dust from roads and construction operations are major sources of emissions, as is sea salt in coastal areas. For the smaller $PM_{2.5}$, direct (primary) emissions from the burning of fossil fuels are the major source. Secondary emissions, which occur when a molecule is transformed through physical or chemical processes, are also important for $PM_{2.5}$. For instance, nitrogen oxides (NO_x) and sulfur oxides (SO_x) can react to form PM (NRC 2004).

The ozone layer that naturally occurs high up in Earth's stratosphere is a good thing, protecting us from harmful UV radiation from the sun. On the other hand, ozone in the atmosphere near the ground is caused by human pollution and is a real danger for human health (NRC 2004). Ground-level ozone causes throat irritation, asthma, and bronchitis (Donahue 2011). It also has negative impacts on natural ecosystems and agriculture, as plant growth and health are reduced at high ozone concentrations (NRC 2004).

Ozone (O_3) is occasionally emitted directly, but is more commonly formed from secondary emissions. For ground-level ozone to form, a complex set of reactions have to take place (figure 8.1). First, you need volatile organic compounds (VOCs), a broad category that includes many different carbon-containing chemicals that will easily evaporate from their liquid form and float away in the atmosphere. VOCs are emitted from cars as well as from various solvents (e.g., paint thinner) and industrial processes. They are also emitted from trees and other vegetation at varying rates, depending on the species involved and the weather conditions.

Second, you need nitrogen oxides (NO_x) to form ozone. NO_x is emitted from the burning of fossil fuels and in many cities is primarily formed from automobiles and power plants. NO_x is a bad thing in its own right, since NO_x emissions contribute to the problem of acid rain. But in the presence of VOCs and sunlight, NO_x will react to form ozone. While all three factors (VOC, NO_x, and light) are needed to form ozone, in different cities different factors may be the one whose concentration is low enough to limit the rate of ozone formation.

This chapter presupposes that health authorities have measured ambient air quality and determined that either PM or ozone concentrations are high enough to imperil public health. In most countries,

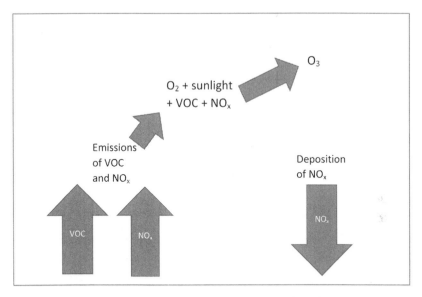

Figure 8.1. Conceptual schematic of ozone formation as well as the removal of ozone and particulate matter by trees.

the environmental protection agency will have conducted an emissions inventory for a city or region. This lists, and sometimes maps, source activities that cause emissions. Each source activity has an emissions factor, which is the amount of emissions per unit activity. For instance, a power plant burning coal will emit a certain quantity of NO_x which is the product of the amount of coal burned (the source activity) times emissions per ton of coal burned (the emissions factor).

Atmospheric transport and chemistry models (table 8.1) can combine spatially explicit information from emissions inventories with meteorological data to map the concentration of pollutants over time and space. For instance, the Urban Airshed Model (UAM), which simulates physical and chemical processes in the atmosphere, is often linked to meteorology data. The output of the UAM would be a grid of pollutant concentration at various points in time. These atmospheric transport and chemistry models can

Table 8.1. Inputs and outputs for ecosystem services models useful for evaluating natural infrastructure for shade provision

	I-Tree	Photochemical model (e.g., Urban Airshed Model)	Dispersion models (a.k.a. atmospheric transport models)
Key data inputs			
Canopy cover	Yes. Contains a tool, I-Tree Canopy, to help in estimation.	Implicitly, as sources of VOCs[a], and for their impact on temperature and pollutant concentration.	Implicitly, as sources of VOCs, and for their impact on temperature and pollutant concentration.
Detailed tree data	Ideally. Contains tools (I-Tree Canopy and I-Streets) to help in mapping. Can use both a sample or complete inventory data.	No	No
Impervious surface data	No	Varies	Varies
Weather data (temperature, wind, humidity, etc.)	Climate zone needed.	Yes	Yes
Key outputs			
Dry deposition of pollutants (site-level)	Yes	No	No
Absorption of ozone (site-level)	Yes	No	No

Table 8.1. (continued)

	1-Tree	Photochemical model (e.g., Urban Airshed Model)	Dispersion models (a.k.a. atmospheric transport models)
Spatially and temporally explicit maps of pollutants	No	Estimates of pollutant reactions and concentrations.	Estimates of dispersion of pollutants over time and space. Often linked or incorporated into photochemical models.
Other notes	Contains models formerly called STRATUM and UFORE.	There are several models in this category, including UAM, CMAQ, CAMx, and REMSAD.	There are several models in this category, including AERMOD and CALPUFF. Micro-meteorology is also sometimes used.

Note: Most tree planting projects to improve air quality will use 1-Tree to calculate the benefits of tree planting. Often, health or environmental agencies will have measured or modeled ambient pollutant concentrations at several locations in a city, which can be used in conjunction with 1-Tree. Only in rare cases, where spatially explicit models of the benefits of tree planting on air quality are needed will photochemical or dispersion modelling be conducted as part of a tree planting project.

[a]VOCs: volatile organic compounds.

then be calibrated against measurements of ambient air concentrations. In developed countries, such spatially explicit information on pollutant concentration exists thanks to modeling efforts by health or environmental authorities. In the absence of such detailed information, cities planning tree planting programs must infer pollutant concentrations from the scattered ambient air measurements that exist.

Natural vegetation affects air quality in several complicated ways. First, as an emitter of VOCs, trees can worsen the problem of ground-level ozone (table 8.2). Some species like sweetgum (*Liquidambar styraciflua*) have high emissions, while others like ginkgo (*Ginkgo biloba*) have very low emissions (Karlik and Pittinger 2012). The standard model for estimating VOC emissions from plants is the I-Tree model. It contains a module that estimates leaf area and canopy structure from standard tree inventory data. This information is then used to estimate VOC emissions, as a function of a species' leaf area, its species-specific VOC emissions rate, air temperature, and the amount of photosynthetically active radiation (PAR).

The presence of trees also increases the amount of shade. As discussed in chapter 7, this can decrease air temperature. Trees directly slow the rate of ozone formation by limiting the light needed during the chemical reaction that forms ozone. Shade also slows the emission of VOCs by those leaves farther down in the canopy that are shaded. Both effects are considered in I-Tree, which models ozone formation in discrete canopy strata (I-Tree 2014).

Particulate matter is removed by trees through dry deposition, which is when particles in the atmosphere deposit themselves on a surface, decreasing the atmospheric concentration. Other pollutants like ozone will directly be absorbed by a plant's leaves, in the process reducing the pollutant's concentration in the atmosphere. I-Tree estimates the amount of O_3, SO_2, NO_2, CO, PM_{10}, and $PM_{2.5}$ removed by trees. One key parameter is the concentration of the pollutant: at higher atmospheric concentrations, the rate of dry

Table 8.2. High and low VOC-emitting species

High-emitting species	Low-emitting species
Sweet gum (*Liquidambar styraciflua*)	White birch (*Betula alba*)
White oak (*Quercus alba*)	Ginkgo (*Ginkgo biloba*)
Red oak (*Quercus rubra*)	Magnolia (*Magnolia grandifolia*)
Eucalyptus (*Eucalyptus globulus*)	Serviceberry (*Amelanchier alnifolia*)
White popular (*Populus alba*)	Hornbeam (*Carpinus betula*)

Source: Based on Karlik and Pittinger 2012.
Note: (VOC) volatile organic compound.

deposition or absorption is greater. Another is the leaf area: more leaf area offers more surface area on which dry deposition or absorption can take place.

I-Tree models the flux of pollutants from the atmosphere to the tree, in grams per square meter per second, as

$$F = Vd \times C$$

where Vd is the deposition velocity (meters per second) and C is the pollutant concentration (grams per cubic meters) (I-Tree 2014). Deposition velocity is in turn a function of aerodynamic, boundary layer, and canopy resistances. The structure of a tree's canopy varies among species, which affects canopy resistance. Moreover, weather conditions such as wind speed and photosynthetically active radiation (PAR) affect aerodynamic and boundary layer resistance. For the dry deposition of particulate matter, the frequency with which rain falls affects how often leaves are washed off, thus freeing up their surface area for more dry deposition to occur.

The standard ecosystem service modeling approach is to map the location of trees in a GIS (geographic information systems) format, along with information on tree characteristics (e.g., species type, diameter at breast height). From atmospheric transport models, site-specific estimates of C can be obtained. I-Tree is then used to calculate the benefits that trees produce on a certain sites. One can then sum up the benefits that all trees provide, either currently or under some future scenario. For example, Nowak et al. (2013) quantified $PM_{2.5}$ removal for ten US cities using I-Tree. They found that the net annual removal amounts for one hectare of canopy cover varied from 1.3 kg in Los Angeles to 3.6 kg in Atlanta. For Atlanta, trees in total remove 64.5 metric tons, 0.25 percent of the total $PM_{2.5}$ load.

Common Threats and Common Solutions

As discussed in chapter 7, the largest threat to the ecosystem services that street trees provide is the continuing loss of trees over time in many cities. Trees are lost because of continued urban development, or because the mortality rate of street trees is higher than the rate at which new trees are planted. The net loss of trees in many cities means that air purification will decrease. In addition, as many cities grow there are greater emissions of ozone and PM. The net effect of the two trends (fewer trees and more emissions) is to increase atmospheric concentrations of ozone and PM.

At the same time, as the evidence mounts of health impacts of PM and ozone even at very low concentrations, government agencies continue to tighten standards. For instance, the US EPA has moved from a 0.08 ppm standard to a 0.075 ppm standard and is likely to move this further downward to 0.06 ppm. The maximum permitted level of $PM_{2.5}$ in a twenty-four-hour period was 65 $\mu g/m^3$ and is now 35 $\mu g/m^3$. These stricter standards mean more cities are struggling to reach air quality standards. Many of the relatively low cost technological solutions have already been applied, and the remaining set of grey infrastructure solutions are relatively expensive.

Many cities are thus looking for additional strategies to meet air quality standards, and large-scale tree planting could be one such strategy. New forests would increase shade, decrease temperatures, and increase dry deposition and absorption of pollutants. On the other hand, new forests will also increase VOC emissions some-what. All else being equal, tree planting to reduce ozone is a better strategy in NO_x limited environments than in VOC-limited cities, since the incremental addition of VOC from trees does not signifi-cantly increase the rate at which ozone is formed. Of course, urban trees have lots of other cobenefits for urban residents, which may also motivate planting.

In the United States, the structure of the Clean Air Act may pro-vide some financial incentives that give value to the benefits nature provides. For a set of criteria air pollutants (ozone, PM, CO, NO_x, SO_2, and Pb), the EPA has to set National Ambient Air Quality Standards (NAAQS) based on scientific data about the pollutant's impact on human health. For areas that fail to meet these standards ("nonattainment"), the relevant state must file a State Implementa-tion Plan (SIP) that describes how they will meet the NAAQS. SIPs contain many measures that try to reduce emissions from both mo-bile and stationary sources of pollution. SIPs usually are based on a lot of modeling work, to show that the proposed measures will indeed help the area comply with the NAAQS.

Tree planting was recognized by the US EPA as an emerging or voluntary measure that might, in principle, be part of a SIP. Tree planting might be directly done by a state, county, or municipal government to help reach attainment. Alternatively, some SIPs have already set up a cap on emissions of NO_x, VOCs, or PM. Total emis-sions in the airshed must be below the cap, and permits are needed to emit the regulated gases. In principle, tree planting could gener-ate credits that have a real value under the permitting system.

However, while several US cities like Houston and Sacramento have begun exploring putting tree planting in their SIP, none have yet succeeded in doing so. The rules of the EPA set a fairly high bar that any measure in a SIP must meet (USFS 2014). Among these, any measure must have quantifiable and precise estimates of its benefits. The science done by the US Forest Service and partners, embodied in I-Tree, arguably meets this standard. Any measure in a SIP must be additional (i.e., the tree planting would not have occurred without the listing in the SIP). The measure must be permanent for the time period that the benefit will be claimed. Finally, any emerging measure cannot replace other existing regulations, a provision that might invalidate claiming credit for tree planting under existing cap-and-trade permitting mechanisms. Despite these regulatory hurdles, there is increased interest by many cities in tree planting as an air quality mechanism, and I have hope that in the near future tree planting will become a standard part of SIPs.

Valuation of Air Purification Natural Infrastructure

Much of the economic value of decreasing air pollution comes from avoided health care costs that would have been paid if the air was dirtier. Asthma, for instance, affects around 25 million Americans, resulting in medical bills as well as missed work and school days (CDC 2011). Studies have also found that particulate matter decreases the productivity of workers when they are at work, an effect which is particularly acute for outdoor workers such as farmhands. Several studies have tried to add up all these various costs and come up with a total cost for a disease. For instance, asthma costs the United States around $3,300 per person with asthma per year, totaling around $50 billion in medical expenses (CDC 2011). Other, more detailed, studies have tried to estimate which fraction of the cases of a disease are due to air pollution, as opposed to other causes. For instance, studies have estimated that around 30 percent of childhood asthma is due to air pollution exposure (NRDC 2014). One of the largest costs of increased air pollution is increased mortality. One study estimated that globally 2.1 million deaths occur every year due to $PM_{2.5}$ (Silva et al. 2013). Within a particular society this increased mortality can be valued using the concept of the statistical value of a life. The public health field also uses the metric of disability-adjusted life year (DALY), essentially the sum of the years of healthy life lost due to a disease, and statistical values of a DALY have been estimated as well. This business of putting an economic value on a human life is controversial, because many believe that every human life is precious in a way that money cannot quantify. Nevertheless, it is widely used by policymakers, who must somehow make the difficult decision of how much society should spend to reduce air pollution.

A natural infrastructure project that reduces ozone and particulate matter concentrations relative to some status quo scenario, what the ozone and particulate matter concentration was without conservation intervention. This incremental difference in air pollution concentrations can be quantified in economic terms. I-Tree uses published average US median values of how a one metric ton reduction in pollution avoids medical costs and mortality (USFS 2013). This quantity is then multiplied by the metric tons of a pollutant removed. Outside the United States, the median values used by I-Tree are likely not appropriate, and other values would have to be used.

A more detailed study of the air pollution benefits of a natural infrastructure project could draw from more detailed public health and epidemiology studies. These studies often provide an empirical relationship between pollutant concentration and health impacts. A particular city's ambient air quality measurements can then be used with these empirical relationships to calculate the health burden an air pollutant imposes. One could use atmospheric transport models to construct spatial estimates of ambient air concentrations before and after the construction of the natural infrastructure project. Spatial information on human population distribution can then be used with these before-and-after concentrations to determine the reduction in health burdens due to the natural infrastructure project.

Air pollution also has impacts on ecosystem health, which imposes real economic costs. For instance, high concentrations of ozone slows the growth of both forests and crops. Various studies have tried to quantify the economic costs of these ecosystem impacts, with particular research attention given to the impacts of acid rain on sensitive ecosystems and the economic costs that air pollution puts on agricultural producers (NRC 2004). A full accounting of the benefits of a natural infrastructure strategy might take into account avoided ecosystem service impacts, although the available science may not be sufficient to estimate benefits in a quantitative, rigorous way.

Another approach to valuing the benefits of a reduction in air pollution is to value the grey infrastructure alternatives. When a city faces mandates by a government agency like the US Environmental Protection Agency, they then try to find the cheapest way to meet the mandate. If tree planting is cost effective relative to the other grey infrastructure strategies that would have to be used to meet the mandate, then it should seriously be considered. For instance, a study by Kroeger et al. (2014) looked at tree planting in the Houston area, using the I-Tree model to calculate the quantity of ozone and its precursors removed by a forest restoration project. The forest restoration project is cost competitive with other ways companies can meet their obligations under the SIP, if the use of the land for reforestation is free or very low cost.

Implementation

All of the challenges faced by cities implementing any sort of tree planting program will be a challenge for natural infrastructure programs for air quality. Often a city must mobilize action by many private landowners. The solution is often working with community groups or other key actors that can influence many landowners. Cities also struggle with the long-term maintenance costs of trees and try to get individual landowners or community groups to agree to accept those maintenance costs. See chapter 7 for further discussion of these common challenges of tree planting programs.

Some considerations are unique to a tree planting program for air quality, however. Ideally, trees would be planted where pollutant concentrations are highest, as the higher the concentration, the faster the rate of dry deposition and absorption. But as the Houston study illustrates (Kroeger et al. 2014), it is also important to find places with a low opportunity cost of reforestation, essentially large parcels of degraded land that are currently unutilized. The spatial overlap of these two considerations often leads to suburban or rural areas downwind of an industrial area of a city. Alternatively, street trees can be located quite close to pollution sources, but can be quite costly to install per tree, and therefore their planting generally cannot be justified solely on the basis of their air quality effects.

Another issue unique to tree planting for air quality programs is selecting trees that emit relatively few VOCs. For many temperate regions, this means merely avoiding particular tree species. In some ecoregions, however, the native vegetation may generally emit a lot of VOCs. In these ecoregions, restoration opportunities may emit so much VOC that they increase ozone concentrations overall.

Finally, the biggest internal challenge for many city governments may be defining a coherent tree planting strategy that meets multiple goals. Different municipal agencies may have very different reasons for planting trees. For instance, the parks department may want to increase recreational access and aesthetic beauty, which leads to tree planting in different places than does air quality considerations. Sustainability or comprehensive plans are a good place to find commonality among these different conceptions of what tree planting can or should do. Realistically for many cities, air purification may be a secondary goal of tree planting, after aesthetic and recreational goals.

Monitoring

One of the simplest ways cities monitor their tree plantings is to just keep track of what was planted where (implementation metrics). Planted trees need to be monitored over time, to assess tree mortality rates and quantify whether the tree's canopy and leaf area is maturing as fast as expected. This is the minimum information needed to check whether trees are delivering the expected air quality benefit. Mortality monitoring may be particularly important for a program under a SIP, which is required to show permanence over the time period for which credit for ozone mitigation is given.

Cities could then take the measured information on canopy and leaf area (often inferred from tree diameter, species type, and height) and use I-Tree to calculate estimated ecosystem service benefits from these trees. The assumption in doing this is that tree planting is truly additional (i.e., the trees would not have been planted without the program, so the air pollution reduction in the status quo case is effectively zero for that plot of land).

Much more challenging is detecting changes in ambient air quality due to a tree planting program. The ambient air quality at a sensor is a function of everything happening upwind. It is often difficult to know what the air quality would have been in the counterfactual case without tree planting. It is helpful to the monitoring program to have sensors very close to the planted stand that make relatively local measurements of air quality nearby (e.g., measurements at a lower height, since air above the canopy is relatively well mixed). It's also helpful to have before-and-after measurements at the site of planting, as well as at a similar control site where no tree planting is anticipated (i.e., a BACI design: see chapter 7).

It will generally not be possible to directly measure the benefit of tree planting on air quality at the scale of an entire watershed. Too many other things can change ambient air concentrations, such as changes in the amount of emissions or changes in weather patterns. However, detailed atmospheric transport models can be used to evaluate two scenarios, the actual and the counterfactual. This would allow isolation of the relatively small changes in forest cover relative to everything else that changed in the airshed. Such modeling can also show the spatial distribution of benefits that tree planting provided, which are likely greatest right next to and downwind of the planting site.

Summary

London, Houston, Sacramento, and many other cities globally are justifying tree planting programs based, in part, upon the air quality benefits those trees provide. The science of the average reduction in air pollution per tree is relatively well characterized, and tools like I-Tree make estimation of benefits relatively easy. However, modeling the effect of this reduction on spatial patterns of air pollution concentrations remains a complicated task for specialists. Probably the biggest factor limiting the widespread use of trees to reduce air pollution is the current structure of air quality regulations in many countries, and skepticism among regulators that natural infrastructure is reliable enough to allow it to meet regulatory requirements. I am optimistic that this skepticism eventually can be overcome. Certainly, as the health impacts of even low levels of particulate matter and ground-level ozone become clear, many more cities will be looking for strategies to meet every tightening of air quality standards, and so many of them will turn to trees as part of the solution.

Chapter 9

Aesthetic Value

D URING SUMMER 2007, a research team went all around Portland, Oregon, visiting more than 3,000 homes. At each house, they
counted the number of trees in the front yard and along the sidewalk. They wrapped a tape around each tree to measure its circum-
ference, and visually assessed its condition. Actually, calling it a
team is a bit too generous a description. As the paper wryly notes,
"all the data collection was conducted by one student," which might
make this one of the more repetitive jobs a student might ever hold
(Donovan and Butry 2010).

The point of this student spending a summer wandering around
Portland was to quantify something that is often invisible: the
beauty of a street tree. What the researchers in Portland found is
that having healthy, attractive trees in front of a house has a real
tangible value when you decide to sell the house. Having street
trees increased the median sale price of houses by around 3 percent,

which in Portland amounts to roughly $9,000. The presence of street trees also reduced the time a property was on the market by a few days, as a more attractive house with trees sold quicker than one without it. The Portland team's findings, while admirable in their academic precision, would come as no big surprise to realtors, who often talk about a home's curb appeal.

Economists have been working for decades to quantify the way trees and nature affect house price (e.g., Anderson and Cordell 1988). This body of research gives us insight into how much we actually value something as ineffable as the beauty of a tree. Most of the time, our aesthetic appreciation of a tree is hard to quantify. But when real estate is bought or sold, our preference for beauty is revealed. Economists call this specific type of revealed preference analysis, using price data to estimate the value of something hidden, "hedonic analysis." Revealed preference methods are one of two ways to quantify the value of the hidden. The other is called "contingent valuation," and involves basically asking people how much you would have to pay them to, for instance, cut down a tree in front of their house.

Adding up all the benefits that the trees of Portland give to residential property owners, the study's authors find that presence of trees adds $54 million annually to the estimated value of properties (Donovan and Butry 2010). In comparison, they estimate that annual maintenance costs of trees in Portland, borne by both the private and public sectors, amounts to $4.6 million. That's a 12:1 ratio of benefits to costs, a very good return on investment by almost any standard. Why then do property owners not plant more trees? As with most ecosystem services, externalities are the culprit. Almost half of the benefit of a tree occurs outside the parcel where it occurs. As a property owner, I would bear all the costs of planting and maintaining a tree, and reap only part of the benefit.

Cities like Portland are beginning to realize the value of street trees. Donovan and Butry (2010) estimated that the presence of trees increases property values in Portland and thus the city's tax revenues by $15.3 million. Property values are, of course, just one manifestation of our preference for the beauty of a tree, albeit a nicely tangible one. Neighborhoods with parks and open space might be more popular places to live. And cities with beautiful views of natural areas might attract more residents.

This chapter describes the exciting economics research that quantifies these aesthetic benefits of nature. I present the characteristics of natural infrastructure that maximize its aesthetic benefits, as well as implementation strategies to create that infrastructure. Perhaps most important, I discuss how to finance the creation of such infrastructure.

Mapping Important Services for Aesthetic Value

The aesthetic beauty of natural habitat influences humans over a variety of scales. One useful distinction is between individual trees scattered along a street, and parcels of green space in relatively continuous blocks. Street trees now seem like a standard component of most cities, but it is worth noting that in the medieval period most cities in Europe had no trees. Street trees were an innovation of the Dutch, who used them to line canals, and the idea spread outward to other countries. Similarly, the idea of having "open space" in a city, whether blocks of natural habitat or created spaces with lawns and gardens, is relatively new. In the medieval period, most greenspace belonged to royalty, and only slowly in England and France did greenspace come to be seen as a public amenity rather than a private perk (Lawrence 2008).

Street trees and other individual trees scattered in developed areas provide a variety of services: wildlife habitat, shade, noise control, and much more. Aesthetic beauty is just one of these ecosystem services. The hedonic analysis performed by Donovan and his wandering student Butry (2010) measures people's willingness to pay for the sum of all of these ecosystem services. Nevertheless, aesthetic value is often the most important service in financial terms.

In order to map the ecosystem service benefits that street trees provide, the first step is to take an inventory of what trees exist. The software package I-Streets provides a good way to do this. It allows for easy entry of either a complete inventory of a city's trees or, alternatively, a representative sample. Inventory can be conducted with a field survey or with remotely sensed imagery (I-Tree 2011).

Arborists have developed a standard way of valuing individual landscaping trees. These values are often used for appraisals in a legal context. If your neighbor, for instance, accidentally kills a tree on your property, compensation can be determined using the guidance by the Council of Tree and Landscape Appraisers (CTLA 2000). For small trees, this appraised value is based on their replacement costs:

$$\textit{Tree value} = \textit{replacement cost} \times \textit{species rating} \times$$
$$\textit{condition rating} \times \textit{location factor}$$

Bigger trees cost more to replace, and tables of industry average costs as a function of diameter are available (Cullen 2007). Often an average of $48 per square inch of cross-sectional area is assumed. For instance, a 20-inch-diameter tree has a cross-sectional area of $\pi(20/2)^2 = 314.2$ inch^2, for a value of $15,082. The species rating goes from zero to one, with one being more desirable (table 9.1). The condition and location factor similarly scale from zero to one and record respectively how healthy a tree is and how prominently featured in the landscaping of a property (table 9.2). For large trees that cannot be replaced at that size, a "trunk formula" is used to calculate the value lost to a landowner.

Economists have tended to look down on the CTLA methodology as rather subjective. One of the first papers to use hedonic pricing, however, compared it to the CTLA method (Morales, Micha, and Weber 1983). The two valuations are remarkably consistent. The CTLA method found that the presence of street trees increased

Table 9.1. Species score for the Council of Tree and Landscape Appraisers (CTLA) method of tree valuation

Class 1—100%

Red maple (*Acer rubrum*), ginkgo (*Ginkgo biloba*), tulip popular (*Liriodendron tulipifera*), white oak (*Quercus alba*), dogwood (*Cornus florida*), American holly (*Ilex opaca*), scarlet oak (*Quercus coccinea*)

Class 2—80%

Magnolia spp. (*Magnolia* spp.), white pine (*Pinus strobus*), Bradford pear (*Pyrus calleryana*), red oak (*Quercus rubra*), hemlock (*Tsuga canadensis*), beech (*Fagus grandifolia*)

Class 3—60%

Buckeye (*Aesculus glabra*), honey locust (*Gleditsia triacanthos*), hophornbeam (*Ostrya virginiana*), hickory spp. (*Carya* spp.), river birch (*Betula nigra*)

Class 4—40%

Sycamore (*Platanus occidentalis*), redbud (*Cercis canadensis*), Norway maple (*Acer platanoides*)

Class 5—20%

Tree-of-heaven (*Ailanthus altissima*), boxelder (*Acer negundo*), mulberry (*Morus* spp.), black locust (*Robinia pseudoacacia*)

Source: Adapted from Garton and Tankersley 2014.

Notes: Higher scores indicate more valuable trees. Species lists and scores vary somewhat between states, but are generally similar. Scores represent an informal average of public opinion, although individual opinion and value might vary substantially—I quite like mulberries, for example!

prices by around 10 percent, while a hedonic analysis estimated the difference at 17 percent. The literature on hedonic valuation has tended to focus on how proximity to street trees influences cost (the location factor), rather than the size, condition, or species factors that the CTLA method includes. The clear finding from dozens of hedonic studies is that people pay more for street trees nearby, and that beyond a few hundred feet, street trees have little discernable effect on property values.

Open space extent and location are often defined by geographic information systems (GIS), either from a vector-based parcel map or a raster-based satellite imagery. The definition of open space has

Table 9.2. Effect of location and condition on tree value following the Council of Tree and Landscape Appraisers (CTLA) method

Location	Location Score %	Condition	Condition Score %
Arboretum	10	Sound tree with no disease	100
Average residential landscape	80	Minor insect or disease problems	80
Parks, city streets	60	Broken branches and other moderate problems	60
Out-of-city highway	40	Trunk scars and early stages of decay present	40
Native woods	20	Advanced decay of trunk	20

Source: Table adapted from Garton and Tankersley 2014.

Note: Higher scores indicate more valuable trees. While presented here in the same table, location and condition are evaluated separately for each tree, and it is possible to get a high score on one metric and a low score on another.

varied a lot from study to study, and of course affects the results of a hedonic analysis greatly (McConnell and Walls 2005). Sometimes any undeveloped parcel is counted as open space, including highly constructed spaces like golf courses. More commonly, open space is defined as areas of natural habitat, while constructed greenspaces are placed in a second category called parks.

A set of easily calculated GIS variables is often used to map how much a particular parcel of open space matters to a particular house's price. Sometimes straight-line distance ("as a crow flies") is used, and sometimes walking distance is used, following along the street and path network to get a more accurate sense of how easy it is to get from the house to the open space. Alternatively, scientists measure the amount of open space in a buffer zone around a property. Common buffer distances range from 100 m to 1 km (McConnell and Walls 2005). The common finding is that proximity matters: people will pay more to live close to open space. The only important longer-distance interactions seem to involve very significant natural areas that people will actively travel a long distance to see, although this kind of interaction can then arguably be seen as a kind of recreation.

There have now been enough studies of the effect of greenspace on house prices that the body of literature has been surveyed by several review papers. Open space, on average, is worth about $1,550 ha/yr (Brander and Koetse 2011). While this is a significant amount of money, note that one big street tree can easily be worth ten times as much. In short, trees on or just adjacent to a parcel are much more valuable than more distant open space. Even for open space, proximity matters: each 10 m closer a parcel is to open space increased home price by 0.1 percent.

One key finding of this hedonic literature on open space is that when population density is high, there tends to be less open space, and we are willing to pay more for it (Kroeger 2008). In other words, we are willing to pay more for a resource when it is scarce. On average, a 10 percent increase in population density leads to a 5 percent increase in open space value. Many studies also find that it matters what open space could become in the future. Permanently protected land is worth more, presumably because home buyers feel some assurance they will be able to enjoy the open space in the future. Conversely, private land may be developed, and thus become less valuable to a landowner, or even a disamenity if the development is ugly enough.

Even farther away spatially, another set of studies show that views of quite distant but pretty scenery can have real value. One study by Tryvainen and Mittinen (2000) found that houses with views of the forest in Finland are worth 5 percent more. Other studies have found similar effects for beautiful views of mountains, lakes, or coasts. Again, land protection seems likely to make a view more valuable, while if the view could be degraded or obscured in the future it is considered less valuable.

Sometimes in studying the value of a view, it is defined subjectively, with researchers deciding whether each parcel has a view of a particular amenity or not, based on site visits or expert opinion.

Other studies have tried to more objectively define the quality of a view on a continuous scale. In a GIS, viewshed tools can be used to calculate the proportion of the view from a property that takes in an amenity. Some studies such as Sander and Polasky (2009) find this a better explanatory variable.

These different kinds of nature may compensate for each other. For instance, a study by Mansfield and colleagues (2005) examined home prices in the Raleigh-Durham metro area as a function of either greenness on the parcel (e.g., tree cover) or greenness nearby (e.g., open space). Both types of greenness positively affected home prices. However, the effects were compensatory: parcels with high in-parcel greenness were less affected by proximity to open space. Compensation effects mean that landowners want a little natural beauty near their parcel, but once that desire is met, further increases in nature don't increase home prices as much. There is a hopeful implication here for urban planners: street trees can to some extent substitute for the open space that is often lacking in dense urban neighborhoods.

Another fascinating idea that emerges from the literature is of nature as a mediating factor. One study in Texas, for instance, found that house prices were lower next to a commercial development like a strip mall, presumably because of the noise and unpleasantness of the commercial development. Trees blocking the view of the commercial area mediated this disamenity. Here, people are willing to pay more to have a view of trees when it stands in the way of an ugly view than a neutral view (Ellis, Lee, and Kweon 2006).

Common Threats and Common Solutions

As with all the ecosystem services that derive from street trees, the biggest threat to service provision is simply their loss over time. As discussed in chapter 7, the average American city lost 2.7 percent of its forest cover over the last decade. Open space also tends to decline over time as metro areas develop. In both cases, the benefits nature provides are not fully incorporated into private markets, so there is no reason to expect private developers to adequately provide street trees or (especially) open space.

Another threat facing cities is the hidden expense that new development can impose on a town. In many cases, the cost of providing municipal services (sewer, water, electricity, etc.) to new developments is substantial, and new tax revenues only partially offset these costs. This is particularly true for low-density suburban developments, which because of their highly dispersed nature have a high per-unit cost of supplying with municipal services. Each development then can worsen a city's financial position. In situations like this, open space protection can seem appealing simply because it limits new development.

To mitigate the slow loss of street trees over time, many cities institute street tree planting programs. While such programs require money and can be hard to finance, they are relatively easy to administer, in that they create natural infrastructure on public land, the road right-of-way. Motivating action on private lands is harder. Sometimes the regulatory powers of a city are used, through programs like tree protection ordinances. Street tree programs are reviewed more fully in chapter 7.

Protecting open space is another common strategy that municipalities pursue. Parcels are purchased to protect the aesthetic good that the open space provides. Using the GIS techniques mentioned earlier, parcels can be prioritized for protection based on their aesthetic value. This is often done using some proxy measurement, such as the number of people within some buffer distance of an open space parce. To achieve an economically efficient prioritization of protection, ideally a parcel's cost and the threat of its development would both be considered during prioritization. See Groves (2003) or another textbook on conservation planning for more information.

Open space can mean different things to different people, and so municipal efforts to protect open space can take several different forms. Three basic types of open space protection programs are most common. Natural area protection programs aim to protect the last remaining parcels of open space. Agricultural area protection programs are ostensibly about agricultural production, but often are motivated by a desire to maintain agricultural vistas. Finally, open space may be acquired as part of a recreational opportunities program, although in this case a significant change in land use may occur as vacant land is developed to expand its recreational opportunities.

Finally, cities sometimes act to protect scenic views for their residents. If the attractive feature is small, it is often protected as a park. For large features, cities commonly restrict development to maintain views. It is rare to ban development outright, but often building characteristics (e.g., height) are limited to minimize impact on viewsheds.

Valuation of Aesthetic Natural Beauty

Hedonic valuation of street trees and open space is one of the best studied ecosystem services profiled in this book. In part this is because economists love studying datasets that have actual prices in them, such as data on house prices, since such datasets can provide strong evidence of the value of ecosystem services. Despite the rich literature on the hedonic value of nature in a city, there are relatively few tools that allow people to estimate its aesthetic value. Often, valuation involves "benefit transfer," when the empirical results of one study are assumed to apply to another site. If Seattle wanted to estimate the value of street trees, it could take the regression equations developed by Donovan and Butry (2010) in Portland and apply it in Seattle. Assuming the socioeconomic environment is similar between the two cities, the assumptions underlying the benefits transfer is probably appropriate.

There is a tendency in the literature on the aesthetic value of nature in a city to calculate the total value of nature, implicitly contrasting the current state of affairs with a hypothetical scenario where all the nature in a city disappears. More meaningful is to define two scenarios: the conservation scenario, where nature in the city is maintained or expanded, and the status quo scenario, which in many cities means a slow decline in urban nature's extent. The status quo scenario is usually constructed by measuring the rate of trees or open space lost over some time period, and then extrapolating that trend into the future. Valuation is conducted on land-cover maps from the conservation action and status quo scenarios, and the difference in ecosystem service provision between the two scenarios is the gain to society from the conservation action scenario.

For street trees, a necessary first step is to conduct an inventory, either field based or remote sensing based (table 9.3). For field-based surveys, it is often possible to collect the data needed to use the CTLA method. Alternatively, if a hedonic study exists in a similar location, benefits transfer can be used to estimate value. Whether the CTLA method or benefits transfer is used, one hard step is quantifying which trees might have died in the scenario of no conservation action. One simple strategy is to assume a certain proportion of trees die, picking out the dead trees randomly from the complete inventory of trees in a city.

The I-Streets software (I-Tree 2011) provides a fairly easy framework in which to do valuation via benefits transfer. The software has an interface that can be used to help conduct a complete inventory of street trees in the city. If time or available resources only permit a partial inventory of trees, the software can be used to conduct a statistically valid sample. Valuation in I-Streets is a linear function of "resource units," in this case multiplying leaf-surface area by the change in property values per unit of leaf-surface area. The function is based on Anderson and Cordell's (1988) study in Athens, Georgia (USA). I-Streets methodology should be considered accurate only in places culturally and economically like Athens, Georgia.

Valuation of open space is always done using benefits transfer, as there is no equivalent of the CTLA methodology for open space. A

Table 9.3. Inputs and outputs for ecosystem services models useful for evaluating the aesthetics of natural infrastructure

	Council on Tree and Landscape Appraisers (CTLA) methods	I-Tree (Stratum)	Property Premium Model	Valuing scenic views via benefits transfer
Key data inputs				
Tree location and characteristics	Yes, enough to estimate scores (see tables 10.1 and 10.2)	Yes. Contains tools (I-Tree Canopy and I-Streets) to help in mapping. Can use both a sample or complete inventory data.	No	No
Open space parcel boundaries	No	No	Yes	Location of scenic view needed
Building and parcel boundaries	No, except for location score (see table 10.2)	No	Geospatial information on at least one focal parcel needed	Information needed if focal parcel has the scenic view
Key outputs				
Street tree aesthetic value	Yes	Yes	No	No
Open space value	No	No	Yes	No
Value of view	No	No	No	Yes
Other notes	Based on expert opinion	Based on benefits transfer	Based on meta-analysis of multiple papers	Based on a user-defined benefits transfer

Note: For street tree valuation, I-Tree is often used, particularly its submodel, I-Streets. For open space and parkland valuation, the Property Premium Model is one useful model. There is no model for valuing scenic views, which requires benefit transfer from a research study in a similar area.

good metareview of the literature conducted by Resources for the Future calculated an average regression relationship for the United States (Kroeger 2008). This regression equation is incorporated into the Property Premium Model, a simple spreadsheet-based tool for open space valuation. The user inputs the size of the open space parcel, its proximity to the home being valued, as well as the other open space within a certain buffer distance of the home. Characteristics of the open space parcel are also input, such as whether the parcel was protected or not, as well as the type of land cover (forest, wetland, etc.). The Property Premium Model then estimates the value of the open space parcel to one particular home parcel. The methodology in the Property Premium Model could be applied to many parcels in a GIS fairly easily, using basic spatial analysis techniques such as buffering.

The valuation of views has no software available to simplify the task. Usually, a benefits transfer approach is adopted. The definition of a view from the transferred study is then used to define which parcels have a beneficial view. Depending on the transferred study, this may be a simple binary classification of parcels (with a view versus not), or a more complex calculation using the Viewshed command in a GIS. The Natural Capital Project's Scenic Quality Provision model provides a good example of how to apply this methodology, albeit one focused on coastal views.

The hedonic valuation studies cited in this chapter are biased toward those conducted in the United States. Partially this is just a function of where I work and the studies I am aware of, but it is a problem with the overall literature on hedonic valuation. Far more studies of revealed preference have been conducted in the United States (and to a lesser extent, Europe) than in other places. It can be hard to find appropriate benefit transfer studies for places like developing countries. Indeed, in cultures significantly different from the United States, street trees or open space may have entirely different connotations.

Implementation

Funding for street tree planting generally comes from municipal funds, ideally general revenues raised through taxes. Sometimes tree planting is funded through special parks and recreation bonds, which may require voter approval. Whatever the funding mechanism, it often is easier to finance new capital costs (tree planting) rather than operations and maintenance costs (maintaining trees). In many cities, this leads to a persistent shortfall in maintenance funds, causing a higher rate of tree mortality than is necessary. It is a best practice to budget for the increased maintenance costs when beginning a major tree planting effort.

Open space acquisition is generally funded through bonds, although occasionally general revenues are used. Often bond packages that protect open space with relatively natural land cover have a variety of other goals, such as providing recreational opportunities or maintaining agricultural production. Some decision-making mechanism is needed to reconcile these various goals, as potential parcels for acquisition may be very valuable for some goals and not others. The Trust for Public Land maintains a database of conservation ballot measures in the United States (LandVote), many of which authorize bonds to fund open space acquisitions. In 2013, $339 million in conservation funding was approved by voters.

Acquisition of open space is sometimes fee-simple, where the municipality purchases all the rights to a parcel. This type of purchase is particularly appropriate when one of the goals of open space acquisition is public access. Alternatively, conservation easements are purchased, which restricts certain rights to a parcel (e.g., preventing development) while allowing the current owner to retain some rights. Easements are of course cheaper than fee-simple acquisition and are appropriate when the goal is merely to restrict development. For instance, agricultural preservation programs are usually by conservation easements, allowing farmers to retain the right to farm even while they sell off their development rights.

For programs aimed at protecting aesthetic benefits, remember that land cover and parcel status affect the perceived aesthetic benefits from the parcel. Protected areas are perceived as having more aesthetic value than unprotected areas, and forest areas are perceived as having more aesthetic value than wetlands. While not fully explored in the literature, it is likely that parcels protected by a conservation easement have less aesthetic value than those protected fee-simple, particularly in cases where the existence of an easement is not widely known.

Monitoring

Mostly cities in the United States and Europe now maintain records on street trees, sometimes just recording the species of the tree and when it was planted. This database can also maintain information of tree growth (diameter at breast height) and health. The parallel for open space is a database of which parcels are protected and where, as well as information on any changes in land-use or stewardship practices over time. Such a database is also important for scheduling periodic field visits to parcels under conservation easement, to make sure the terms of the conservation easement are being followed.

With tree inventory data tracked over time, it becomes possible to model the aesthetic benefits over time. I-Streets provides a useful framework to track aesthetic benefits. Even if all of the assumptions of the benefit transfer are not fully met (e.g., the incremental effect of a unit leaf-surface area on a house price is different), if the parameters of the regression are held constant over time then at least the rough trend in aesthetic benefits is tracked. For open space, one could in principle run the Property Premium Model over time, applying the model in a GIS framework to that year's open space parcel map.

Another level of monitoring rigor would be to see the effect of a particular conservation action on home prices. This may be hard to do until several years after the conservation action, since it may take a while for the action's value to affect a house's sale price. Ideally, sales price data would be available before and after the conservation actions. Moreover, a sample of sales of comparable houses will be needed both near and far from the conservation action, so that the faraway sites can serve as a control. This level of rigor will likely only occur if there are academic partners involved who are interested in leading the analysis, but the widespread electronic availability of home sale records makes it increasingly more feasible.

Alternatively, a survey could collect information on residents' satisfaction with a particular conservation action. Ideally, survey pre- and postconservation action would be conducted, although in practice this is rare. Even if only postconservation surveys are available, however, it can provide an indication if the conservation action has a perceived benefit to citizens. Designing a good survey instrument is challenging, and interested readers should consult a technical source for more advice (e.g., Rea and Parker 2005).

Summary

More and more cities are following the lead of Portland, Oregon, and quantifying the aesthetic value of their street trees in economic terms. In a sense this is just putting a precise number on something cities have managed for a long time: the beauty of their streetscapes. However, this precise number has given new impetus to tree planting efforts in many cities. After all, the economic data suggest that a mature tree has very significant aesthetic value, and indeed the value of this ecosystem service often is greater than the value of other ecosystem services discussed in this book. But at the same time, the average city in the United States lost tree cover over the last decade. So even though there is a positive economic return on street tree planting from the aesthetic value alone, the country is underinvesting in maintaining this natural infrastructure. This can be seen as a sad parallel to the underinvestment in maintaining and renovating grey infrastructure that is also common in many cities. Having the economic information in hand on the value of a street tree can perhaps make it clear to policymakers how misguided this underinvestment is.

Chapter 10

Recreation Value and Physical Health

O VER TWO DECADES AGO, more than 3,000 kids from Los Angeles were selected for a unique study. They were part of the Southern California Health Study, which had multiple goals, but chief among them was understanding the causes of child obesity. The United States was, and still is, in the grip of an obesity epidemic: obesity rates have risen over the past two decades and now the rate is greater than 20 percent nationally. Among kids in Los Angeles, it is 32 percent. What makes the Southern California Health Study special is that it tracks kids over time, permitting an examination of how factors in a kid's family or neighborhood affect their risk of becoming obese.

Because of this special data, Jennifer Wolch and colleagues (2011) have turned Southern California into a focus of research into how access to parks affects kid's health. For each child, they measured whether there was a park within easy walking distance, defined as within 500 meters (0.3 miles). They then compared park access to one measure of obesity, the Body Mass Index (BMI). Kids with better access to parks had consistently lower BMI over the years of the study. The inference is that kids with parks nearby spent energy both walking to the park and then playing there, and this extra bit of exercise kept the kids a little bit thinner.

What is more, Wolch's work showed that access to parks is quite unevenly distributed across Los Angeles. Poorer, mostly Latino and African American neighborhoods had fewer parks nearby. Richer, mostly white neighborhoods had more parks nearby. From one perspective, this is a confounding factor in Wolch's analysis: obesity is correlated with income and ethnicity in the United States, with higher rates of obesity in poorer Latino and African American groups than the general population, for reasons related to diet. Wolch went to great lengths to control for these socioeconomic effects. Even after controlling for these effects, park access was significantly related to obesity. In other words, Latinos and African Americans in poor neighborhoods face a double burden: dietary habits that predispose them to obesity, plus neighborhoods with few recreational opportunities.

In response to concerns about insufficient park access, state voters passed Proposition K in 1996, which authorized state spending to create parks (Wolch, Wilson, and Fehrenbach 2002). Money was to be explicitly targeted to areas with park shortages. Wolch and colleagues built a GIS (geographic information systems) tool and plan, Green Visions, that helped prioritize parcels for acquisition. A review of the spending after the fact shows that money was indeed targeted to poorer neighborhoods in East Los Angeles, although where the money was spent was constrained by where the state received proposals to create parks from municipal officials and community members. That is, rather than picking the optimal parcels for new parks based on a GIS analysis, the state could only strategically choose among the proposals they received.

Just how certain is this link between parks and health? And

how much should urban planning reflect this park health benefit? I spoke with Laurence Roderick, who is running the PHENOTYPE program (Positive Health Effects of the Natural Outdoor environment in TYpical Populations in different regions in Europe), which looks to quantify this benefit for cities in the European Union. Roderick's opinion was that "you cannot assume people will use parks for exercise." Far more significant, in his view, was how much people have to walk in their day-to-day lives: the walkability of the city. "Means of transport has much more of an effect on physical activity than proximity to parks." In cities where people walk more, they are skinnier.

This chapter looks at the evidence for how parks affect physical health, as well as the general importance of walkability. It also describes how to map and quantify the direct use value of parks for recreation. How much do we value being able to play or picnic or relax in a park? This is a classic topic for city planners (e.g., Harper 2009), but recent research allows us to quantitatively map the recreational value of parks.

Mapping Important Services for Recreation

Many benefits of parks—health, value for picnicking, value for playing, and so forth—are part of the "direct use" value of the park. Direct use is often contrasted with indirect use, such as the aesthetic benefits discussed in chapter 9. I will use "recreation" as a synonym for direct use. This is using the term in a broad sense, encompassing activities that involve physical activity (e.g., playing basketball) as well as those that are more sedentary (e.g., barbequing on an outdoor grill). Some, more contemplative uses, such as the mental health benefits of interaction with nature, I leave to the next chapter. Recreation, in the broad sense in which I am using it, is the fundamental reason urban public parks exist. Cities began to see supplying parks for the public use as a way to ensure the common good.

There are of course many different types of parks, and the kind of recreation that predominates varies widely by park. On one extreme, there are little parks in urban neighborhoods. In my neighborhood in DC, for instance, a small park just a couple blocks away is very popular for its children's playground and its dog park. Then there are larger park parcels, sometimes in more suburban locations, that sometimes have large athletic facilities (football fields, for instance). Finally, there are remnant patches of natural habitat, sometimes on quite large parcels. Even these more natural parks generally have trails added, to encourage recreation.

The first task for mapping recreation value is to measure visitation, often in terms of person-days or person-hours spent at a park (table 10.1). These visitation numbers are then multiplied by valuation rates (e.g., $/person-day) to estimate recreation value (see valuation section below). Different types of parks draw visitation from various distances (i.e., the ecosystem services have different transportability or different "servicesheds"). Neighborhood parks, like the one just down the street from me, draw people from a very short distance, generally less than half a mile. On the other hand, large parks or those with specific amenities that are in demand (e.g., a swimming pool) may draw visitors from a long distance.

Visitation to parks appears to have declined over time in developed countries. While there was a growth in per capita visitation rates post WWII, presumably as a by-product of economic growth and an increase in the number of people in the middle class with sufficient "free time," in recent decades, visitation rates have declined. The cause of this decline in visitation is unclear, although it has been variously attributed to "videophilia" (a preference for video games and TV over real-world experiences with nature) and globalization (an increasing fraction of vacations are now international, perhaps reducing visitation domestically but increasing it abroad). Interestingly, Balmford et al. (2009) show that while visitation in developed countries is in decline, it is on the increase in developing countries, presumably due to economic growth and the expansion of the middle class in these countries.

Table 10.1. Inputs and outputs for models useful for evaluating park visitation and recreational value including tools to estimate the walkability of a neighborhood and health benefits from access to parks

	Visitation Model (InVEST)	Parkscore	Benefits transfer for direct use valuation	Walkscore/ Smart Growth American Index	Health Benefits Calculator (TPL)
Key data inputs					
Location of park	Yes	Yes	Yes		Yes
Spatial demographic information	No	Built into calculation of Parkscore	Yes	Built into calculation of metric	Yes
Park characteristics	No	No	Depends on type of benefits transfer		No
Key outputs					
Visitation rate	Yes	Yes (qualitative)	No	No	No
Value of direct use	No	No	Yes	No	No
Walkability	No	No	No	Yes	No
Health value	No	No	No	No	Yes
Other notes	Based on an empirical relationship between park visitation and Flickr geotagged photos.	US data only	Three main techniques: travel cost, contingent valuation, and use value (table 11.2)	Walkscore, based on Google Maps data, is available internationally.[a]	Does not appear to be publically available.[b]

[a]The SGA Index (2003) was calculated for the United States only.
[b]See TPL 2009.

The ideal source for visitation data is park gates that are monitored or charge an entrance fee. This is more commonly the case for large, "nature-type" parks than for urban parks. For one thing, most small urban parks do not have full-time staff on-site. Moreover, most don't charge entrance fees, which would be somewhat at odds with the idea of public parks as serving the common good. Indeed, the paucity of visitation data for urban parks makes it hard to tell whether the general decline in visitation for nature-type parks is mirrored by a decline in visitation of urban parks.

One intriguing new tool models visitation rates off social media data (Wood et al. 2013). The photo-sharing website Flickr has more than 197 million geotagged photos submitted by members. The number of geotagged photos submitted from within a particular park is highly correlated with visitation rates. This empirical relationship is now incorporated into the Visitation model in the InVEST package of the Natural Capital Project. The relationship is more useful for rural, nature-based protected areas than for small urban parks but can be used to provide a good first estimate of visitation rates.

A large number of studies have quantified who visits particular parks and have generally shown that proximity matters greatly. For neighborhood parks that users will walk to, parks must be within 0.62 miles (1 km) of homes for them to be consistently used. For instance, Cohen et al. (2007) surveyed users at eight parks in Los Angeles, and found that 43 percent of users live within 0.25 miles (0.40 km), 21 percent lived 0.5–1.0 mile away (0.80–1.61 km), and only 13 percent lived farther than a mile (1.61 km) away. They did find that increased quality of parks could induce longer distance visitation.

For major cities in the United States, a useful tool is the Trust for Public Land's (TPL) Parkscore. For fifty cities, TPL has mapped the access to parks within a ten-minute walk (a half mile along the road network), and also flags areas of the city that are in need of more parks to rectify the current low access. TPL has also ranked the top fifty cities overall, using a complex metric accounting for the proportion of the population that has sufficient access to a park.

Another important variable controlling park visitation is the number and type of access routes. A study in Dekalb County, Georgia (a suburb of Atlanta), showed that for walking access to a park, access routes connecting to a street with a sidewalk are needed.

Multiple access points are even better at ensuring pedestrian access to a park. As a result of this research, Dekalb County actually purchased several small parcels of land adjacent to existing parks to create new access routes (Robert Wood Johnson Foundation 2011).

Park characteristics are also important controls on visitation rates (McCormack et al. 2010). For instance, if a park is perceived as unsafe, visitation rates will drop dramatically. Research has shown perceived safety is ranked as a more important issue for women than for men. The degree to which park facilities seem clean and new also is important. Finally, all else being equal, parks with more organized activities (e.g., sporting events) have more visitors.

The surrounding neighborhood's demographics also control visitation rates. For instance, since different ethnic groups in Los Angeles have different preferred sports (on average, Latinos prefer soccer, and African Americans prefer basketball), facilities need to match neighborhood demographics to maximize visitation. Age also matters, with parks for children requiring playgrounds while parks for adults require more trails and landscaping.

Overall walkability of a city—how easy it is to walk from destination to destination during a day—is a function of overall urban form. The word "sprawl" is often used to describe a city that is the opposite of walkable. While sprawl has been variously defined, it generally refers to an urban form that requires a car to move between locations (Tacheiva 2010). An older metric of sprawl was defined by Smart Growth America (SGA), combining information from several dozen geospatial data layers (Ewing et al. 2003). A useful new metric is provided by Walkscore.com (figure 10.1), which calculates for a given point on Google Maps the walking distance to various other locations (shops, mass transit, parks). This metric allows for a continuous look at how walkability changes across a city.

These metrics of urban form correlate with how much people walk and hence how healthy they are. For instance, Ewing et al. (2003) reviewed all United States counties and related the Sprawl Index of SGA with reported walking data from the Behavioral Risk

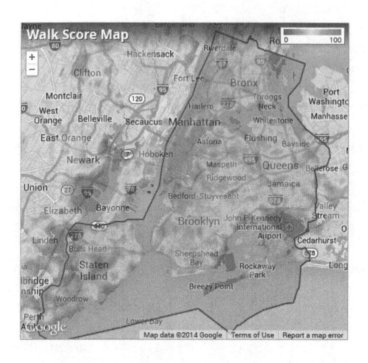

Factor Surveillance System. While there is a highly significant effect, its size is rather small. Comparing New York City, which had the most walking, with Geauga County (a suburb of Cleveland), which had the least, one finds that the average New Yorker did seventy-nine minutes more walking per month. On average, those who live in New York City have 1 unit less of BMI than those in Geauga. For comparison, the average adult in the United States has a BMI of 27, so walkability can at most reduce average BMI by around 4 percent.

Common Threats and Common Solutions

The common threat to recreational access is simply not having enough parks. The National Parks and Recreation Administration proposed a standard of 6–19 acres (2.4–7.7 ha) of parkland per 1,000 people (Cohen et al. 2007). Few cities hit that standard. Los Angeles, for example, has 0.65 acres per 1,000 people. New suburban neighborhoods in the United States have lower amounts of parkland per capita than do older neighborhoods, so in an important sense urban planning has gotten less successful at providing recreational amenities to urbanites. New suburban neighborhoods are also more car centric than older neighborhoods, contributing to the obesity epidemic.

Many cities have tried to overcome the threat by creating new parks. If parcels of open space remain in the urban fabric, these become obvious targets for acquisition and protection, since they

---

Figure 10.1. Walkability in two American cities, as estimated by Walkscore.com, which calculates walking distances from homes to different types of amenities and stores. Top panel: Cleveland, OH. Its suburb, Geauga County, was rated the least walkable county in a study by Ewing et al. (2003). Geauga County is located east of Cleveland. Bottom panel: New York, NY. New York County (i.e., Manhattan) is the most walkable county in the study, and residents have on average 1 unit less of BMI due to this increased walkability.

are relatively cheap and pristine. Alternatively, the focus can be on buying underused, previously developed "brownfield" sites and converting them to parkland. In Los Angeles, for instance, Proposition K funds bought what was previously industrial land to turn it into public parks (Wolch, Wilson, and Fehrenbach 2002).

In some cities, there may be adequate parkland, but the facilities may have degraded over time, making the park less pleasant to visit (McCormack et al. 2010). Negative characteristics of a park, such as dirty bathrooms, broken playground equipment, and unmown grass, can significantly decrease visitation. Expectations about the characteristics of an acceptable park vary among countries, and have also shifted over time. In my neighborhood in Washington, DC, the standard playground equipment put in the parks in the 1970s—a metal slide, some monkey bars, some swings—is now seen as passé. In some countries in the developing world, the minimum standard for an acceptable park might be room for a soccer pitch and a water fountain.

Cities attempt to solve this problem by investing in new recreational infrastructure. In my neighborhood, the little corner park has been renovated to create a giant theme playground with giant treehouses and twenty-foot-tall plastic flowers. While it certainly seems likely that such new super-playgrounds might increase park visitation permanently, most visitors to neighborhood parks are local, so there's an upper limit to how much visitation can be increased by simply upgrading existing facilities. In contrast, adding a new type of facility (e.g., a municipal pool) will be more likely to permanently increase visitation.

Another threat to park visitation is a sense that a park is dangerous. In the United States, fear of crime has increased over time (Gallup 2011). Interestingly, this trend is not driven by a surge in crime rates, which in fact have fallen significantly over the last several decades, but is presumably driven by changes in perception of risk (Oppel 2011). Nevertheless, crime is of course a very real and significant problem in some neighborhoods. Parks in such neighborhoods occasionally serve as locations for drug dealing, prostitution, and other illicit activities.

Communities usually focus on increased policing as a solution to a problem (perceived or real) of park crime. Increased visits by officers to parks are one solution, as is the employment of a park guardian (full time or part time) to watch over the park. Cities may also focus on increased enforcement of so-called nuisance ordinances (preventing public consumption of alcohol in parks, or stopping the homeless from sleeping overnight in the park), on the theory it discourages an atmosphere of lawlessness. Another tactic is to have more organized activities, such as sporting events, at a park. Increased public attendance of these events provides a perception of "safety in numbers" and can also serve to provide a positive reintroduction to the park for some members of the public that were previously afraid to visit.

Valuation of Natural Infrastructure for Recreation

After you have an estimation of visitation at a park, in people-days or some similar unit, the next step is calculating the economic value of that direct use. This economic value is often measured in per-visit terms, in $/people-days or something similar. This economic value, if multiplied by total visitation, gives an estimate of the total economic value of direct use of a park. Three methods are commonly used to estimate the per-visit value of a park.

Perhaps the oldest method is the travel cost method (Clawson and Knetsch 1966). The basic idea underpinning this method is the more I value the experience of visiting a park, the farther I will be willing to travel to visit it. Travel has costs, and if I am willing to bear those costs to visit a park, then the experience at the park must be worth at least that much to me. Costs of travel are usually a mix of direct expenses (gas and tolls, if I am driving) and the time it takes me to get there. While each person values time differently, we all put an implicit value on our time, since we make decisions all the time that involve such a value, like whether to pay more for a faster mode of transit (flying, for example, instead of driving). The travel cost method is only really applicable for parks where visitors have to travel a long way. I personally value my daily visit to my neighborhood park a lot, but my travel costs are negligible since it is only a few blocks from my home. Note also that the travel cost method estimates only direct use value of a park.

Another method is called contingent valuation (Brander and Koetse 2011). Essentially, a survey is used to ask people how much they would be willing to pay (WTP) to have a certain kind of park in existence and accessible to them. Alternatively, surveys could measure people's willingness to avoid (WTA) the loss of a currently extant park. Generally, contingent value methods estimate both direct and indirect values of a park, including things like aesthetic value (chapter 9). Care is needed in the design of the survey instrument (Kopp and Smith 2013), but numerous review articles have shown well-done contingent valuation can accurately estimate people's values (Brander and Koetse 2011).

Finally, the use value method collects information on the average amount spent by visitors to a park. In some cases, this method can be very sophisticated. For instance, the United States National Park Service has done detailed studies of the average hotel and restaurant receipts of visitors, as well as spending on incidentals (e.g., fishing gear or park maps). These figures are codified in the Money Generation Model (Fish 2009) and are used to estimate the value of an average visit to specific parks to the local economy.

In other cases, the use value method can be quite simple in application. The US Army Corps of Engineers, for instance, has developed average use values for generic categories of activities on their lands (USACE 2012). Other United States government agencies have each modified the average use values slightly to fit their specific agency's needs. Some use values relevant to urban parks are shown in table 10.2. While these use values were primarily developed based on data from more "nature-based" parks, they are often applied to urban "developed" parks as well. For instance, Trust for

Table 10.2. Average use values for types of recreation common to urban parks

Activity	Use value ($/person/day)
Bicycling	43
Hiking	61
Picnicking	21
Sightseeing	46
General recreation	48

Source: Based on the Recreation Use Values Database (Rosenburger 2014).

Public Land (TPL) used them to estimate the direct use value of parks in Boston (USA), assuming for instance that a visit to a playground is worth $3.50, and running on a trail is worth $4.00. TPL estimated the total direct use value of Boston's park system at $354 million from 131 million visits (TPL 2009).

Valuating the health benefits of parks remains difficult. TPL's Health Calculator assumes a $250 annual health savings for adults ($500 for the elderly) who have access to parks and thus are assumed to exercise more (Wang et al. 2004; TPL 2009). Using this simple assumption, TPL estimated a $19.8 million health benefit of Sacramento's (USA) park system (TPL 2009). A more detailed study of the health benefits of a city's parks, or even its overall walkability, could use one of the published studies that relate park access or urban form to a health metric like BMI. Other health studies are then available that can value this improvement in a health metric in economic terms. For instance, Wang et al. (2006) estimated that medical and pharmaceutical costs increased by $204 per person per year per unit BMI. Relating this to the finding mentioned above that those in New York City had, on average, one less unit of BMI than those in the most sprawling US county (2003), we might estimate the total value of this effect as

$$\$202/person/yr/BMI \times 8.405 \text{ million people} \times 1 \text{ BMI} = \$1,700 \text{ million/yr.}$$

Implementation

All the solutions presented to increase park access and visitation cost money. The most common solution for United States cities is to take out bonds to finance this investment. Depending on the city and its financial and legal status, the bonds can be either general bonds or special parks bonds, which might require voter authorization. Occasionally, as in Proposition K, the authorizing language of a bond may target money toward specific goals, such as increasing park access for currently underserved neighborhoods.

Another way to finance new park infrastructure is to charge user fees when they enter a park or engage in a specific activity. This is only possible when the park or facility has controlled access, with only one or a few entrances. The park also must have an amenity that people would be willing to pay for. User fees are more often applicable to special facilities people visit only occasionally (e.g., a swimming pool), rather than a simple neighborhood park that might get daily or weekly visits. Most significantly, user fees will discourage some proportion of people from visiting, decreasing the direct use value of a park.

Research shows that the number and quality of organized programs at parks (e.g., sporting events) greatly affect park visitation, and hence the health benefits of parks. Running such programs also costs money, which may occasionally be financed by user fees, but more commonly is part of a city's parks and recreation budget. While such organized programs have real tangible health benefits, it is generally not possible to link these health benefits to a willing payer. Health insurance companies may be hesitant to finance such municipal parks programs, although their presence likely reduces claims against the insurance company.

Monitoring

Perhaps the easiest monitoring effort is simply implementation metrics of how many hectares of parks were created, and where. Most cities would maintain this sort of information as part of their normal operation of the parks department. This database can then be used to estimate park visitation crudely, by using the Recreational Visitation tool of the Natural Capital Project, or by transferring the empirical regression equations developed in another study of visitation. If money is available, a survey of city residents, or observation data from city parks, can more accurately quantify visitation. Once visitation is estimated, a crude valuation of the direct use of a city's parks can be estimated using the use value methodology.

Directly measuring the effect of increased park access on a population's health would be very difficult. Longitudinal data like that available in Wolch (2011) would be required, ideally available before and after the intervention. One would also need enough information on potentially confounding variables to factor them out. For instance, there has been a large rise in obesity over the last two decades, for reasons which have nothing to do with park access. Increased park access will have, at best, limited the increase in obesity somewhat.

Sometimes cities want to get a more accurate estimate of the value of a park visit. This usually involves a survey of residents, either to more accurately estimate spending associated with visits or through a contingent valuation analysis. Design of such a survey requires the help of an economist or other professional in the field. Survey design needs to be sensitive to ethnic and socioeconomic differences in the perception of park value.

Summary

Los Angeles, Atlanta, New York, and many other cities are beginning to see their park and open spaces as part of their public health system, tools to help combat obesity and other diseases. There is now clear evidence that the presence of parks does help to improve the physical well-being of citizens, and this improvement is of significant economic value to society. Tools exist that allow a rapid estimation of roughly how many people visit a park and, using the techniques of benefits transfer, the potential physical health benefits.

Some humility is needed by the conservation community as we promote these benefits, however. Public health officials may consider parks as one of their tools, but it is only one of several they have to combat obesity, and it is likely not their most important one. Moreover, if parks are designed primarily to promote physical health, they will probably be more active spaces (playgrounds, ball fields, etc.), which is a rather different kind of "natural infrastructure" than is traditionally the domain of the conservation movement.

Chapter 11

Parks and Mental Health

Nature is the last thing I would think of upon arriving in bustling Penn Station in New York (fig. 11.1). Every day, 600,000 people stream through this station, pouring into the island of Manhattan for work and then flowing back home in the evening (Randolph 2013). People dart left and right through the crowd, looking for a way to move just a little bit faster from point A to point B. It's a mad ballet of commuters, and a visitor to New York like me feels like a clumsy oaf, disrupting the dance and wasting precious seconds of commuters' time. Time seems to run faster here, and everyone is in a hurry.

A few years ago, Jose Lobo, Luis Bettencourt, and other colleagues at the Santa Fe Institute began a study to try quantifying how living in a city changes the speed of life. People really do walk faster in cities, but more important, cities also accelerate economic growth

Figure 11.1. The hustle and bustle of urban life, as in Penn Station in New York (top), imposes considerable psychological stress on people. Photo courtesy of Matthias Rosenkranz. Urban green spaces, such as Central Park in New York (bottom), provide numerous mental health benefits. Photo courtesy of echiner1.

and innovation (Bettencourt et al. 2007). As Lobo put it when I talked to him, "I think anyone who thinks about the current state of humanity…sooner or later will think about cities." Cities thrive, from Lobo's perspective, because they offer the possibility of more interaction. "Some of these interactions aren't so benign. People get murdered. But some of them are powerful good interactions." Proximity has its benefits. From Penn Station, I am guaranteed that there is someone within two miles (and maybe two blocks) who could provide me with any imaginable product or service.

In a certain sense, cities are quintessentially human. We are creating a space, an artificial world, which allows certain processes—creativity, innovation, interaction—to thrive. Perhaps they are even helping us fulfill our destiny. One of the things that makes our species unique is our ability to reason, to analyze, to think deeply about the world and discern patterns, and then to design ways to change that world when we wish. Our species is called, after all, *Homo sapiens*, which translated from Latin means something like "the thinking man." If thinking is part of our essence, and interactions with other people are the key to increasing our ability to think up new and creative ideas, then cities are a representation of our essence.

However, cities are also shockingly different than the natural environments in which humans evolved. A group of psychologists and evolutionary biologists have begun to prove that the sense of fatigue I feel in Penn Station, that many of us feel in cities, is a very real phenomenon with a deep evolutionary cause. We are, they argue, psychologically not that different from our ancestors who evolved to live on the savannahs of Africa. Our minds evolved to be in a social setting of a few dozen people, with a background of natural noises and sights that only occasionally require our attention. One of the things that is fatiguing about city life is that the brain is constantly trying, at least unconsciously, to guess the motivations and intentions of every person we pass on the sidewalk or subway (Kaplan and Kaplan 1989). Background noises from honking cars

and flashing signs constantly demand attention. If increased interaction is the great positive benefit one gets from being in a city, it
exerts a psychological toll.

This new research into the mental health benefits of access to
nature shows that even a brief time-out in nature can reduce this
psychological toll. Stress levels decrease, and people's ability to focus increases. There is even evidence that time in nature reduces
the symptoms of attention deficit hyperactivity disorder (ADHD)
in children and reduces the odds of domestic violence between
their parents. These mental health benefits of parks are in addition
to the benefits to physical health from recreation (chapter 10) and
the aesthetic benefits (chapter 9). Even views of nature through a
window have some mental benefits.

This chapter is about how parks can let us have the best of both
worlds: a thriving urban environment with plenty of opportunity
for interaction, as well as pieces of nature to nurture the souls of urbanites and give them a chance to recover from the stress of city life.
I present theories about how nature exactly acts to increase mental
health and then discuss how one maps access to this mental health
benefit and values it. Finally, I show how to put this information
into decision making and monitoring.

Mapping Important Services for Mental Health

Research into the mental health benefits of interacting with nature shows that there are both direct and indirect effects (Bratman,
Hamilton, and Daily 2012). Perhaps the best-studied indirect effect
is through physical activity (table 11.1). Many visits to parks and
protected areas involve some physical activity, whether walking or
jogging or playing sports. Physical exercise improves mental health
as well, so all the techniques discussed in chapter 10 to improve
recreational access will also provide mental health benefits. Another
type of indirect benefit to mental health from parks is simply that
they provide a forum for socializing with friends and neighbors.

Table 11.1. Inputs and outputs for ecosystem services models useful for evaluating mental health benefits of natural infrastructure

	Visitation	Indirect mental health benefits: recreational use	Direct mental health benefits: benefits transfer models
Key data inputs			
Location of park	Yes	Yes	Yes
Spatial demographic information	Yes	Yes	Yes
Park characteristics	Yes	Depends on type of benefits transfer	Depends on type of benefits transfer
Key outputs			
Visitation rate	Yes	No	No
Value of indirect mental health benefits	No	Yes	No
Value of direct mental health benefits	No	No	Yes
Other notes		Extrapolates from visitation rate to indirect mental health benefits, based on empirical relationships observed in other studies.	Extrapolates from visitation rate to indirect mental health benefits, based on empirical relationships observed in other studies.

Note: There are no predefined models that allow for spatial estimation of mental health benefits of natural infrastructure. Visitation rates may be quantitatively mapped easily (see chapter 11), which can be a useful first proxy measure of mental health benefits.

Socializing with such close contacts has also been shown to have significant mental health benefits.

Spaces for socializing can be public or private. For our purposes, the focus is on public spaces. To promote socializing, public spaces need not be parks or in any way natural: the traditional plaza or town square serves that function as well. Some of the techniques for quantifying visitation discussed in chapter 10 can also be used for mapping potential places for socializing. For instance, social media sites like Twitter, Flickr, and Facebook provide voluminous data on how many people are using particular parcels of public open space.

Some towns have taken this idea of promoting socializing and interaction even further, and are trying to design "innovation districts." An innovation district is supposed to be a neighborhood where multiple start-ups and entrepreneurs can congregate, gaining benefits from being located near one another (AIA 2013). These benefits from interaction can be due to knowledge sharing between individuals, as well as the creation of a denser labor market—more workers with a specialized skill in one spot makes it easier for firms to find someone with that skill to hire. Spaces to interact are key for a successful innovation district. Research suggests that what matters most is promoting interactions that are one-on-one or in a small group, in a neutral, nonwork space. Natural features such as parks may very well become a best practice for the design of innovation districts, because of their mental health benefits.

There is also clearly a direct effect of nature on human well-being, separate from the indirect effects of exercises and socializing. For instance, Ulrich (1984) looked at how long it took patients to recover after gallbladder surgery. Patients were randomly assigned to rooms with a view of a beautiful natural setting or to rooms with a view of a busy highway. Recovery was quicker for patients who had a view of nature. It clearly wasn't recreation or socializing benefits of public open space that mattered to these patients. What could be causing this more direct effect of nature on human well-being?

There are two dominant theories of how nature has a direct effect on mental health (Bratman, Hamilton, and Daily 2012). One is called attention restoration theory (ART) and was first proposed by Kaplan and Kaplan (1989). Modern life takes a lot of directed attention; judging the intention of passing strangers, monitoring the beeps coming from my smart phone and computer, and avoiding getting lost, all demand my attention as I wander through Penn Station. All this directed attention is tiring, according to ART. A natural setting, by contrast, requires less directed attention. So a visit to a natural setting by an urbanite is a restorative break. For instance, test takers score significantly higher on tests that require direct attention and short-term memory after a visit to a natural setting (Berman, Jonides, and Kaplan 2008). Similarly, the symptoms of ADHD have been shown to be fewer after a break in nature, presumably because the restorative break increases one's ability to pay directed attention to a task, often a challenge to those suffering from ADHD (Kuo and Taylor 2004).

The other dominant theory is called stress reduction theory (SRT). Penn Station certainly increases my stress level, and this theory states that much of life in a city is stressful to most people. Natural settings thus provide a break from that stress, allowing our bodies to relax to normal baseline stress levels. Indeed, studies have shown that stress hormones decrease after a walk in the woods (Ulrich 1983). Note that ART and SRT are not mutually exclusive, but may even interact with each other: stress, for instance, has been shown to reduce our ability for directed attention.

As the Ulrich study shows, even mere views of nature are enough to give mental health benefits. In one famous study of residents of public housing in Chicago, researchers examined how views of nature affected mental health (Kuo and Sullivan 2001). Tenants were randomly assigned to apartments, without regard to views. Those with views of nature reported lower levels of stress in their life. Moreover, there were fewer incidences of domestic violence in apartments with views of nature.

As Bratman and colleagues (2012) note, the ecosystem service in the case of mental health benefits is a unique interaction of a person's mind and the environment. The value of nature for mental health appears to vary by gender as well as age (Barton and Pretty 2010). For men, the greatest benefit appears to be in early adulthood. For women, there are benefits both early and late in life. The mental health benefit also likely varies considerably by culture, and some cultures may even view natural areas as threatening.

The positive effect of nature on mental health varies in magnitude depending on how long a person stays in nature. One review study (Barton and Pretty 2010) that looked at this response effect found that the first five to ten minutes of being in a natural setting give more than half the total mental health benefits. More time in a natural setting continues to give mental health benefits, but with diminishing effects per unit time. Thus, planners looking to map how park access improves mental health in a city have to consider not just those who live near a park, but also those who might briefly pass through the park during their day. On the other hand, some authors argue that long-term, immersive experiences of nature give deeper, qualitatively different mental health benefits that are particularly important for children (Kahn and Kellert 2002).

Another review study suggested that quality of natural areas is more important for the magnitude of mental health benefits than is the quantity (Francis et al. 2012). That is, having more parks near your house is associated less with mental health measures than is having certain key characteristics present in those parks. Chief among these is a relatively quiet part of the park, where reflection and solitude are possible. This trend is consistent with the studies of dose response: a short amount of time in a special place is what is important. This is somewhat contrary to the research into recreation and physical health, where quantity of hours exercised is clearly important in determining physical health.

Still other studies have looked at whether the biodiversity of plants and animals affects the magnitude of the mental health benefits. Fuller and colleagues (2007) did find an association, with more biodiverse parks correlating with greater mental health benefits. However, there is a potentially confounding factor, with large parcels often tending to have greater biodiversity. Large parcels are, of course, unique for other reasons as well. For instance, the chance for solitude may increase in a large parcel.

In short, mapping the mental health benefits of a city's parks remains difficult, and there are no models or software that facilitate such mapping. My recommendation is to focus on mapping park visitation as a proxy measure for mental health benefits. Access for specific, sensitive populations such as schools and hospitals can be given special focus. If there are only a handful of city parks that offer the potential for reflection and solitude, they should be the focus of the visitation analysis. Such an analysis, while far from perfect, is likely to capture the gross spatial pattern of mental health benefits from nature in a city.

Common Threats and Common Solutions

As with many other ecosystem services supplied by natural habitats within the urban core, the key threat to service provision is the gradual loss of street trees and open space over time to development. Common strategies to combat this threat include tree protection ordinances and tree planting programs (see chapter 10 for a discussion). Cities also buy patches of open space to ensure access for their citizens for recreational purposes, and these parks can provide mental health benefits. However, parks that are designed to maximize recreational benefit may not contain sufficient solitude to provide the direct mental health benefit of nature, although athletic fields do provide indirect benefits to mental health through exercise and socialization.

Cities may want to explore targeting conservation actions where they would provide the most mental health benefits to sensitive populations. This way of designing a conservation program fits with a theme of "park access equality," a goal of many cities. For instance, New York City's tree planting program targets planting on blocks with low average tree cover. This helps rectify the shortage of several ecosystem services on these streets, including the mental health benefits that trees provide.

One sensitive population is hospital patients, who can, as the Ulrich study shows, benefit from a little bit of nature in their lives. Some countries have traditions of using natural places as healing spaces. Since Roman times, many spas have contained attached gardens, places for relaxation and contemplation. More and more, hospitals are returning to this practice of having gardens for their patients. For instance, the proposed design for New North Zealand Hospital near Copenhagen wraps the hospital around a large formal garden (de Zeen Magazine 2014). Surrounding the hospital on the outside are woods, ensuring that every room has some sort of nature view.

Another sensitive population is children at school. Some schools are beginning to incorporate outdoor play in natural spaces into their children's day, in the hope that their students will gain in attentiveness from this time in nature. For instance, in Helsinki several forest daycares base their programs on students spending most of their time outdoors in nearby nature reserves (Shaw 2011). Many public school systems, while unable to go to this extreme, are trying to have natural features as part of their landscape design.

While not as beneficial as direct nature access, views of nature still have clear mental health benefits, and protecting viewsheds is another conservation action taken by cities. Viewsheds are often degraded by development or other forms of land clearing. For small-scale views, protecting them is often a matter of preserving and enhancing street trees and other landscaping. Large-scale views are more challenging, as land use of many parcels is important for determining the overall quality of a view.

Techniques for protecting viewsheds are discussed in chapter 10. Most cities use a combination of regulation and land acquisition. Regulation, usually through a city's zoning code, puts limits on building height or appearance, trying to minimize land uses incompatible with the viewshed. Land acquisition can fully prevent development on particularly important parcels. It is unlikely that viewshed protection will be motivated solely by mental health values rather than its value for tourism and aesthetics.

Valuation of Natural Infrastructure for Mental Health

There are relatively few quantitative models that will calculate the mental health benefits of interacting with nature. Because this ecosystem service is inherently the product of an interaction between a person's mind and a natural habitat, it is arguably harder to value than a service like stormwater mitigation (fig. 11.2). Moreover, the mental health effects of interacting with nature are a relatively new field of scientific study, and quantitative valuation models are not as well developed as for other types of ecosystem services. In any event, such quantitative valuation of mental health benefits is often not needed by decision makers. Mental health benefits are more often considered as cobenefits to projects that are primarily about providing aesthetic or recreational benefits.

If more precise valuation is needed, the only available method is through benefit transfer. The benefits quantified in one study would be assumed to apply to a new site, and the models developed in the previous study used at the new site. For this to be a valid inference, the two sites need to be somewhat similar in ecological and cultural contexts. The same definition of park access should be used in both old and new studies, to facilitate the benefits transfer calculation. The old study will also largely dictate which mental health benefits are calculated.

In Australia, a study by Francis and colleagues (2012) surveyed 911 residents of Perth, and found that the residents of neighborhoods with "high-quality" public open space had lower odds of having mental problems. If another city in Australia wanted to build upon this study, they could adopt the same definitions of high quality and park access as used in the Francis study. Assuming the equation estimated in the Francis study is true in the new city,

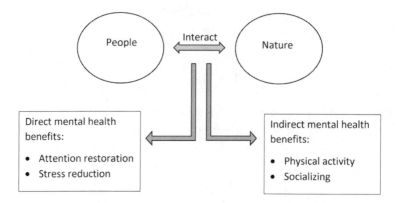

Figure 11.2. The mental health benefits that nature provides are a product of the interaction between an individual and nature, and the quantity of benefits produced depends on both the characteristics of the individual and the characteristics of the natural site. This interaction of an individual and nature provides both direct and indirect benefits to mental health.

one could estimate the mental health benefits of parks in terms of the particular metric used by Francis. If there is a way to relate this metric to the costs that mental illness places on society, then these benefits could be translated to economic terms. For instance, in the United States the annual cost of treating serious mental illness exceeds $300 billion, or around $1,000/person (Insel 2008). Even if such a figure was known for Australia, it may be hard to relate such average per capita figures to scores on the particular metrics used by Francis and colleagues.

The Ulrich study mentioned earlier also provides an example of potential economic benefits. By speeding patient recovery, costs are reduced: for instance, in the United States, one day of hospitalization, on average, costs $1,960 (Kaiser Family Foundation 2013). Thus, if the view of nature reduces hospitalization by 0.74 days per person (on average) it will save roughly $1,500 per patient. Potential extrapolation to other types of surgery would be possible, if a similar proportional reduction in hospitalization could be achieved through viewing nature.

The study on the effects of exposure to nature on those with ADHD cited earlier could be another example of benefits transfer. More than two million kids in the United States may have ADHD (Kuo and Taylor 2004). Note, however, that access to nature only reduces the symptoms of ADHD but doesn't remove the disorder. It is unclear how valuable a mere reduction in symptoms could be. However, it could potentially be very valuable: some school systems spend millions accommodating students with ADHD.

As can be seen in comparison with other ecosystem services in this book, valuation of mental health benefits is imprecise. It is my belief, however, that it is still well worth doing, since such information can point decision makers in the right direction. Often the alternative to a rough, ballpark estimation is for decision makers to assume, implicitly or explicitly, that the mental health benefits are zero. Mental health benefit information, while difficult to quantify precisely, is important to give policymakers a sense of what direction they should go. Often the incremental cost of putting nature into a project like a school may be small, and mere awareness that there are mental health benefits from access to nature may motivate the inclusion of a natural element in the project.

Implementation

One key challenge cities face in implementing nature projects to provide mental health benefits is that there is often no institution that views it as its mandate to explicitly fund such projects. Mental health departments care about promoting mental health, of course, but they may not have a mandate or budget to protect or restore natural habitat. Hospitals and schools may care about their immediate surroundings enough to fund nature projects there. For the rest of the city, there is no institution that can pay to provide this mental health benefit. Interaction, as we have seen, is key to this marvelous invention we call a city. But while there are numerous economic forces that will push to increase the pace of interactions in a city, there are no real counterbalancing institutions that will ensure that our cities have natural places where one can rejuvenate.

Sustainability planning or comprehensive planning can often be a good place for intangible values like mental health benefits to enter into the planning process. In principle, "orphan" ecosystem services (those without an institutional champion) can be included in the list of things considered by the plans. Mental health benefits can then be considered along with the other benefits of parks when decisions about park creation and maintenance are being made. Sustainability or comprehensive planning is also the right level for consideration of targeting conservation action to help increase the access of sensitive populations to nature. However, it should be acknowledged that many cities, particularly in the developing world, have little experience creating such comprehensive plans. Moreover, in many cities, the comprehensive plan is often ignored in practice by many institutions.

A second challenge that many cities face when trying to use nature for mental health is simply a sense that intangible issues like mental health are somehow not as "real" or important as tangible factors. A hospital may be far more willing to spend on a new piece of medical equipment than on landscaping, simply because the cost and benefits of the equipment are more easily calculated, and seemingly more tangible. Going along with this is a cultural bias toward viewing mental health differently than physical health. A polluting factory is seen as a clear public health threat to air quality. A new development obstructing people's views of nature is seen as at most an inconvenience, even if the loss of the forest reduces provision of mental health benefits.

One way institutions address this bias against mental health, is with education campaigns. Some hospitals, for instance, have begun to ask doctors to tell patients to visit a courtyard or garden, where appropriate, given a patient's condition.

Monitoring

Because the science of nature's effect on mental health is relatively nascent, there are few examples of monitoring the effects of a conservation intervention on mental health. Most published studies have been observational, with the exception of a few whose unique circumstances essentially ensure random assignment to groups (e.g., a hospital randomly assigning patients to a room). New conservation interventions by cities could in principle be monitored, although this may go beyond the level of funding available to, and the rigor demanded by, most cities.

For true monitoring to be possible, information on mental health from at least two points in time would be needed. One survey prior to the intervention would set the baseline, while the survey after the intervention would provide information on the treatment effect. The effect size is the difference between the before and after indices of mental health. However, there is potential for problems with multiple survey measures on the same subject over time, so an expert in this sort of survey design should be consulted (Blair, Czaja, and Blair 2013).

There is also a need for some sort of control data. As in the Ulrich study example, the random room assignment essentially creates this control set (i.e., those placed randomly in rooms without a nature view). For the planting of new trees or the creation of new parks, it is often more difficult to have true control sets. Often, mental health data from other similar neighborhoods without the conservation intervention are used as controls.

While detailed monitoring of mental health outcomes of conservation actions is hard, it is possible to have metrics of mental health provision over time to aid decision making. My recommendation is that all towns should track over time street trees and parcels of greenspace in a GIS (geographical information systems) framework. This allows the calculation of metrics of park access. Since these metrics correlate with mental health provision, their trend provides useful information to decision makers. And spatial information can be used to inform where future park creation should be targeted, in an adaptive management framework.

Summary

The relationship between parks and mental health is one of the least scientifically explored ecosystem services described in the book, and there are few cities that have park creation programs solely focused on mental health. However, an increasing number of institutions like schools and hospitals are taking this relationship into account as they design their facilities. The scientific literature makes clear that there are deep and profound links between the presence of nature and our mental health, yet the tools to quickly quantify this relationship in economic terms are relatively limited, compared with other ecosystem services addressed in this book. Many cities would do well to focus on park access for all their residents and assume that mental health benefits come with park access, as well as physical health and aesthetic benefits, rather than trying to precisely quantify mental health benefits in economic terms.

Chapter 12

The Value of Biodiversity in Cities

Sᴀɴ Dɪᴇɢᴏ ʜᴀᴅ ᴀ ᴘʀᴏʙʟᴇᴍ. It was a rapidly growing city, accumulating almost a million new residents in the 1990s and early 2000s (UNPD 2011). But the landscape was also home to lots of rare plants and animals, having one of the highest levels of biodiversity in the United States. Many of the rare species were listed as endangered and had protection under the Endangered Species Act, which requires critical habitat for rare species to be conserved. This had the potential to really constrain the expansion of San Diego into the surrounding lands, hurting the economic development of the city. A particular worry was that if each rare species' critical habitat was defined separately, the resulting patchwork of critical habitat designations would prove difficult to administer or plan around.

The solution came to be called the Multi-Species Conservation Plan (MSCP) (City of San Diego 2014). The planning process considered the habitat requirements for eighty-five species covered by the Endangered Species Act. The plan delineated the Multi-Habitat Protected Area (MHPA), around 900 square miles of land, only a portion of which is in San Diego proper. The critical habitat in the MHPA would be protected from development in a collaboration between federal, state, and local officials. Much of the responsibility for figuring out how to protect the MHPA was devolved to San Diego municipal officials, who had to figure out how to protect this large area while also planning for the city's fast growth.

Some of the MHPA (66 percent) is now publically owned protected land. The City of San Diego has made a commitment to expand conservation and now has committed funding to protect another 28 percent of the land in the MHPA. For the remaining privately owned parcels in the MHPA, development is limited by zoning code to 25 percent of the parcel, and must be in the least ecologically sensitive portion of the parcel. If a parcel owner wants to further develop his parcel, mitigation swaps are possible through a process called Boundary Line Adjustment: the owner must pay to protect a parcel elsewhere of similar size and ecological value. Finally, parcels adjacent to the MHPA are subject to a set of zoning regulations to make sure their land use does not damage the rare species in the MHPA.

As is often the case in conservation, the limiting factor is money. Funding for the protection of the MHPA is split between federal, state, and local agencies. Local funding comes primarily from the Habitat Acquisition Fund (HAF). Every new development in San Diego pays an impact fee to offset the city's cost of supporting the new development, and a portion of the impact fee goes into the HAF. There are also private mitigation banks which, for a fee, will protect habitat as swaps for parcels developed in the MHPA.

The San Diego case is an extreme example of a common struggle for many cities. Many cities want to maintain the biodiversity in remnant patches inside the urban core as well as in the surrounding natural areas. This may be because of regulatory obligations like the Endangered Species Act. Or it may simply be because some of the citizens care enough about biodiversity to advocate for its protection. Whatever the reason, conservation of biodiversity is important for many cities, and they are willing to pay for it.

This chapter is about biodiversity conservation in cities. In a sense, planning to protect biodiversity in cities is similar to conservation planning generally, about which there is a large literature (e.g., Groves 2003; Sarkar et al. 2006). However, the urban context poses at least two unique problems for conservation planners that will be discussed: biotic homogenization and habitat fragmentation. I point toward tools that allow planners to account for these unique problems. I also discuss how to quantify the economic value of biodiversity to citizens, to put it in economic terms as we have for the other ecosystem services considered in this book. As we shall see, in principle, biodiversity information can be put in economic terms and incorporated into planning, just as any other ecosystem service can.

Mapping Biodiversity and Planning for Its Conservation

Urban development necessarily destroys natural habitat, so planning to maximize biodiversity in the face of habitat loss is always a challenge. The challenge is a very important one for cities to grapple with, however, since cities are preferentially located in high biodiversity areas. Cities have tended to form near transportation corridors, which historically were primarily oceans and large, navigable rivers. Coasts and floodplains are also places of high biodiversity, raising the conflict between urban growth and biodiversity. Moreover, human population density tends to be higher in high productivity landscapes, where it is easier to grow food, but high productivity areas also are areas of high biodiversity (Luck 2007). The spatial correlation of cities and high biodiversity means the direct impact of cities on biodiversity is much larger than one might expect from their urban footprint. For instance, my colleagues and I showed that cities occupy only 2 to 4 percent of Earth's land surface, but impact around 13 percent of the earth's vertebrates (2008).

Species may be usefully put into three categories (McKinney 2002, 2006, 2008; Forman 2014). *Avoiders* (sometimes called sensitive species) are species that decrease in abundance or even disappear near urban areas. *Adapters* are species that can persist in remnant patches even when surrounded by urban areas, often by modifying their behavior to take advantage of the surrounding urban area. *Exploiters* are species that are much more prevalent and abundant in urban-dominated landscapes than in more natural settings.

As urban development proceeds and natural habitat is lost, the remaining natural habitat is more and more surrounded by urban development. Avoider species are lost, and total avoider species richness goes down. On the other hand, exploiters increase, and total exploiter richness increases. The total species richness of a patch or even a city may thus decrease or increase, depending on the relative numbers of avoiders lost and exploiters gained. But as avoider species are often local endemics, while exploiter species are often common cosmopolitan organisms, the net effect globally of urban development is to decrease biodiversity. As a corollary, this process of endemic avoider loss and cosmopolitan exploiter increase leads to biotic homogenization: species composition between two cities is more similar than between two rural areas, because the cities share this common cosmopolitan set of species. As species composition changes, so too does ecosystem function, and Groffman and others (2014) have shown that for some functions the process of urbanization homogenizes the level of ecosystem function.

The goal of most biodiversity protection actions by cities is thus to prevent avoider species loss. Principally, this is done by protecting remnant patches of key natural habitat from development. This is what the MHPA represents in San Diego: a plan to protect key habitat for some endemic species that would likely be extinct if their habitat was lost. Conservation efforts in cities also sometimes focus on limiting the arrival of new exploiter species, on the theory that new invasive nonnative species might outcompete some of the avoider species. San Diego's efforts to use their zoning power to limit land use near the edges of the MHPA might be seen in this light, creating a buffer area of moderate human use around the core protected area.

Conservation planning in an urban context must also take into account the extreme habitat fragmentation that takes place (Saunders, Hobbs, and Margules 1991). While fragmentation occurs naturally for a few habitat types (e.g., high-altitude forests in the deserts of the American Southwest, so-called sky islands), it becomes much more prevalent in man-made landscapes such as urban areas (Swenson and Franklin 2000). The concept of fragmentation is an analogy: You have small remnant patches of vegetation separated by a matrix of inhospitable habitat (fig. 12.1). Such an analogy is appropriate for most avoider species that are limited to the native habitat, but less so for adapters and exploiters, which can use the matrix urban area for their day-to-day lives (Haila 2002). Fragmentation is traditionally conceived of as having three main effects. First, habitat area is necessarily lost as a city expands and fragmentation proceeds. One of the most famous relationships in ecology is the species-area curve; less habitat area, fewer species on average (Desmet and Cowling 2004). The exact shape of this curve depends on the habitat and the species involved, with species with large home ranges being most sensitive to a loss in habitat area.

A second component of fragmentation is edge effects: the change in abiotic and biotic conditions that occurs near the edge of a habitat patch (Murcia 1995; Woodroffe and Ginsberg 1998). Abiotic changes include increases in light and temperature, decreases in relative humidity, and the deposition of increased pollutants (e.g., Dignan and Bren 2003). Biotic changes can include invasive species, which often come to natural habitat patches via the surrounding matrix habitat. They can also be more idiosyncratic: for instance, songbirds tend to sing in different pitches near road edges, so their

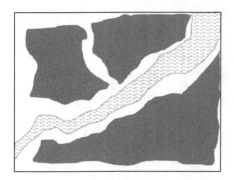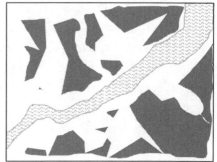

Figure 12.1. Schematic diagram of habitat fragmentation, before (left panel) and after (right panel) urbanization. Grey areas are natural habitat that is fragmented by urban areas, here represented as the white background. A river flows through the center of the diagram, naturally fragmenting some habitat patches. Note that total habitat area necessarily decreases with urbanization-induced fragmentation. Moreover, a greater proportion of each habitat patch is near an edge, increasing edge effects. Finally, the habitat is broken into a greater number of patches, and the patches are farther from each other, decreasing habitat connectivity.

songs can be heard over the road noise (Nemeth et al. 2013). Edge effects can penetrate from tens of meters to 1 kilometer into a habitat patch, depending on the effect (McDonald et al. 2009). Many small patches, which necessarily have a higher perimeter-to-area ratio, have their entire area affected by edge effects. This renders them useless for many avoider species.

The third component of fragmentation is the loss of connectivity between patches (Tischendorf and Fahrig 2000). Many species need access to multiple patches, either to cobble together a sufficient home range, to find a mate, or to migrate. As urban development proceeds, the intervening habitat gets more hostile, more difficult to traverse. This separates individuals into separate populations, preventing gene flow and migration. Sometimes corridors are described as ways to maintain connectivity. What is a useful, viable corridor varies by species, of course, as a corridor for a salamander under a road (e.g., a pipe that allows safe passage) will look really different from a corridor for a mountain lion (e.g., a large greenway along a river ravine).

Several software packages are useful for quantifying the components of fragmentation, whether in an urban or a rural context (table 12.1). Fragstats is perhaps the simplest, and is certainly an old standby of the landscape ecology community. It calculates lots of landscape metrics, and some of them are quite useful for studying fragmentation. For instance, the perimeter-to-area ratio and the amount of core habitat available in a set of habitat patches can be useful for studying edge effects, while mean distance between patches can be useful for studying loss of connectivity. If a city has different development scenarios under consideration, then the fragmentation statistics of the remaining remnant patches under each scenario can be calculated. There are now several software packages specializing in delineating corridors and their importance in a landscape, including FunConn, Conefor, CorridorDesign.org, and Graph AB. If a city has different development scenarios in mind, then the impact of these development scenarios on patch connectivity can be quantified. The RAMAS software package combines the corridor delineation function with a metapopulation model, tracking population growth in each patch and dispersal among them. Detailed models like RAMAS can be useful in situations where a particular focal species is important (e.g., species listed as endangered by the government) and for which detailed population and life history information is available.

Conservation planning is a well-studied topic, and in this short chapter I cannot hope to do more than point the reader toward a few key principles and some good reference works (Groom, Meffe, and Carroll 2005; Groves 2003). Fundamentally, the task of conservation planning is an optimization problem: select the patches for conservation that achieve some conservation objective (e.g., minimize the loss of avoider species) for the minimal cost (Sarkar et al. 2006). The first general principle identified in the conservation planning literature is the idea of complementarity between patches selected for conservation: the species list of one patch should not be entirely identical to the species list of another patch, but instead should complement it, so that in total a large number of species

Table 12.1. Inputs and outputs for models useful for biodiversity conservation planning

	Fragstats	Connectivity models	Metapopulation models (e.g., RAMAS)	Conservation planning software	Biodiversity valuation
Key data inputs					
Land cover	Yes	Yes	Yes	Yes	No
Habitat quality information or barriers to dispersal	No	Maybe	Yes	Maybe	No
Valuation information from a WTP study	No	No	No	No	Yes
Key outputs					
Landscape metrics of fragmentation	Yes	Varies	Varies	Varies	No
Connectivity metrics	Some simple metrics	Yes	Yes	No	No
Demographic information	No	No	Yes	No	No
Optimal conservation plans	No	No	No	Yes	No
Existence value	No	No	No	No	Yes
Other notes	Easy to use	Several models in this category include FunConn, Conefor, CorridorDesign.org, and Graph AB	Models integrate a demographic model with information on patch connectivity and area	Several models in this category include Marxan, ResNet, and Target	Uses benefits transfer from a similar study

are protected. Related to the idea of complementarity is the idea of irreplaceability. If a patch has species that occur only in it, then it should be selected for conservation. So the simplest optimization problem that could be considered by a conservation planner is finding the minimal set of patches, those that protect the target level of biodiversity in the minimum total area.

Smarter analyses will incorporate another principle of conservation planning: vulnerability. Different parcels have different chances of being converted to another land use, perhaps through urban development, and by losing their biodiversity. The effectiveness of conservation action is thus measured against the expected loss of biodiversity without conservation action, which can be defined as the vulnerability (probability of habitat conversion) times the biodiversity loss, if conversion occurs. In an urban planning context, this is often assessed using build-out analyses, assuming that in the long term everything that is currently allowed to be developed by a town's zoning code will be developed, and analyzing the habitat patches lost. Alternatively, statistical models of the probability of development occurring over a certain time period (e.g., the next decade) can be used (McDonald 2009). Whatever the methodology used, the incorporation of vulnerability into conservation planning will significantly improve conservation effectiveness, for the simple reason that the protection of high biodiversity sites that have low vulnerability is unlikely to prevent much biodiversity loss.

Finally, analyses should consider parcel cost. Different parcels of natural habitat cost different amounts, both because they vary in area and also because the per-area cost can vary considerably across a planning landscape. Land near the center of the city is often more expensive than land near the city's periphery. The objective function being optimized thus should be meeting some target threshold for expected biodiversity loss (e.g., zero biodiversity loss). The ideal solution is at the minimum possible cost, so more expensive pixels are less likely to be selected than less expensive ones.

There are numerous software tools for solving this optimization problem. One of the most common is Marxan (table 12.1).

Marzone is an extension of Marxan, which allows for multiple objectives (e.g., biodiversity and ecosystem service provision) to be solved for at once. Other packages include ResNet and Target. Note that in the real world, it is rare that the optimized solutions provided by these packages are the sole determinant of conservation planning decisions. Rather, other real-world factors (legal status on different lands, willingness of landowners to make a deal, political and funding opportunities) all make the implementation of conservation strategy deviate from these idealized solutions. Nevertheless, the optimized solutions provide a smart place to start a discussion about what should be conserved where.

Common Threats and Common Solutions

This chapter has focused on the biggest direct impact of urban growth on biodiversity, which is biodiversity loss due to habitat conversion associated with new urban development. Globally, the total urban area is expected to triple between 2000 and 2030 (Elmqvist et al. 2013). Estimates of the biodiversity impact of this expansion vary depending on the taxa, but are around 13 percent for vertebrates (McDonald, Kareiva, and Forman 2008). Regardless of the taxa, however, biodiversity loss is highly concentrated spatially. Twenty ecoregions globally will have more than half of the biodiversity lost directly to urban growth. Cities, of course, also have lots of indirect effects on biodiversity, particularly through how natural resources are sourced to the city. These indirect effects are not the focus of this chapter, although note that some of the other chapters in this book that relate to natural resource use (e.g., drinking water, chapter 3) consider this broader urban footprint of consumption.

Once the basic information on biodiversity and habitat fragmentation are available, this information can be used to inform other planning decisions a city makes. For instance, if certain parcels are selected as key natural habitat in a city's conservation portfolio, this designation can be put into a comprehensive or master plan. Particularly when these plans can influence the actual zoning code, they can have tremendous power to protect rare elements of biodiversity. Cities may also choose to incorporate biodiversity information into an overall sustainability plan, where biodiversity protection will have to be considered alongside things like energy efficiency and resilience. Or, like San Diego, they may have a stand-alone biodiversity plan, mandated by species protection laws. Plans are only meaningful if they can actually affect what habitat is developed, of course, so before putting biodiversity information into such planning processes it is important to get agreement on the incentives and regulations that will be used to affect landowner decisions. If biodiversity conservation is to protect habitat that would have otherwise been lost, there is necessarily an opportunity cost. Land that could have been used for urban development is now being left in its native habitat instead.

Another solution that cities use is programs that allow the transfer of development rights (TDRs). Usually, rules are set up so that part of the landscape is prioritized for land protection, and landowners in this protected part of the landscape are compensated by getting development rights for other sites. Mitigation banks, such as those used in San Diego, operate under a similar logic. The idea is that only a certain amount of habitat will be lost, because a finite amount of development permits will be issued. To develop land within with MHPA, you need to buy a permit from a mitigation bank that shows that an ecologically equivalent parcel elsewhere will be protected.

Many of the other chapters in this book are about ecosystem services that cities depend on, and how payment for ecosystem service schemes can be created that maintain the flow of these services. Such schemes will also tend to protect biodiversity because they give value to particular parcels of natural land cover and tend to maintain them. The extent that biodiversity overlaps spatially with ecosystem service provision varies, depending on the landscape and ecosystem service under consideration (Chan et al. 2006). Natural habitat may be quite good for carbon sequestration or air filtration for instance, but for recreational services, altered parkland (e.g., baseball fields) may be better than natural habitat.

Often, requirements to protect biodiversity are foisted upon cities by national or provincial governments. Command-and-control legislation tends to define biodiversity loss as something to be minimized or avoided, regardless of the cost (Polasky 2008). Thus, cities' conservation planning is often in the context of rules and targets set by others. Command-and-control legislation can lead to very sharp consequences for a city. If a parcel is truly irreplaceable in a biodiversity sense, and biodiversity loss is unacceptable, then development will effectively be banned outright on the site. In the case of the MHPA in San Diego, development isn't strictly banned on private landholdings but is sharply limited by the zoning code.

Valuation of Biodiversity

Why does society put such emphasis on the protection of biodiversity? Why are governments willing to write laws that promote biodiversity protection and in effect set aside land from development, with significant opportunity costs? Broadly speaking, there are two categories of reasons that biodiversity is valued. The first is instrumental values: the benefits to our well-being that we receive from the existence of biodiversity. Ecosystem services are a type of instrumental value, since they by definition are the ecosystem functions that provide some real benefit to human well-being. The second is intrinsic values, values that do not depend on the practical benefit to people, but instead are somehow inherent to the species or habitat itself. These intrinsic values would, in some sense, exist even without humans.

Intrinsic values often arise from moral principles, and vice versa. It seems to many people, including myself, that somehow the right thing to do is to protect biodiversity, apart from any benefit to human beings. Moral principles may lead, in theory, to almost infinite value being placed on biodiversity: if it is the right thing to do to protect biodiversity, then it is always morally good to spend whatever it takes to prevent the loss of a species. But in real life, different moral principles conflict, which require trade-offs and legal judgments. We may think that it is always worthwhile to protect biodiversity but also believe in a landowner's right to have, within some reasonable limits, the ability to control what happens on their land. These two beliefs may conflict, and sorting out their relative weight is a complex philosophical or legal analysis.

The Endangered Species Act is an example of a law based primarily on the intrinsic value of biodiversity (Polasky 2008). Under the original law, in general and in most cases, actions that jeopardized an endangered species were illegal, regardless of the cost. However, when a single population of a single snail species held up a major hydroelectric plant, the law was amended to allow for exemptions for actions that would jeopardize endangered species but were in the national interest. And in practice, decisions to list species as endangered, as well as critical habitat designations, are influenced by public comment from affected stakeholders. Controversial and costly listings tend to be delayed and to be challenged in court (Ando 1999).

The instrumental value of biodiversity is somewhat more amenable to being quantified in dollar terms. Most of the other chapters in this book are about how to quantify one particular type of instrumental value (ecosystem services). To the extent that biodiversity is needed for each of these services to be provided, biodiversity can be said to support the ecosystem service provision and hence has value (MEA 2003). More directly, the sheer existence of biodiversity has value to many people. I feel happy knowing that polar bears still exist in their native habitat, even though I may never see them there. Indeed, I might be willing to give money to a conservation group that is trying to protect polar bears, so they can continue to exist in their native habitat.

Existence value has primarily been measured using contingent valuation techniques, which essentially ask people how much they would be willing to pay (WTP) to avoid the loss of a species or willing to accept (WTA) as compensation for the loss of a species. One review (Loomis and White 1996) found a range of WTP from $6 to $95 per household per year to protect a single species. More charismatic species, such as tigers and polar bears, are generally worth more than snails or beetles. Interestingly, contingent valuation studies that measure WTP to avoid the loss of a whole suite of species (e.g., all beetles) generally have found numbers in a similar range to those for single species (Polasky, Costello, and Solow 2005). It is thus not clear exactly what contingent valuation studies of biodiversity measure. By being willing to give money, survey respondents could be signaling support for environmental protection generally, or simply enjoying the "warm glow of contributing to a worthy cause."

Nevertheless, contingent valuation studies show that the existence value of biodiversity is clearly positive and is nonnegligible. For instance, suppose San Diego citizens value at $10/person/year the mere existence of the eighty-five (endangered or threatened) species covered by the MHPA. Since there are 1.4 million people in San Diego, this implies a willingness to pay for conservation of around $14 million per year. In actual fact, payment into the HAF is much less, around $140,000 per year (City of San Diego 2014), although this is supplemented by state and federal spending. Total costs to protect the MHPA were estimated as $339 to $411 million in 1996 dollars, and actual costs have been significantly higher due to the real estate boom that has raised land prices.

Most cities will not need to explicitly estimate their citizens' willingness to pay for biodiversity conservation, since they will instead try to incorporate biodiversity information into their planning process, which weighs many subjects of concerns to citizens and tries to find an acceptable overall solution. If a city does want such an estimate, they have to resort to the benefits-transfer method of valuation. This requires finding a study that looks at a similar element of biodiversity. Moreover, the study will hopefully have done contingent valuation in a similar socioeconomic context. The contingent valuation will then be applied to the new city, providing an estimate of biodiversity value which, while rough, is sufficient to make decisions for conservation. This sort of ballpark number can be very useful when setting funding goals for conservation.

Implementation

The first, and most important act for many cities, is simply having biodiversity information assembled and analyzed, as described in the Mapping section above. Just having a map of key conservation areas can often cause change in numerous city planning processes and zoning decisions. These key conservation areas also can become targets for future conservation actions by the city.

Once key biodiversity areas are located, the next step is figuring out how to protect them. Many cities end up using a mix of the solutions described earlier: changing comprehensive and master plans, altering zoning codes, directly protecting some parcels, and so forth. Deciding on the ideal mix of solutions depends on the regulatory and legal context in which a city finds itself. San Diego's strategy was dictated, in large part, by the structure of the Endangered Species Act and its counterpart in California law. On the other hand, a city working to protect species or habitats that are not covered by legal statutes may use more voluntary measures in their mix of solutions.

Once a mix of solutions is decided on, funding is usually needed to carry them out. Some strategies like zoning changes are relatively cheap. Changes in zoning only directly cost the city the incremental costs of enforcement, although they of course can force significant opportunity costs on to landowners. Similarly, tradable development permits may have a relatively small cost for the city for program monitoring but may be a significant expense for those who end up needing to purchase permits. Land protection, however, often requires significant amounts of money, particularly since the cost of land is so high in urban centers. Land protection in the United States is often funded with open space bonds, whether general revenue or special use bonds, which allows the relatively large cost of land purchase to be repaid over many years.

San Diego has chosen to fund the HAF through an impact fee. These are commonly charged to developers to offset infrastructure costs incurred by the city as a result of new development. In essence, San Diego is treating habitat protection as part of the essential activities of the city, just like laying new sewer pipes or building new roads. By law, new developments have to comply with the Endangered Species Act, and payments to the HAF help ensure that they do so.

Monitoring

Biodiversity monitoring is a well-developed field with specialized textbooks (Sutherland 2006; McComb et al. 2010). The easiest task is usually determining if a rare species or community, sometimes called an "element occurrence," remains present on a parcel. An occasional site visit often suffices, particularly for sessile animals, which are easy to survey in their permanent locations. Animals and other organisms that move about are more difficult to survey, requiring monitoring schemes that have a good probability of detecting the target organism if it is present.

Collecting data on the population and demography of a rare species is harder, generally requiring a longer site visit and more intensive monitoring procedure. The goal is to understand variability in population number over space (i.e., among parcels) and time, and so multiple samples are needed. These kinds of spatiotemporal data, while harder to collect, are crucial to understanding the population viability of rare species in an urban context. There are established monitoring procedures for both animals and plants that natural resource managers in cities can draw upon (Morris and Doak 2002).

The monitoring needs of a city thus will be determined by the goals of its biodiversity protection program. For species regulated by the Endangered Species Act or similar laws, a fairly complete and thorough population viability analysis is needed. For other species, simple presence/absence information often suffices.

Even these sorts of presence absence lists can be powerful tools for historical analysis. For instance, one study looked at plant species composition in a wooded parkland in the urban Boston area for almost 100 years (Drayton and Primack 1996). During this time, 155 species out of 422 were lost, despite the parcel being fully protected, while another 64 species of cosmopolitan exploiter species were added. Presumably this is an example of the biotic homogenization phenomenon in action, and it provides a good case study of why land protection does not necessarily mean that all species that live on the parcel will be viable over the long term.

Summary

Many cities like San Diego make protection of biodiversity a key goal of their parks and open space protection program, for either regulatory or moral reasons. Indeed, as urban population and urbanized area grow dramatically over the next few decades, this approach will be key to avoiding significant biodiversity loss, particularly in cities whose surrounding natural habitat harbors high biodiversity or endemism. The existence value of biodiversity can be thought of as an ecosystem service and quantified in economic terms, and even simple extrapolations of published studies suggest that public willingness to pay for biodiversity is quite significant in aggregate. For many cities, however, such economic valuation will not be needed, and traditional conservation planning techniques can be used to site urban parks. Biotic homogenization and habitat fragmentation are uniquely intense in cities, however, and must be dealt with in any conservation planning effort, if it is to be a success.

Chapter 13

Putting It All Together

THE PRECEDING CHAPTERS EACH focused on an individual ecosystem service, describing how to map important habitats for service provision, how to value the service, and how to implement and monitor ecosystem service programs. Having completed our whirlwind tour of key ecosystem services in cities, what is next? For some cities that have focused primarily on one ecosystem service, this may be the endpoint. Perhaps they have developed a good conservation program around that one ecosystem service and are content just to maintain and refine this program over time. However, cities that have identified multiple ecosystem services of importance may want to find a way to merge information and programs from disparate ecosystem services into one coherent vehicle.

In chapter 2, I presented a simple framework for working on ecosystem service provision to urban residents. Each stage of the framework is one that cities must pass through, either explicitly or implicitly, as they conduct ecosystem service work. The first stage was defining the problem or policy issue that natural infrastructure is to address. This could be defined using a resiliency analysis (chapter 2), which would help define the key steps that must be taken to maintain or enhance a city's resiliency. Or the problem or policy issue could be defined relative to a city's broad goals, as set out, for instance, in a sustainability or comprehensive plan.

In the second stage of the framework, cities define key ecosystem services that could help solve the problem or policy issue. These often follow easily from the problems identified by a resiliency analysis, which often also lists key steps the city could take to improve its resilience. Some of these steps will involve the creation or alteration of grey infrastructure. For instance, many cities near coasts are responding to climate change by moving critical infrastructure like electrical substations away from low-lying areas. But many of the steps identified will depend upon maintaining or enhancing ecosystem service provisions to urban residents, the central focus of this book. Stage 2 thus helps define a list of one or more key ecosystem services that must be considered to achieve resiliency or the city's broader priorities.

The rest of the framework is shown in figure 13.1. In stage 3, cities list critical natural systems for providing ecosystem services. During stage 4, cities identify opportunities for action, either strategies that mitigate threats or strategies that can increase service provision. In stage 5, cities assess their different options and settle upon a plan for each ecosystem service, asking granular questions such as, Which specific parcels should be protected, and by what agency?

In stage 6, cities implement their plans, and then monitor their outcomes over time. Stage 6 isn't so much an endpoint as a beginning. Smart cities allow monitoring data to affect program management, so it can become more efficient over time. They also create future plans in light of monitoring results, so that mistakes in the past are not replicated in the future. This is the so-called adaptive

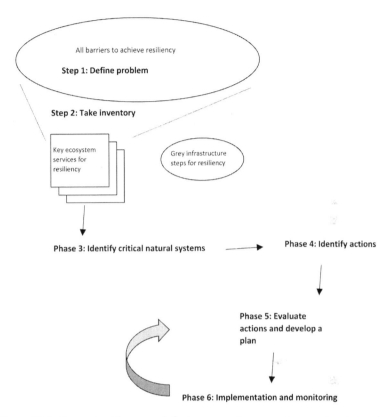

Figure 13.1. Conceptual framework for incorporating ecosystem services into urban planning and decision making. See chapter 3 for a detailed discussion.

cycle, about which a great deal has been written (Allan and Stankey 2009; Salafsky et al. 2002; Stem et al. 2005). In a certain broad sense, cities have always used adaptive management when providing services to their residents like clean water, changing laws, policy, and institutional structure when needed to streamline service delivery. It is my belief that cities will similarly need to learn over time how best to run something like a "natural infrastructure utility," ensuring adequate provision of ecosystem services to urban residents (McDonald et al., forthcoming).

One key reason why cities may want to bring together information and plans from multiple ecosystem services is to craft a compelling overall natural infrastructure vision. For the general public, quantitative information on one particular ecosystem service may not be enough. If all of the city's plans for different ecosystem services are conducted, what is the cumulative effect? What will the city look like? What will it feel like to live in this greener, more resilient city?

One forum for communicating that vision may be future comprehensive or sustainability plans. Each ecosystem service plan may be one layer in the overall map, and just this common presentation on one map has communication value. Putting the information on one map also tends to begin the process of tweaking each ecosystem service plan or program to align it with the city's overall goal, as misalignments are often glaringly apparent when placed side by side on the same map. Finally, a common map gives urban officials a chance to make the most compelling possible case for why ecosystem service programs are essential to solve the problem or policy issue identified in stage 1.

Another advantage of a city bringing together information from multiple ecosystem services is it allows the estimation of the cumulative benefits of all the ecosystem services. This is sometimes called "stacking" of ecosystem service benefits. Each ecosystem service may not be valuable enough by itself to motivate action, but together there might be a compelling case for action. For instance, my own research on urban drinking water supplies suggests that only occasionally will source watershed conservation make economic sense for a utility, in the sense that if a utility had to pay for all the costs of conservation, then the costs would outweigh the benefits to the utility (McDonald and Shemie, 2014). But in most cases, when ecosystem service benefits to other stakeholders are considered, source watershed conservation makes sense.

Finally, putting information on multiple ecosystem services together can spur coordination among agencies. Sometimes synergistic actions can supply multiple ecosystem services at once. For instance, natural infrastructure programs for stormwater mitigation can also have freshwater biodiversity benefits. Conversely, coordination can help avoid antagonistic actions, where provision of one service harms provision of other services. For instance, in desert ecosystems planting trees provides shade to urban residents but may increase municipal water use, a trade-off that must be managed.

Natural Sets of Ecosystem Services

Now that I've discussed the reasons why it is helpful to bring together information from multiple ecosystem services, I offer some thoughts on how best to go about the task. One way to approach the task is to consider sets of ecosystem services together (table 13.1). Certain sets of ecosystem services naturally go together. They may be provided by the same habitat, or be thematically related, so good reasons exist to consider them together during planning.

Table 13.1. Clusters of ecosystem services

	Hydrological services	Services from natural habitat patches	Services from natural infrastructure
Ecosystem services	Drinking water provision	Air purification	Shade and urban heat island mitigation
	Floodwater mitigation	Coastal protection services	Recreation
	Stormwater mitigation	Biodiversity persistence	Aesthetic beauty
			Physical and mental health
Type of area providing service	Upstream contributing area, more often natural habitat for drinking water and floodwater and natural infrastructure for stormwater.	Remnant natural habitat, although occasionally constructed natural infrastructure, plays this role.	Constructed natural infrastructure, although occasionally natural habitat, plays this role.

One clear natural set is the hydrologic services. Drinking water provision, floodwater mitigation, and stormwater mitigation often are considered together. Projects to maintain or enhance this set of ecosystem services all involve manipulating the quantity or quality of water flowing downhill. The serviceshed of each ecosystem service is thus simply the upstream contributing area of the drinking water intake, floodplain, or stormwater intake.

However, the serviceshed of these three services is not the same. Drinking water intakes are often located upstream from the city center, and their source watersheds sometimes contain large blocks of natural habitat, which can be the focus for conservation. On the other hand, stormwater intakes are usually located in the urban center, out of necessity, and have much smaller, more developed upstream areas. This can lead to the creation of natural infrastructure patches within the urban fabric. Floodplain sourcesheds can be either large or small, and a range of conservation strategies, from land protection or habitat restoration to de novo natural infrastructure, are used.

But when the servicesheds for the different hydrological services overlap, conservation actions need to be harmonized across the services. In general, individual actions that help with one service are unlikely to directly oppose provision of other services. For instance, actions to reduce erosion to protect a city's water supply are unlikely to worsen problems with flooding. However, because the best places to work vary from service to service, more optimal plan designs may be obtained if they are jointly considered. For instance, planners may pick parcels that meet multiple needs (e.g., floodplain reconnection and restoration may reduce flood risk while also protecting drinking water.

Another set of ecosystem services are primarily provided by remnant habitat patches. These patches provide habitat for biodiversity as well as air purification services, including carbon sequestration. Remnant habitat near coastlines is also crucial for coastal protection services. All of these services have in common that a relatively large area of habitat, at least as contrasted with things like shade provision, which can be gained from a single street tree. Habitat restoration is a common strategy for this set of ecosystem services, particularly for coastal habitats that have been disproportionately impacted by human development.

Again, it is rare for provision of one service in this set to directly conflict with provision of another service. However, one can imagine situations where there is a conflict. For instance, carbon sequestration might be maximized by planting trees, which if it occurred in native grasslands would be a net negative for biodiversity. More common are situations where the services are only partially correlated. Again, efficiencies in planning can often be found using information from all the ecosystem services, since parcels can be chosen that meet multiple objectives.

I should acknowledge again here that the line between natural habitat and man-made natural infrastructure can be blurry and indistinct. When a coastal wetland is substantially restored, is that a natural habitat patch again? When a constructed space such as Central Park in New York City begins to house biodiversity, does it become natural habitat? As mentioned in chapter 1, there is a continuum of naturalness. Groups that are most interested in natural resource and biodiversity conservation may work primarily at the more natural end of the spectrum, while those most interested in urban design and landscape architecture may work, out of necessity, at the man-made end of the spectrum.

Finally, there is a set of ecosystem services that primarily come from this man-made end of the spectrum, which I have been calling green infrastructure in this book. The green infrastructure can be parks of various sizes, or simply a row of street trees. Provision of shade, recreation, aesthetic beauty, and physical and mental health benefits all fall within this set. In certain cases, of course, natural habitat provides one or more of these services. But because of the scale at which these services operate and the compact nature of many urban cores, constructed green infrastructure is often key for these services.

Control of these constructed spaces often falls to the city's parks and recreation department. This agency often takes the lead in planning for the multiple benefits natural infrastructure can provide. However, as has been shown in previous chapters, different ecosystem services have different stakeholders which should be invited into the planning process. Public health officials, for instance, may be interested in the role of parks in reducing obesity.

Indeed, each of these sets of ecosystem services has different sets of stakeholders that advocate for them. This is true in terms of having different agencies that care about these ecosystem services, but it is also true at the individual levels. The task then for a city is to minimize any barriers to collaboration among stakeholders interested in a particular set of ecosystem services. For instance, for the hydrological services, watershed basin planning commissions are one possible way to bring stakeholders together and minimize the transaction costs of collaboration.

Creating a Resilient City

All this talk about ecosystem services can seem dry and academic. *Ecosystem services* is a term coined by environmental economists who wanted to put nature's benefits on a par with other goods and services in the economy. I have used the term in this book because it is standard in the field now, and it makes clear the economic value of nature's benefits. But I hope you, the reader, haven't lost sight of the fact that always behind ecosystem services are people's lives. Each of the chapters in this book tries to present practical ways to use nature to improve people's lives, through very tangible things like clean air or clean water or a beautiful vista. Taken together, the various chapters in this book provide a guide to using nature to build a more resilient city, one that doesn't just survive but thrives.

In short, these natural infrastructure techniques help us move toward building our conception of the ideal city.

The twenty-first century will be the urban century, as more of humanity will live in cities than ever before. This vast urbanization is happening because cities are so successful at what they do. The concentration of people in cities leads to increased interaction, which leads to dramatic increases in productivity. Innovation and invention also increase in cities, as ideas and people interact at a frenetic pace. Cities, these constructed urban landscapes in which the majority of us live, are in a certain sense quintessentially human. We have built a habitat that gives fullest expression to our need to interact and communicate and discover.

However, cities are also very damaging to the environment. The concentration of people in an urban area also means a concentration of environmental impact, whether in terms of natural resource use or in terms of pollution. Cities depend on the natural world for resources they need to survive, but they also can degrade facets of this same natural world on which they depend. As was discussed in chapter 11, the urban environment itself is in some ways a very unnatural place for people to live. Living in a city for a long while puts people's physical health in jeopardy, although movements to supply clean water and sanitation and clean air have lessened this strain (McGranahan 2007). However, living in a city still puts tremendous mental stress on people, for our species simply didn't evolve for this hyperwired, hyperconnected urban landscape.

This book is about using conservation for cities and provides the tools and techniques for cities to actively preserve and expand the natural infrastructure on which they depend. I believe that conservation for cities, and particularly the preservation of a vibrant network of natural infrastructure, can get humanity out of its urban conundrum. We can gain the benefits of an urban existence, while keeping our urban life pleasant and livable. We can enjoy the benefits that concentration of population brings while also protecting or enhancing the ecosystem services cities depend on. Indeed, I believe that the most successful cities in the twenty-first century will do the best job of protecting the ecosystem services on which they depend.

Some humility is needed by ecologists and conservationists in this urban endeavor, however. Each city will have to identify itself the key steps it must take to ensure a resilient, successful future. Only some of these steps will involve the use of natural infrastructure. I often joke about nature-based solutions being the "10 percent solution." Often, the majority of steps taken to achieve resilience will involve changes to grey infrastructure. Nevertheless, while ecologists and conservationists should be humble about our role, we should also be proud. Just as a water utility or a sanitation department became an essential part of a successful city government in the nineteenth and early twentieth centuries, it is my belief that a successful natural infrastructure program will be an essential part of a smart city government in the twenty-first century.

Cities as Advocates for Conservation of Wild Nature

In 1901 an expedition of ninety-six prominent San Franciscans toured Yosemite's magnificent valley, as part of the first High Trip of the Sierra Club. They went to see for themselves the landscape that John Muir had equated to the beauty of a cathedral, but also to plan how to protect that landscape from development and degradation. The valley itself was already protected, but Muir and others wanted a more complete and comprehensive conservation for the entire area, under the control of the federal government rather than the state of California. In the end, they were successful, with the federal government taking control of the management in 1906.

Yosemite is symbolic of wild nature, and yet the members of that 1901 expedition were by and large urbanites, city dwellers all fighting to protect a landscape that was quite different from where they lived. Time and again, those in cities have been at the forefront of protecting natural places far outside the city walls. On first glance, this can seem a little odd. Wild natural areas are often conceived of as the very opposite of urban areas. To put it another way, what would life be like in San Francisco without Yosemite? On a practical level, it would seem that the destruction of a landscape some 170 miles distant would have had little effect on day-to-day life in San Francisco. So why did some prominent San Franciscans feel they would lose something of value if Yosemite disappeared?

Historically, the movement to create parks and greenspaces within cities has been allied with the movement to protect wilder areas very far from city centers. Periods where one movement has been active are also periods where the other movement has been active. The movement to green cities aimed to provide parks for recreation and reflection, lest our minds and souls atrophy. The movement to protect wild nature made similar arguments in favor of its protection, except they emphasized the particularly refined "sublime" experience that contemplation of wild areas allowed, arguing that even a brief interaction with such areas could have a deep impact on man's character (Nash 2001).

To see the links between the two movements, examine the trends in land protection over the years in the United States. Some of the earliest protected areas were originally common land in urban areas, such as Boston Common, which has had various degrees of protection since the seventeenth century. Commons were originally used for grazing animals, but in the nineteenth century most of them, including Boston Common, were converted to urban parks for pleasure and recreation. The first national parks in more wild areas appeared in the late nineteenth century, starting with the creation of Yellowstone in 1872. The late nineteenth century is also the beginning of rapid urbanization in the United States, with the population living in cities increasing from 25 percent in 1870 to 40 percent in 1900. At the time of the Great Depression (1930s), 56 percent of people lived in cities. One of the most iconic public works programs of that period was the Civilian Conservation Corps, which helped create the infrastructure for a whole set of national parks, such as Skyline Drive in Shenandoah National Park. By the end of World War II and the great economic expansion of the 1950s, the United States was 64 percent urbanized (US Census Bureau 2002). The 1950s and 1960s saw a rapid expansion of protected areas in the United States, particularly through increasing the protection status of federal lands, such as by making resource-use areas into designated monuments or wilderness areas. Thus, the period of fastest urbanization in the United States has also been the period of greatest land protection in areas far from city boundaries.

I would also argue that urbanization has been a helpful factor for the environmental movement more broadly. The creation of the modern "sanitary city" can be seen as the first environmental movement (Melosi 2008), driven by a desire to improve living conditions. The first goal often was to develop clean water sources, for urban residents, as well as to develop a way to move sewage out of cities. A secondary goal was to improve local air quality, sometimes by banning the burning of coal.

Many of the major environmental laws of the twentieth century also were predominately supported by the urban population. The Clean Water Act, passed in 1972, went beyond drinking water quality concerns to set goals for most water bodies to be fishable and swimmable for future generations. The Clean Air Act, passed in 1963 and substantially increased in scope in the following decades, set air quality goals for entire regions, helping cities solve regional air problems that went beyond their particular jurisdictions. The Endangered Species Act (1973) set a goal of the persistence of all biodiversity, even a species whose habitat was so remote that it was unlikely to even be seen by most urban environmentalists. While correlation is not causation, it is at least clear that the rapid urbanization of the 1960s and 1970s was not a barrier to the growth of the modern environmental movement (Cohen 1988).

For the organization where I work, The Nature Conservancy, urban dwellers have always been our base of support. The same would be true for most environmental nongovernmental organizations

(NGOs). A majority of donations come from a handful of very important cities (in the United States, those include New York, Chicago, and San Francisco). Indeed, the concentration of financial and political power in a few megacities means that attitudes in these cities are very important for environmental NGOs. How citizens in these cities feel about conservation is crucial for the continuing success of environmental NGOs, even those that primarily operate in rural areas.

For many of the developing countries globally, the twenty-first century will be their urban century, and it will involve a shift to cities at least as profound as the urban shift of the twentieth century was in the United States. An additional two billion people will reside in cities (UNPD 2011). It is an open question whether all these new urbanites will also be a good thing for the environmental movement. Will urban growth in China drive increased attention toward the creation and enforcement of environmental laws? Will urban growth in Africa drive increased interest in conservation?

The American humorist Mark Twain once said that "history doesn't repeat itself, but it rhymes." I believe that as the great urbanization of the twenty-first century continues, there will be echoes of past trends in the United States and Europe. Thirty years from now, we will look back on the period of rapid urban growth as the time of the greatest growth in the environmental movement in the developing world. But I should acknowledge that cultural context matters, and it may be that the shared culture of the United States and Europe, particularly the romantic ideal of wilderness (Nash 2001), uniquely shaped their response to urbanization. Technology has also changed dramatically, and it is possible that in a world of TV and computer screens, nature may hold less emotional power than it did in an earlier era. It is my belief that having bits of natural infrastructure in the city can make its citizens care more about the health of nature in the broader world. People's sympathies don't end at the city's borders, and those who advocate urban parks will also advocate for conservation elsewhere. An active "conservation for cities" program can thus do more than improve the lives of those in cities: it can connect them with the broader environment.

I wrote this book not just to make cities more resilient but also, I must confess, with an ulterior motive. It is my hope that a new, smarter, more targeted round of natural infrastructure in cities will help hook a new generation on conservation. If "past is prologue," as Shakespeare put it, then this seems to me a likely possibility. An urbanized humanity could just turn out to be a great thing for the health of the earth's broader environment.

Parting Thoughts

The language of ecosystem services that I have exploited through-out this book carries with it an assumption that public decisions are made from a utilitarian perspective. Quantifying ecosystem services in utilitarian terms is an important practical skill, for these are often the terms on which important planning decisions are made. But there is another way to frame conservation in cities to preserve or enhance ecosystem services: as actions to promote the common good. Conservation for cities helps create or maintain natural in-frastructure in service of that common good, that vision of a more perfect and just society. Framed this way, it is clear that conser-vation for cities is part and parcel of the enduring tasks of land-scape architects, urban planners, and natural resource managers. The new science and tools of ecosystem services merely allow us a clearer, more precise vision of what steps must be taken to preserve the common good.

Many in the environmental community view our species' current massive urbanization with sadness, as part of what Bill McKibben terms the "end of nature" (1989). McKibben argued that we have reached the point where every square meter of land, every eco-system process, has been altered by humans, and thus there is no real nature left. Cities, from this perspective are the endpoint, the death of nature, in the sense that they are wholly created spaces that we have designed for ourselves. I have argued in this book that while wild nature is increasingly rare, nature and natural processes still deeply matter for cities. Our natural infrastructure may not be nature in the sense McKibben means, for it is human agency that has chosen to maintain or create it, but it is still a damn sight more natural than the alternatives of concrete and steel, of more grey infrastructure. Rather than viewing the twenty-first century as the end of something, I prefer to see it as a beginning. We are creating a new world, an urban world.

This urban world could be a dystopia, if we let it. We could let the surface waters of Earth become massively polluted, and then build complex water treatment plants when we need some tolerably clean water to drink. We could let the air get so polluted that, like Mexico City in the 1990s, we need special booths that will give us relief with a breath of fresh air. We could retreat increasingly into our virtual world of the Internet and TV and all the rest, and forget about how beautiful the real world used to be. This is the dystopian future that many environmentalists fear, and it could happen, if we let it. My belief is that we will move toward this dystopian world if we continue to treat the landscape as just an incidental, disposable thing, rather than something more special.

I believe, though, that there is an alternative way to view our relationship with the landscape. Rene Dubois once spoke about the "wooing of the Earth" (Dubois 1980). Rather than being the masters of the earth, bending it to our will, Dubois envisioned humanity as a lover of the earth. Dubois' idea was to approach any decision on how to use a landscape with love and respect in our heart. There are things we need from the landscape, including ecosystem services, but there are also things that Earth needs from us. Rather than completely bending nature to our will, we could bend our will to match nature's pathways, at least a little bit. It is my belief that the science of ecosystem services gives us some of the crucial tools to follow these other pathways, if we have the love to follow them.

We have become an urban species, whether *Homo sapiens* are ready or not for this transformation. If we choose to ignore nature's pathways, if we treat the landscape as a disposable thing, then we can have our dystopia. If we choose to create our urban world thoughtfully, wooing Earth, we can have another more beautiful and humane world. In a sense, we will choose the urban world we create, and we will get the urban world we deserve. Far from being an end, our new urban world of the twenty-first century can be the beginning of something beautiful, if we chose right.

References

AIA. 2013. *Cities as a Lab: Designing the Innovation Economy.* Washington, DC: American Institute of Architects.

Alcott, E., M. Ashton, and B. Gentry. 2013. *Natural and Engineered Solutions for Drinking Water Supplies: Lessons from the Northeastern United States and Directions for Global Watershed Management.* Boca Raton, FL: CRC Press.

Allan, C., and G. Stankey. 2009. *Adaptive Environmental Management: A Practitioner's Guide.* Kindle Store: Amazon Digital Services.

Alonso, W. 1964. *Location and Land Use: Toward a General Theory of Land Rent.* Cambridge, MA: Harvard University Press.

Anderson, L., and H. Cordell. 1988. "Influence of Trees on Residential Property Values in Athens, Georgia (U.S.A.): A Survey Based on Actual Sales Prices." *Landscape and Urban Planning* 15: 153–64.

Ando, A. 1999. "Waiting to Be Protected under the Endangered Species Act: The Political Economy of Regulatory Delay." *Journal of Law and Economics* 42(1): 29–60.

APA. 2002. *Growing Smart Legislative Guidebooks: Model Statutes for Planning and the Management of Change.* Chicago, IL: American Planning Association.

Arnfield, A. J. 2003. "Two Decades of Urban Climate Research: A Review of Turbulence, Exchanges of Energy and Water, and the Urban Heat Island." *International Journal of Climatology* 23: 1–26.

Associated Press. 2012. "What We Know about Superstorm Sandy a Month Later." Associated Press, November 29.

Balmford, A., J. Beresford, J. Green, R. Naidoo, M. Walpole, and A. Manica. 2009. "A Global Perspective on Trends in Nature-Based Tourism." *PLoS Biology* 7(6): e1000144.

Barton, J., and J. Pretty. 2010. "What is the Best Dose of Nature and Green Exercise for Improving Mental Health? A Multi-study Analysis." *Environmental Science & Technology* 44: 3947–55.

BBC News. 2011. "Boris Johnson Sticks by Gluing Pollution to Roads." BBC News, November 17.

Beck, M., B. Gilmer, Z. Ferdaña, G. T. Raber, C. Shepard, I. Meliane, J. Stone, A. Whelchel, M. Hoover, and S. Newkirk. 2013. "Increasing the Resilience of Human and Natural Communities to Coastal Hazards: Supporting Decisions in New York and Connecticut." In *The Role of Ecosystems in Disaster Risk Reduction*, edited by Renaud, Sudmeier-Rieux and Estrella. Tokyo: United Nations University Press.

Bedient, P., W. Huber, and B. Vieux. 2012. *Hydrology and Floodplain Analysis*. New York: Prentice Hall.

Bell, M., D. Davis, and T. Fletcher. 2004. "A Retrospective Assessment of Mortality from the London Smog Episode of 1952: The Role of Influenza and Pollution." *Environmental Health Perspectives* 112(1): 6–8.

Berke, P., D. Godshalk, and E. Kaiser. 2006. *Urban Land Use Planning*. 5th ed. Champaign: University of Illinois Press.

Berman, M. G., J. Jonides, and S. Kaplan. 2008. "The Cognitive Benefits of Interacting with Nature." *Psychological Science* 19: 1207–12.

Bettencourt, L., J. Lobo, D. Helbing, C. Kuhnert, and G. West. 2007. "Growth, Innovation, Scaling, and the Pace of Life in Cities." *Proceedings of the National Academies of Science* 104(17): 7301–6.

Blair, J., R. Czaja, and E. Blair. 2013. *Designing Surveys: A Guide to Decisions and Procedures*. Washington, DC: SAGE.

Boyd, J., and S. Banzhaf. 2006. "What Are Ecosystem Services? The Need for Standardized Accounting Units." In *RFF DP 06-02*. Washington, DC: Resources for the Future.

Brander, L., and M. Koetse. 2011. "The Value of Urban Open Space: Meta-analyses of Contingent Valuation and Hedonic Pricing Results." *Journal of Environmental Management* 92: 2763–73.

Bratman, G. N., J. Hamilton, and G. Daily. 2012. "The Impacts of Nature Experience on Human Cognitive Function and Mental Health." *Annals of the New York Academy of Sciences* 1249: 1183–6.

Brinkley, D. 2007. *The Great Deluge: Hurricane Katrina, New Orleans, and the Mississippi Gulf Coast*. New York: Harper Perennial.

Carpenter, Stephen, Brian Walker, J. Marty Anderies, and Nick Abel. 2001. "From Metaphor to Measurement: Resilence of What to What?" *Ecosystems* 4: 765–81.

CDC. 2011. *Asthma in the US*. Atlanta, GA: Centers for Disease Control.

Chan, K., M. Shaw, D. Cameron, E. Underwood, and G. Daily. 2006. "Conservation Planning for Ecosystem Services." *Proceedings of the Library of Science—Biology* 4(11): 2138–52.

Che, X. Z., A. English, J. Lu, and Y. D. Chen. 2011. "Improving the Effectiveness of Planning EIA (PEIA) in China: Integrating Planning and

Assessment during the Preparation of Shenzhen's Master Urban Plan." *Environmental Impact Assessment Review* 31(6): 561–71.

City of San Diego. 2014. *2013 MSCP Annual Report*. San Diego: City of San Diego.

Clawson, M., and J. Knetsch. 1966. *Economics of Outdoor Recreation*. Baltimore: John Hopkins University Press.

Cohen, D. A., T. L. McKenzie, A. Sehgal, S. Williamson, D. Golinelli, and N. Lurie. 2007. "Contribution of Public Parks to Physical Activity." *American Journal of Public Health* 97(3): 509–14.

Cohen, M. 1988. *The History of the Sierra Club, 1892–1970*. San Francisco: Sierra Club Books.

CTLA. 2000. *Guide for Plant Appraisal*. Champaign, IL: Council of Tree and Landscape Appraisers/International Society of Arboriculture.

Cullen, S. 2007. "Putting a Value on Trees—CTLA Guidance and Methods." *Arboricultural Journal* 30: 21–43.

DC Water and Sewer Authority. 2002. *WASA's Recommended Combined Sewer System Long Term Control Plan*. Washington, DC: DC Water and Sewer Authority (now called DC Water).

de Zeen Magazine. 2014. "Herzog & de Meuron Win Contest for Danish Forest Hospital." www.dezeen.com: *de Zeen Magazine*.

Desmet, P., and R. M. Cowling. 2004. "Using the Species-Area Relationship to Set Baseline Targets for Conservation." *Ecology and Society* 9(2): 11.

Dignan, P., and L. Bren. 2003. "Modelling Light Penetration Edge Effects for Stream Buffer Design in Mountain Ash Forest in Southeastern Australia." *Forest Ecology and Management* 179(1–3): 95–106.

Donahue, J. 2011. *An Empirical Analysis of the Relationships between Tree Cover, Air Quality, and Crime in Urban Areas*. Graduate School of Arts and Sciences, Georgetown University, Washington, DC.

Donovan, G., and D. Butry. 2010. "Trees in the City: Valuing Street Trees in Portland, Oregon." *Landscape and Urban Planning* 94: 77–83.

Drayton, B., and R. B. Primack. 1996. "Plant Species Lost in an Isolated Conservation Area in Metropolitan Boston from 1894 to 1993." *Conservation Biology* 10(1): 30–39.

Dubois, R. 1980. *The Wooing of Earth: New Perspective on Man's Use of Nature*. London: Charles Scribner's Sons.

Edzwald, J. K., and J. E. Tobiason. 2011. "Chemical Principles, Source Water Composition, and Watershed Protection." In *Water Quality and Treatment: A Handbook on Drinking Water*, edited by J. K. Edzwald. New York: McGraw Hill.

Ellis, C., S.-W. Lee, and B.-S. Kweon. 2006. "Retail Land Use, Neighborhood Satisfaction and the Urban Forest: An Investigation into the Moderating and Mediating Effects of Trees and Shrubs." *Landscape and Urban Planning* 74: 70–78.

Elmqvist, T., M. Fragkias, J. Goodness, B. Güneralp, P. J. Marcotullio, R. I. McDonald, S. Parnell, M. Schewenius, M. Sendstad, K. Seto, and C. Wilkinson. 2013. *Urbanization, Biodiversity, and Ecosystem Services: Challenges and Opportunities, a Global Assessment.* New York: Springer.

Enrnst, C. 2004. "Protecting the Source: Conserving Forests to Protect Water." *Journal of the American Water Works Association* 30(5): 3–7.

EPA. 2002. *Consider the Source: A Pocket Guide to Protecting Your Drinking Water.* Washington, DC: US Environmental Protection Agency.

———. 2011. *Green Long-Term Control Plan-EZ Template: A Planning Tool for Combined Sewer Overflow Control in Small Communities.* Washington, DC: US Environmental Protection Agency.

———. 2012. "Basic Information: Heat Island Effect." Washington, DC: US Environmental Protection Agency. Accessed at http://www.epa.gov/heatisld/about/index.htm.

———. 2013a. "Green Infrastructure Modeling Tools." http://water.epa.gov/infrastructure/greeninfrastructure/gi_modelingtools.cfm. US Environmental Protection Agency.

———. 2013b "San Antonio Agrees to $1.1 billion Upgrade Sewer Systems to Comply with Clean Water Act." US Environmental Protection Agency.

———. 2014a. "Combined Sewer Overflows (CSO)." US Environmental Protection Agency 2014 [cited 22 September 2014]. http://water.epa.gov/polwaste/npdes/cso/.

———. 2014b. Reducing Urban Heat Islands: Compendium of Strategies (draft). Washington, DC: US Environmental Protection Agency.

Eubanks, C., and D. Meadows. 2002. *A Soil Bioengineering Guide.* Washington, DC: United States Department of Agriculture Forest Service.

Ewing, R., T. Schmid, R. Killingsworth, A. Zlot, and S. Raudenbush. 2003. "Relationship between Urban Sprawl and Physical Activity, Obesity, and Morbidity." *American Journal of Health Promotion* 18(1): 47–57.

FEMA. 2013. *Hurricane Sandy Recovery Efforts One Year Later.* Washington, DC: Federal Emergency Management Agency.

Fish, T. 2009. "Assessing Economic Impacts of National Parks." *Park Science* 26(2): Article #322.

Fitts, C. 2012. *Groundwater Science.* Waltham, MA: Academic Press.

Forman, R. T. T. 2014. *Urban Ecology: Science of Cities*. Cambridge, UK: Cambridge University Press.

Francis, J., L. Wood, M. Knuiman, and B. Giles-Corti. 2012. "Quality or Quantity? Exploring the Relationship between Public Open Space Attributes and Mental Health in Perth, Western Australia." *Social Science and Medicine* 74: 1570–77.

Fuller, R., K. Irvine, P. Devine-Wright, P. Warren, and K. J. Gaston. 2007. "Psychological Benefits of Greenspace Increase with Biodiversity." *Biology Letters* 3(4): 390–94.

Gallup Polls. 2011. "Most Americans Believe Crime in the U.S. is Worsening." New York: Gallup Polls.

Gartner, T., J. Mulligan, R. Schmidt, and J. Gunn. 2013. *Natural Infrastructure: Investing in Forested Landscapes for Source Water Protection in the United States*. Washington, DC: World Resources Institute.

Gilmer, B., and Z. Ferdaña. 2012. "Developing a Framework for Assessing Coastal Vulnerability to Sea Level Rise in Southern New England, USA." In *Resilient Cities*, edited by K. Otto-Zimmermann. New York: Springer.

Groffman, P., J. Cavender-Bares, N. Bettez, J. M. Grove, S. J. Hall, J. B. Heffernan, S. Hobbie et al. 2014. "Ecological Homogenization of Urban USA." *Frontiers in Ecology and the Environment* 12(1): 74–81.

Groom, M. J., G. Meffe, and C. Carroll. 2005. *Principles of Conservation Biology*. Sunderland, MA: Sinauer Associates.

Groves, C. 2003. *Drafting a Conservation Blueprint: A Practitioner's Guide to Planning for Biodiversity*. Washington, DC: Island Press.

Haila, Y. 2002. "A Conceptual Genealogy of Fragmentation Research: From Island Biogeography to Landscape Ecology." *Ecological Applications* 12(2): 321–34.

Hanley, N., J. Shogren, and B. White. 2013. *Introduction to Environmental Economics*. Oxford: Oxford University Press.

Hansen, M. C., P. V. Potapov, R. Moore, M. Hancher, S. Turubanova, A. Tyukavina, D. Thau et al. 2013. "High-Resolution Global Maps of 21-Century Forest Cover Change." *Science* 342 (6160): 850–53, http://earthenginepartners.appspot.com/science-2013-global-forest.

Hanson, C., J. Ranganathan, C. Iceland, and J. Finisdore. 2012. *The Corporate Ecosystem Services Review: Guidelines for Identifying Business Risks and Opportunities Arising from Ecosystem Change*. Washington, DC: World Resources Institute.

Hardin, G. 1968. "The Tragedy of the Commons." *Science* 162(3859): 1243–45.

Harper, J. 2009. *Planning for Recreation and Parks Facilities: Predesign Process, Principles, and Strategies.* State College, PA: Venture Publishing.

Hémon, D., and E. Jougla. 2003. Surmortalité liée à la canicule d'août 2003—Rapport d'étape. Paris: Institut national de la santé et de la recherce médicale (INSERM).

Higgins, J. V., and A. Zimmerling. 2013. *A Primer for Monitoring Water Funds.* Arlington, VA: The Nature Conservancy.

Insel, T. 2008. "Assessing the Economic Costs of Serious Mental Illness." *American Journal of Psychiatry* 165(6): 663–65.

IPCC. 2013. *Climate Change 2013: The Physical Science Basis.* Geneva, Switzerland: Intergovernmental Panel on Climate Change.

I-Tree. 2011. *Reference Cities—The Science behind I-Tree Streets (STRATUM).* Syracuse, NY: US Forest Service.

———. 2014. *UFORE Methods.* Syracuse, NY: US Forest Service.

Kahn, P., and S. Kellert. 2002. *Children and Nature: Psychological, Sociocultural, and Evolutionary Investigations.* Cambridge, MA: MIT Press.

Kaiser Family Foundation. 2013. *Hospital Adjusted Expenses per Inpatient Day (2011).* Washington, DC: Kaiser Family Foundation: http://kff.org/other/state-indicator/expenses-per-inpatient-day/.

Kaplan, R., and S. Kaplan. 1989. *The Experience of Nature: A Psychological Perspective.* New York: Cambridge University Press.

Kaplan, T. 2013. "Homeowners in Flood Zones Opt to Rebuild, Not Move." *New York Times*, April 26.

Karlik, J., and D. Pittinger. 2012. *Urban Trees and Ozone Formation: A Consideration for Large-scale Plantings.* Davis: University of California.

Kawamura, S. 1991. *Integrated Design of Water Treatment Facilities.* New York: Wiley.

Kelley, R. 1989. *Battling the Inland Sea: Floods, Public Policy, and the Sacramento Valley.* Berkeley: University of California Press.

Kolstad, C. D. 2000. *Environmental Economics.* New York: Oxford University Press.

Kopp, R., and V. K. Smith. 2013. *Valuing Natural Assets: The Economics of Natural Resource Damage Assessment.* Oxford, UK: Routledge.

Kousky, C. 2014. *The National Flood Insurance Program: Directions for Reform.* Washington, DC: Resources for the Future.

Kousky, C., S. Olmstead, M. Walls, A. Stern, and M. Macauley. 2011. *The Role of Land Use in Adaptation to Increased Precipitation and Flooding: A Case Study in Wisconsin's Lower Fox River Basin.* Washington, DC: Resources for the Future.

Kousky, C., and M. Walls. 2013. *Floodplain Conservation as a Flood Mitigation Strategy: Examining Costs and Benefits*. Washington, DC: Resources for the Future.

Kroeger, T. 2008. *Open Space Property Value Premium Analysis*. Washington, DC: Defenders of Wildlife.

Kroeger, T., F. J. Escobedo, J. Hernandez, S. Varela, S. Delphin, J. Fisher, and J. Waldron. 2014. "Reforestation as a Novel Abatement and Compliance Measure for Ground-Level Ozone." *Proceedings of the National Academy of Science*: doi: 10.1073/pnas.1409785111.

Kuo, F., and F. Sullivan. 2001. "Aggression and Violence in the Inner City: Effects of Environment via Mental Fatigue." *Environment and Behavior* 33(4): 543–71.

Kuo, F., and A. Taylor. 2004. "A Potential Natural Treatment for Attention-Deficit/Hyperactivity Disorder: Evidence from a National Study." *American Journal of Public Health* 94(9): 1580–86.

Lawrence, H. W. 2008. *City Trees: A Historical Geography from the Renaissance through the Nineteenth Century*. Charlottesville: University of Virginia Press.

Lefebrve, A. 2003. "French Government Tries to Quell Scandal over Heat Wave Deaths." World Socialist Web Site, 18 September 2003.

Lehner, B., K. Verdin, and A. Jarvis. 2008. "New Global Hydrography Derived from Spaceborne Elevation Data." *Eos, Transactions of the American Geophysical Union* 89(10): 93–94.

Lide, Cang. 2013. "Saving Urban Water." *China Daily USA*, July 11, p. 8.

Loomis, J., and D. White. 1996. "Economic Benefits of Rare and Endangered Species: Summary and Meta-analysis." *Ecological Economics* 18: 197–206.

Luck, G. W. 2007. "A Review of the Relationships between Human Population Density and Biodiversity." *Biological Reviews* 82(4): 607–45.

Maidment, D., D. Brookshire, J. W. Brown, J. Dorman, G. Galloway, B. Imam, W. Lathrop et al. 2009. *Mapping the Zone: Improving Flood Map Accuracy*. Washington, DC: National Academies Press.

Mansfield, Carol, Subhrendu Pattanayak, Will McDow, R. I. McDonald, and P. N. Halpin. 2005. "Shades of Green: Measuring the Value of Urban Forests in the Housing Market." *Journal of Forest Economics* 11(3): 177–99.

Masson, V. 2000. "A Physically Based Scheme for the Urban Energy Budget in Atmospheric Models." *Boundary Layer Meteorology* 94: 357–97.

McComb, B., B. Zuckerberg, D. Versely, and C. Jordan. 2010. *Monitoring Animal Populations and Their Habitats: A Practitioner's Guide*. New York: CRC Press.

McConnell, V., and M. Walls. 2005. *The Value of Open Space: Evidence from Studies of Nonmarket Benefits*. Washington, DC: Resources for the Future.

McCormack, G., M. Rock, A. Toohey, and D. Hignell. 2010. "Characteristics of Urban Parks Associated with Park Use and Physical Activity: A Review of Qualitative Research." *Health & Place* 16: 712–26.

McDonald, R. I. 2009. "Ecosystem Service Demand and Supply along the Urban-to-Rural Gradient." *Journal of Conservation Planning* 5: 1–14.

McDonald, R. I., R. T. T. Forman, P. Kareiva, R. Neugarten, D. Salzer, and J. Fisher. 2009. "Urban Effects, Distance, and Protected Areas in an Urbanizing World." *Landscape and Urban Planning* 93: 63–75.

McDonald, R. I., B. Guneralp, W. Zipperer, and P. Marcotullio. Forthcoming. "The Future of Global Urbanization and the Environment." *Solutions*.

McDonald, R. I., P. Kareiva, and R. Forman. 2008. "The Implications of Urban Growth for Global Protected Areas and Biodiversity Conservation." *Biological Conservation* 141: 1695–1703.

McDonald, R. I., and D. Shemie. 2014. *Urban Water Blueprint: Mapping Conservation Solutions to the Global Water Challenge*. Washington, DC: The Nature Conservancy: nature.org/waterblueprint.

McGranahan, G. 2007. "Urban Transitions and the Spatial Displacement of Environmental Burdens." In *Scaling Urban Environmental Challenges: From Local to Global and Back*, edited by P. Marcotullio and G. McGranahan, 18–44. London: Earthscan.

McKibben, B. 1989. *The End of Nature*. New York: Random House.

McKinney, M. L. 2002. "Urbanization, Biodiversity, and Conservation." *Bioscience* 52(10): 883–90.

———. 2006. "Urbanization as a Major Cause of Biotic Homogenization." *Biological Conservation* 127(3): 247–60:

———. 2008. "Effects of Urbanization on Species Richness: A Review of Plants and Animals." *Urban Ecosystems* 11: 161–76.

MEA (Millennium Ecosystem Assessment). 2003. *Ecosystems and Human Well-Being: A Framework for Assessment*. Washington, DC: Island Press.

Melosi, M. V. 2008. *The Sanitary City*. Pittsburgh: University of Pittsburgh Press.

Milbrant, E., M. Thompson, L. Coen, R. Grizzle, K. Ward, and S. Lartz. 2013. *Community-Based Restoration of Oyster Habitat: A Project to Evaluate Its Success, Associated Effects on Water Quality and Seagrass Health in a Recently Modified, Substrate-Limited Southwestern Florida Embayment*. Sanibel, FL: Sanibel-Captiva Conservation Foundation Marine Laboratory.

Montgomery, M., R. Stren, B. Cohen, and H. E. Reed. 2003. *Cities Transformed: Demographic Change and Its Implications in the Developing World*. Washington, DC: National Academies Press.

Morales, D., F. Micha, and R. Weber. 1983. "Two Methods of Valuing Trees on Residential Sites." *Journal of Arboriculture* 9: 21–24.

Morris, W., and D. Doak. 2002. *Quantitative Conservation Biology: Theory and Practice of Population Viability Analysis*. Sunderland, MA: Sinauer Associates.

Murcia, C. 1995. "Edge Effects in Fragmented Forests—Implications for Conservation." *Trends in Ecology & Evolution* 10(2): 58–62.

NAS (National Academies of Science). 2009. *Mapping the Zone: Improving Flood Map Accuracy*. Washington, DC: National Academies Press.

NASA. 2012. "European Heat Wave: Image of the Day." National Aeronautics and Space Administration, Earth Observatory: http://earthobservatory.nasa.gov/IOTD/view.php?id=3714. 2003 [cited 15 May 2012].

Nash, R. 2001. *Wilderness and the American Mind*. 4th ed. New Haven: Yale University Press.

Nemeth, E., N. Pieretti, A. Zollinger, N. Geberzahn, J. Parteceke, A. C. Miranda, and H. Brumm. 2013. "Bird Song and Anthropogenic Noise: Vocal Constraints May Explain Why Birds Sing Higher-Frequency Songs in Cities." *Proceedings of the Royal Society B-Biological Sciences* 280(1754): 20122798.

New York City. 2011. *PlaNYC: A Greener, Greater New York*. New York: The City of New York.

Nowak, D. J., S. Hirabayashi, A. Bodine, and R. Hoehn. 2013. "Modeled PM2.5 Removal by Trees in Ten U.S. Cities and Associated Health Effects." *Environmental Pollution* 178: 395–402.

Nowak, D. J., and E. J. Greenfield. 2012. "Trees and Impervious Cover Change in U.S. Cities." *Urban Forestry & Urban Greening* 11: 21–30.

NRC (National Research Council). 2004. *Air Quality Management in the United States*. Washington DC: National Academies Press.

NRDC. 2012. *Financing Stormwater Retrofits in Philadelphia and Beyond*. New York: National Resources Defense Council.

———. 2014. *Asthma and Air Pollution*. Washington, DC: Natural Resources Defense Council.

NWF, Smart Growth America, and NatureServe. 2005. *Endangered by Sprawl: How Runaway Development Threatens America's Wildlife*. Washington, DC: National Wildlife Federation.

Oke, T. R. 1982. "The Energetic Basis of the Urban Heat Island." *Quarterly Journal of the Royal Meteorological Society* 108: 1–24.

Oppel, R. 2011. "Steady Decline in Major Crime Baffles Experts." *New York Times*, May 23.

Opperman, J., G. Galloway, J. Fargione, J. Mount, B. Richter, and S. Secchi. 2009. "Sustainable Floodplains through Large-Scale Reconnection to Rivers." *Science* 326: 1487–8.

Polasky, S. 2008. "Valuing Nature: Biophysical or Monetary Measures?" In *Economics and Conservation in the Tropics: A Strategic Dialogue*. Conference proceeding: http://citeseerx.ist.psu.edu/viewdoc/summary?doi =10.1.1.205.8987.

Polasky, S., C. Costello, and A. Solow. 2005. "The Economics of Biodiversity." In *Handbook of Environmental Economics*, edited by Jeffrey Vincent and Karl-Goran Maler. New York: Elsevier.

Prasad, N., F. Ranghieri, F. Shah, Z. Trohanis, E. Kessler, and R. Sinha. 2009. *Climate Resilient Cities: A Primer on Reducing Vulnerabilities to Disasters*. Washington, DC: The World Bank.

Preston, S. D., R. Alexander, and D. Wolock. 2011. "Sparrow Modeling to Understand Water-Quality Conditions in Major Regions of the United States: A Featured Collection Introduction." *Journal of the American Water Resources Association* 47(5): 887–90.

Randolph, E. 2013. "Transplanting Madison Square Garden." *New York Times*, March 28.

Rawlinson, J. G. 2005. *Creative Thinking and Brainstorming*. Mumbai: Jaico.

Rea, L., and R. Parker. 2005. *Designing and Conducting Survey Research: A Comprehensive Guide*. New York: Wiley.

Reckhow, K., M. N. Beaulac, and J. Simpson. 1980. *Modeling Phosphorous Loading and Lake Response under Uncertainty: A Manual and Compilation of Export Coefficients*. Washington, DC : US Environmental Protection Agency.

Richardson, H. W. 2013. *The New Urban Economics: And Alternatives*. New York: Routledge.

Robert Wood Johnson Foundation. 2011. "Georgia Community Making Parks More Accessible." Online at: http://www.rwjf.org/en/about-rwjf /newsroom/newsroom-content/2011/09/winning-strategies-in-the

-fight-against-childhood-obesity/georgia-community-making-parks -more-accessible.html.

Robine, J., S. Cheung, S. Le Roy, H. Van Oyen, C. Griffiths, J. Michel, and F. Herrmann. 2003. "Death Toll Exceeded 70,000 in Europe during the Summer of 2003." *Comptes Rendus Biologies* 331(2): 171–8.

Rockefeller Foundation, and ARUP. 2014. *City Resilience Framework*. New York: Rockefeller Foundation.

Room for the River. 2014. Riumte voor der ivier (English). The Netherlands 2014 [cited 1 June 2014]: http://www.ruimtevoorderivier.nl /english/.

Salafsky, N., R. Margoluis, K. H. Redford, and J. G. Robinson. 2002. "Improving the Practice of Conservation: A Conceptual Framework and Research Agenda for Conservation Science." *Conservation Biology* 16(6): 1469–79.

Salcido, R. 2012. "The Success and Continued Challenges of the Yolo Bypass Wildlife Area: A Grassroots Restoration." *Ecology Law Quarterly* 39: 1085–1134.

Sander, H. A., and S. Polasky. 2009. "The Value of Views and Open Space: Estimates from a Hedonic Pricing Model for Ramsey County, Minnesota, USA." *Land Use Policy* 26(3): 837–45.

Sarkar, S., R. L. Pressey, D. P. Faith, C. R. Margules, T. Fuller, D. M. Stoms, A. Moffett et al. 2006. "Biodiversity Conservation Planning Tools: Present Status and Challenges for the Future." *Annual Review of Environment and Resources* 31: 123–59.

Saunders, D. A., R. J. Hobbs, and C. R. Margules. 1991. "Biological Consequences of Ecosystem Fragmentation: A Review." *Conservation Biology* 5: 18–32.

Schwirtz, M. 2013. "Report Cites Large Release of Sewage from Hurricane Sandy." *New York Times*, April 30.

Shaw, A. 2011. "Back to Nature Begins Early." This is Finland. http:// finland.fi/Public/default.aspx?contentid=230992&nodeid=41807& culture=en-US.

Silva, R., J. West, Y. Zhang, S. Anenberg, J-F. Lamarque, D. Shindell, W. Collins et al. 2013. "Global Premature Mortality Due to Anthropogenic Outdoors Air Pollution and the Contribution of Past Climate Change." *Environmental Research Letters* 8(3): 034005.

Stem, C., R. Margoluis, N. Salafsky, and M. Brown. 2005. "Monitoring and Evaluation in Conservation: A Review of Trends and Approaches." *Conservation Biology* 19(2): 295–309.

Sutherland, W. J. 2006. *Ecological Census Techniques: A Handbook*. Cambridge, UK: Cambridge University Press.

Swenson, J. J., and J. Franklin. 2000. "The Effects of Future Urban Development on Habitat Fragmentation in the Santa Monica Mountains." *Landscape Ecology* 15: 713–30.

Tacheiva, G. 2010. *Sprawl Repair Manual*. Washington, DC: Island Press.

Tallis, H., and S. Wolny. 2011. "Including People in the Mitigation Hierarchy: Mapping Ecosystem Service Winners and Losers in Colombia." Paper read at Ecological Society of America, Austin, TX., August 7–12.

Tallis, H., R. Goldman, M. Uhl, and B. Brosi. 2009. "Integrating Conservation and Development in the Field: Implementing Ecosystem Service Projects." *Frontiers in Ecology and the Environment* 7(1): 12–20.

Tallis, H. T., T. Ricketts, A. D. Guerry, S. A. Wood, R. Sharp, E. Nelson, D. Ennaanay et al. 2013. *InVEST 2.5.6 User's Guide*. Stanford, CA: The Natural Capital Project.

Tallis, M., G. Taylor, D. Sinnett, and P. Freer-Smith. 2011. "Estimating the Removal of Atmospheric Particular Pollution by the Urban Tree Canopy of London, under Current and Future Environments." *Landscape and Urban Planning* 103: 129–38.

TEEB. 2011. "TEEB Manual for Cities: Ecosystem Services in Urban Management." www.teebweb.org: The Economics of Ecosystems and Biodiversity.

Tischendorf, L., and L. Fahrig. 2000. "On the Usage and Measurement of Landscape Connectivity." *Oikos* 90(1): 7–19.

TPL. 2004. *Protecting the Source*. Washington, DC: Trust for Public Land.

———. 2009. *Measuring the Economic Value of a City Park System*. Washington, DC: Trust for Public Land.

Tyrvainen, L., and A. Miettinen. 2000. "Property Prices and Urban Forest Amenities." *Journal of Environmental Economics and Management* 39: 205–23.

Ulrich, R. 1983. "Aesthetic and Affective Response to Natural Environment." *Human Behavior and Environment: Advances in Theory and Research* 6: 85–125.

———. 1984. "View through a Window May Influence Recovery from Surgery." *Science* 224: 420–21.

UNPD. 2011. *World Urbanization Prospects: The 2011 Revision*. New York: United Nations Population Division.

USACE. 2012. *Unit Day Values for Recreation, Fiscal Year 2012*. Washington, DC: US Army Corps of Engineers.

US Census Bureau. 2002. Demographic Trends in the 20th Century. Washington, DC: US Census Bureau.

USFS. 2013. *I-Tree Eco User's Manual* (v4.1.0). Washington, DC: United States Forest Service.

——. 2014. *Strategic Tree Planting as an EPA-Encouraged Pollutant Reduction Strategy: How Urban Trees Can Obtain Credit in State Implementation Plans.* Syracuse, NY: US Forest Service.

Valderrama, A., L. Levine, E. Bloomgarden, and C. Kaiser. 2013. *Creating Clean Water Cash Flows: Developing Private Markets for Green Stormwater Infrastructure in Philadelphia.* New York: National Resources Defense Council.

Vandertorren, S., P. Bretin, A. Zeghnoun, L. Mandereau-Bruno, A. Croisier, C. Cochet, J. Riberon, I. Siberan, B. Declercq, and M. Ledrans. 2006. "August 2003 Heat Wave in France: Risk Factors for Death of Elderly People Living at Home." *European Journal of Public Health* 16(6): 583–91.

Vandentorren, S., F. Suzan, S. Medina, M. Pascal, A. Maulpoix, J. Cohen, and M. Ledrans. 2004. "Mortality in 13 French Cities during the August 2003 Heat Wave." *American Journal of Public Health* 94(9): 1518–20.

Waidler, D., M. White, E. Steglich, S. Wang, J. Williams, C. Jones, and R. Srinivasan. 2009. *Conservation Practice Modeling Guide for SWAT and APEX.* College Station: Texas A&M University.

Wang, F., T. McDonald, J. Bender, B. Reffitt, A. Miller, and D. Edington. 2006. "Association of Healthcare Costs with Per Unit Body Mass Index Increase." *Journal of Occupational Environmental Medicine* 48(7): 668–74.

Wang, F., T. McDonald, L. Champagne, and D. Edington. 2004. "Relationship of Body Mass Index and Physical Activity to Health Care Costs among Employees." *Journal of Occupational Environmental Medicine* 46(5): 428–36.

White, R. E. 2005. *Principles and Practice of Soil Science: The Soil as a Natural Resource.* New York: Wiley.

Wischmeier, W. H., and D. D. Smith. 1978. *Predicting Rainfall Erosion Losses—A Guide to Conservation Planning.* Agriculture Handbook No. 537. Washington, DC: US Department of Agriculture.

Wolch, J., M. Jerrett, K. Reynolds, R. McConnell, R. Chang, N. Dahmann, K. Brady, F. Gilliand, J. Su, and K. Berhane. 2011. "Childhood Obesity and Proximity to Urban Parks and Recreational Resources: A Longitudinal Cohort Study." *Health & Place* 17: 207–14.

Wolch, J., J. Wilson, and J. Fehrenbach. 2002. *Parks and Park Funding in Los Angeles: An Equity Mapping Analysis.* Los Angeles: Sustainable Cities Program, University of Southern California.

Woodroffe, R., and J. R. Ginsberg. 1998. "Edge Effects and the Extinction of Populations inside Protected Areas." *Science* 280(5372): 2126–28.

Wood, S., A. D. Guerry, J. Silver, and M. Lacayo. 2013. "Using Social Media to Quantify Nature-Based Tourism and Recreation." *Scientific Reports* 3:doi:10.1038/srep02976.

Wouters, H., K. De Ridder, M. Demuzere, D. Lauwaet, and N. P. M. van Lipzig. 2013. "The Diurnal Evolution of the Urban Heat Island of Paris: A Model-based Case Study during Summer 2006." *Atmospheric Chemistry & Physics* 13: 8525–41.

Index

Page numbers followed by "f" and "t" indicate figures and tables.